Refusing to Be Made Whole

REFUSING TO BE MADE WHOLE

Disability in Black Women's Writing

Anna LaQuawn Hinton

University Press of Mississippi / Jackson

Margaret Walker Alexander Series in African American Studies

The University Press of Mississippi is the scholarly publishing agency of the Mississippi Institutions of Higher Learning: Alcorn State University, Delta State University, Jackson State University, Mississippi State University, Mississippi University for Women, Mississippi Valley State University, University of Mississippi, and University of Southern Mississippi.

www.upress.state.ms.us

The University Press of Mississippi is a member of the Association of University Presses.

Any discriminatory or derogatory language or hate speech regarding race, ethnicity, religion, sex, gender, class, national origin, age, or disability that has been retained or appears in elided form is in no way an endorsement of the use of such language outside a scholarly context.

Copyright © 2025 by University Press of Mississippi
All rights reserved
Manufactured in the United States of America

∞

Library of Congress Control Number: 2024055931

Hardback ISBN: 9781496855039 | Paperback ISBN: 9781496855046
E-pub Single ISBN: 9781496855053 | E-pub Institutional ISBN: 9781496855060
PDF Single ISBN: 9781496855077 | PDF Institutional ISBN: 9781496855022

British Library Cataloging-in-Publication Data available

Contents

Acknowledgments vii

Introduction: Refusing to Be Made Whole 3

Chapter 1: If I am Crazy, Can I Be of Sound Mind?:
Representation, Disability, and Black Women's Novel Aesthetic 25

Chapter 2: Black Community, Crip Communities of Care 56

Chapter 3: Cripping Motherhood 85

Chapter 4: Sexual Healing 108

Conclusion: Towards a Crip Technoscience of the Spirit 123

Postscript 134

Notes 137

Index 163

Acknowledgments

I would like to give thanks and praise and honor to God, the Creator.

As well as honor my unknown ancestors. I am the manifestation of their most ambitious freedom dreams.

I am grateful to be buoyed by the Prayers of my known ancestors, especially My Nana, Yvonne Smith. Even though we talk often, I miss your physical presence every day. I feel you and the impact of your prayers on my life every day. Throughout the long process of writing this book, I've longed to lay my head on your lap one last time. I am also grateful to my granddaddy, Willie Smith, My Granddaddy George, George Wheat; and my Daddy, Robert Ferrell. May His Peace be with you, until we meet again.

This book has been made possible by the faith and mentorship I have received throughout my education journey from those who have transitioned before the completion of this book. I'd like to honor and thank my Virginia State University undergraduate mentor, Freddy Thomas, whose faith and investment in me provided material sustenance and planted and nourished the seed that this was a vocation in which I could succeed. I'd like to thank my beloved friend and mentor, Martha Satz, who introduced me to disability studies and who maintained faith in me until the very end. Finally, I'd like to thank my dearest mentor and champion, Dr. Cheryl A. Wall, who forged pathways and opened doors. May you all rest in power.

The earliest seeds of this book were planted at Virginia State University, and I'd like to express gratitude for the guidance and encouragement of Meredith Polk, Dr. Lilly Bailey, and Dr. William Hobbs.

This book began as my dissertation I started at Southern Methodist University, where I continue to grow and thrive under the guidance of Dr. Darryl Dickson-Carr, Dr. Angela Ards, and the late Dr. Martha Satz, who served on my dissertation committee. I thank my professors and colleagues at the Taos writing workshops, where several of these chapters were workshopped, including, but not limited to, Dr. Bruce Levy, Dr. Beth Newman, Dr. Timothy Rosendale, Dr. Laurin Miskin, Dr. Kathrine Boswell, Dr. Kari Nixon, Dr.

Christopher Stampone, Dr. Summer Hamilton, Dr. Anna Nelson, Kathrine Harceclode, Liz Duke, and particularly my cohort and writing companions Kelsey Kiser, Andrew Forrester, Chelsea McKelvey, and Seth McKelvey.

I am grateful for the space that a postdoctoral fellowship in the English department at Rutgers University, under Dr. Cheryl Wall's mentorship, provided to write and workshop this book. I am especially grateful for the encouragement and generous feedback from Dr. Evie Shockely, Dr. Carter Mathes, Dr. Erica Edwards, Dr. Melanie Hill, and Dr. Stéphane Robolin.

I'd like to offer a special thanks to Dr. Therí Pickens, who has blazed trails in the field, opened professional doors, and has been a dear friend. Through my work, I've been blessed with the chance to connect with so many people who have contributed to this book in a variety of ways. These included, but are by no means limited to, Alison Kafer, Sami Schalk, Jess Waggoner, Akemi Nishida, Susan Burch, J. Logan Smilges, La Marr Jurelle Bruce, Kameelah L. Martin, Jina B. Kim, Sony Coráñez Bolton, Kelsey Henry, Delia Steverson, Anna Mollow, Heather Watkins, Leslie Frye, Timothy Lyle, Dennis Tyler, Julie Avril Minich, Steven Knadler, Moya Bailey, M. Remi Yergeau, Robert Volpicelli, Will Mosley, Anthony Boyndton II, Tyeshia Thompson, Janelle Hobson, Leroy Moore, Vilissa Thompson, Carol E. Henderson, Stacie McCormick, and many others.

I am grateful for my colleagues at the University of North Texas and the resources provided through the university, such as the Scholarly Creative Award and the Faculty Writing Group organized and hosted by Kat Aoyama. I am forever grateful for the support from my friends, colleagues, and mentors in La Colectiva—Mariella Nuñez-Janes, Brenda Barrio, Valerie Martinez-Ebers, Sandra Mendiola, Lok-Sze Wong, Angie Cartwright, Alicia Cruz as well as from the Black Faculty Network—Dorothy Bland, Jackie Walker, John Edwards, Yolanda Mitchell.

I am particularly thankful for the writing companionship and friendship of Joanna Davis-McEligatt, Priscilla Ybarra, Jennifer Gómez Menjívar, Aja Martinez, Karine Narahara, and Sasha Sanders.

I'd also like to express special thanks and gratitude to my colleagues from the College Language Association (CLA). CLA has been a professional buoy in the turbulent waters of academia and imposter syndrome. I would especially like to thank the 2019 (now) current Executive Committee, Dr. Jervette R. Ward, Dr. Mckinley Melton, Dr. Janaka B. Lewis, Dr. Jason Hendrickson, Dr. Donna Akiba Sullivan Harper, Dr. Constance Bailey, Dr. Donovan Ramon, Dr. Shauna Morgan, Dr. Reginald Bess, Dr. Jose Batista. Y'all have inspired and supported my work, professional development, and personal growth.

Acknowledgments

I would like to thank the editors at the University Press of Mississippi, particularly Lisa McMurtray who supported this work early, early on in the writing and publishing process.

I am so thankful for my family. I am especially thankful for the support, prayers, kikies, and spaces to work during a transitional time in my life that Kesha McNeil and Tonya Spivey provided. Y'all, along with Crystal Pringle, Regina Duggins, were supportive at a much-needed time. I'd like to thank Barry Smalls and Deborah Smalls-Brown, and my aunts Debra Williams, Glenda Whittington, and Robin Wheat—y'all have been other mothers to me, and I thank you and love you. I'd like to thank my siblings, Bre'Onca Ferrell and Caleb Howard. I'd like to thank my mother-in-law, Tracey Toney, for being so kind, caring, understanding, and supportive.

This book would not be possible—I would not be possible—without the unwavering love of my mommy, Georgina Wheat-Ferrell. I hope I make you proud.

I'd like to thank my wonderful spouse, Krystal Toney, for being such a supportive life-partner and best friend. Our road has not been easy, but it has been the testing ground for the healing power of choosing to act in and with love. Finally, I dedicate this book to Ella, my beautiful, awesome daughter. You have been here through every incarnation of this book. You have been my most consistent and enthusiastic cheerleader. You are a role-model of bravery and authenticity. I love you so deeply. Thank you.

Refusing to Be Made Whole

Introduction
Refusing to Be Made Whole

Toni Cade Bambara's novel *The Salt Eaters* (1987) opens with the protagonist, Velma Henry, on a stool, assed out after attempting suicide by taking pills and putting her head in an oven. She is being treated at the Academy of the Seven Healing Arts' Southwest Community Infirmary, a multiracially and ethnically owned and operated institution that combines biomedical treatments and healing practices from various non-Western cultures. Velma is surrounded by interns, there to observe and learn, as well as doctors and a select group of community members known as "The Twelve, or The Master's Mind." Also present and central to Velma's treatment team is folk healer and conjurer Minnie Ransom. While Ransom is there to support and guide her out of her stupor, it is Velma who must work through the trauma that led her to suicide in the first place: a disintegrating marriage, strained family life, an unfulfilling career, burdensome activist work, and constant acts of violent misogynoir, the specific form of racism and sexism that Black women face.[1] Additionally, Velma is confused and frightened by her burgeoning spiritual powers. Like many Black women, Velma has been physically, mentally, and spiritually broken by a racist and sexist society, which is compounded by, as the novel suggests, a predisposition to depression and suicide. Illness and healing, for Velma, is multifaceted. Illness involves a complex matrix of societal and interpersonal harms as well as natural bodymindspirit diversity. Healing involves attending to Velma's acute injuries, prioritizing her mental health by balancing her responsibilities and not overburdening herself, accepting and adjusting to her spiritual gifts, and participating in a larger effort to make a seismic shift away from a world rampant with hate towards Black women. Ransom and the other healers envisage Velma's wholeness as crucial for not only self-actualization but also communal uplift in the struggle to save a world on the verge of apocalypse. In other words, treatment is not an individualized, medical experience but a collective striving for wellness of body, mind, and spirit. Healing is not meant to reproduce the normate body, what Rosemarie Garland-Thomson has defined as the idealized subject only emergent through its contrast with those who have stigmatized attributes,[2] but to equip people with the wellness needed to fight for a more just world.

Bambara's *The Salt Eaters* is only one text among the corpus of Black women's writing where debilitating violence and spiritual healing are thematically central. While these themes emerge in the earliest works by Black women, this is particularly evident in the literature Black women have produced from the 1970s to the present day. Why do psychically and physically maimed central characters—as opposed to the more commonly found disabled marginal figure—proliferate Black women's writing, both fiction and nonfiction? Why are spirituality and healing so deeply enmeshed in these works? And why, in a culture concerned with rehabilitation and cure, does healing always seem so incomplete in Black women's writing? Why, despite all the rituals and laying on of hands, is disability cum the nonnormative bodymindspirit so recalcitrant? Where and how does this fit in their visions of liberation? The aim of this book is to explore how these Black women writers have theorized injury and healing, debilitation, disability, and cure in and through their writing.

In *Refusing to Be Made Whole: Disability in Black Women's Writing*, I argue that contemporary Black women writers, like Toni Cade Bambara, present becoming disabled as a traumatic and violent experience of Black womanhood. In their essay, life-writing, and fiction, the material consequences of misogynoir are violently writ on Black women's body, mind, and spirit. Nevertheless, Black women embrace disabled Black womanhood by turning to Africanist spiritual understandings of wholeness. These writers often appeal to a mix of African traditional religions (ATRs), African-derived religions (ADRs), and Indigenous-American belief systems that understand debilitating injury and illness as not only physical and mental but also spiritual, as not just an individual problem but a symptom of communal discord. These spiritual belief-systems reclaimed and revised by these writers have more complex and capacious understandings of the body, sickness, and wellness; thus, Black women use these belief systems to reimagine healing in ways that make space for a variety of bodymindspirits. In so doing, these writers frustrate the tendency to equate healing with cure and wholeness with a return to a normate body. I maintain that disability is not only a major theme in contemporary Black women's writing but that it also shapes the formal elements characteristic of the Black women's literary tradition. The dialogic, recursive, open-ended, cyclical nature of Black women's writing results from a way of knowing and being that not only refuses wholeness of body and mind but also narrative. In what follows, I expand on and layout the contours of this book's arguments in three sections that represent the major argumentative arc. In the first section, I discuss racialization and gendering as a debilitating process in both life and literature. Next, I discuss healing through Africanist spirituality. This section introduces two terms that I theorize and employ throughout: my use of *bodymindspirit* and my theorization of Black cultural locations of disability. The final section before the chapter breakdowns talks about disability and Black women's aesthetic practices as central to the theorizing of race, gender, and disability and the healing praxis of the literature. Each of these sections is a concentric discussion of extant conversations, methods, and issues that come together to inform and inflect the shape of this introduction as well as each chapter of this book.

Inscribing Race, Inscribing Gender: Disabled Black Womanhood and Becoming

As a field, Africana literary studies has produced a robust body of theory and criticism about the sick, injured, maimed, brutalized, and traumatized Black female bodymindspirit in Black women's writing. Scholars like Hortense Spillers, Rebecca Wanzo, Deborah King, and Tameka Carey identify how misogynoir is violently and physically inscribed on Black women's bodymindspirit. As Rebecca Wanzo asserts, "... the play of domination is continually imprinted on black women's bodies and ... the nexus of identity and pain is continually shaping black female identity."[3] Misogynoir is not only physically and mentally damaging in Black women's literature, but the process of becoming injured as a result of misogynoir is a foundational experience of Black womanhood. Drawing on theories and methods from the field of critical disability studies, I read the broken bodymindspirit in Black women's literature as a disability. The field of disability studies exposes and challenges the expectations, attitudes, and assumptions we have about bodies. Foundational to this work, disability studies reconfigures definitions of disability from a tragic flaw and disfunction of the bodymindspirit that should be treated and ideally cured through biomedical intervention, the medical model of disability, to an understanding of disability as a complex interaction among bodies, environments, and societal attitudes and expectations, also known as the social model of disability. Within this frame, disability is no longer a fact of the body; instead, its produced by inaccessible environments, institutionalized stigma, and political disenfranchisement. As such, critical disability studies scholars not only theorize bodies with traits typically considered a disability, such as limb difference, sensory differences, and mobility impairments, but it also considers how one's body—able-bodied or disabled—shapes experience, thought, and belief, as well as cultural production and politics. Disability studies identifies and challenges ableism, the preference for the able body and mind, and discrimination based on perceived disability, as an institutionalized and systemic practice of oppression informative of and informed by other oppressive ideologies and practices like racism and heterosexism.

Debilitation is part of the racializing process, and a Black feminist disability studies methodology enables us to recognize this, but also that Black feminists have discerned this in their theorizing. Historically, Blackness has been constructed as a disability, as a form of bodymindspirit difference in contradistinction to whiteness (re: healthy and able-bodied) as an ideal. The racist discourse used to denigrate Blackness and justify Black people's subjugation relied on ableism for its argumentative thrust. From law to philosophy to medicine, the intellectual disciplines were dedicated to proving a racial hierarchy through the language of deficit and deficiency. Moreover, the ableist construction of Blackness as a disability validated violent racial domination that often impaired the Black bodymindspirit. As Hortense Spillers so poignantly provokes in her now foundational essay in Black studies, "Mama's Baby, Papa's Maybe: An American Grammar Book," might we consider the atrocities of the transatlantic slave trade not crimes against the body—the theft of bodies but as "high crimes against the *flesh* as the person of African females and African males registered the wounding."[4] This wounding is not merely historical or discursive—although it is surely both of those things, but material, embodied. Spillers goes on to comment on the "all day long" violence of the plantation:

> The anatomical specifications of rupture, of altered human tissue, take on the objective description of laboratory prose- eyes beaten out, arms, backs, skulls branded, a left jaw, a right ankle, punctured; teeth missing, as the calculated work of iron, whips, chains, knives, the canine patrol, the bullet. These undecipherable markings on the captive body render a kind of hieroglyphics of the flesh whose severe disjunctures come to be hidden to the cultural seeing by skin color.[5]

Nirmala Erevelles quite perceptively recognizes the "beaten out," "branded," and "punctured" flesh of enslaved Black folk as disability.[6] Spillers's analysis, taken with Erevelles's critical observation, unearths several important truths: (1) the process of racialization is a process of wounding the flesh. (2) The wounded, debilitated flesh indicates one's subjugated status, what Spillers articulates as the difference between "captive and liberated subject positions." (3) Race—Blackness—then renders this disability invisible. This, as scholars such as Michelle Jarman, Ellen Samuels, and Sami Schalk argue, exposes race and disability as mutually constitutive. However, as Therí A. Pickens quite significantly counters, Blackness and disability, especially as it encounters whiteness and able-bodiedness, cannot exist on "the same temporal plane," disabled Blackness inevitably gets "evacuated from history."[7] While Spillers argues that this process "transfers from one generation to another" in "its various *symbolic substitutions*," I maintain that the process of racialization still renders itself as crimes against the flesh: the climate of anti-Blackness continues to corporeally mutilate Black bodymindspirits.[8] Disproportionate rates of poverty, poor housing conditions, environmental racism, medical racism, reproductive injustice, and state violence, to name a few, continue to debilitate Black bodies. Thus, when we claim that the "violence of anti-Blackness produces Black existence,"[9] we must recognize, to politically mobilize, this anti-Black violence as disabling.

Methodologically, *Refusing to Be Made Whole* seeks not so much to put Black studies and disability studies into conversation—as Pickens has also noted, they have already had theoretical and thematic overlaps—but to use theories of Blackness and disability already present and presented by Black women writers to critically (re)engage themes, issues, and conflicts foundational to the study of contemporary Black women's writing without, as tends to happen, "[severing] the two for political expediency."[10] As it stands, this "political expediency" emerges because of two faulty impulses. In Black literary studies and Black activism generally, the impulse has been to react defensively to accusations of Blackness as a disability through disavowal. In so doing, as Douglas Baynton points out, Black scholars and activists fail to critique disability as grounds for subjugation. Indeed, this passively accedes and takes for granted that it is.[11] This reflects a larger critical trend within Black studies and Black feminist studies specifically—what Jennifer C. Nash has identified as the field's defensiveness.[12] Defensiveness as a critical and political tactic is ultimately ineffective. As Pickens notes, it results in scholarly "stagnation." The field gets stuck in a set of methodologies that then fails to account for the complex and nuanced ways race, gender, and disability unfold in the literature.[13] It distracts from continuing to grow new critical methodologies, theories, and readings.[14] Most importantly, to borrow the language of venerated Black feminist ancestor Audre Lorde, it seeks to dismantle the master's house with the master's tools.[15] In *Refusing to Be Made Whole*, I concentrate on how Black women have defined what liberation means for themselves to borrow the words of another venerated Black feminist ancestor.[16] What I find is that Black women's literature is concerned with speaking truth to life on how Black womanhood continues to be marked on the flesh; yet, Black women also strive to find ways not to remain stuck in and by this violence. As Bambara so frankly states, "When the experts (white or Black, male) turn their attention to the Black woman," they tend to "focus so heavily on what white people have done to the psyches of Blacks, that what Blacks have done to and for themselves is overlooked. . . ."[17] While I discuss misogynoir, I do so through the theorizing of these Black women, centering their interests and perspectives. While critical disability studies provides a legible language to discuss this body of work, I focus on how Black women have theorized their bodies.

In disability studies, the faulty impulse that emerges is to privilege certain readings of bodies (and reject others) that align with the cultural and historical politics of forging an identity around disability, as James Berger significantly points out.[18] More specifically, disability studies tends to disavow texts and theories that view disability as a liability, connect disability with suffering and tragedy, and/or present disability as undesirable. Far too often, this is achieved by decentering, or altogether ignoring, how people become disabled—and usually for good reason. Focusing on the cause of disability, Jill C. Anderson argues positions disability as an accident, "as unintentional, undesirable, marginal, deviations from idolized norms of fitness." Instead, "[disability] studies rejects the assumptions that underlie this view, foremost by affirmatively valuing disability experience and accepting bodily diversity not as accidental but as essential to society."[19] Disability studies's revision of common assumptions about disability by laying claim to disability as bodily diversity is an important foundational belief informing the social model of disability. While I fundamentally believe that disability is a natural form of bodily diversity, liberation for oppressed people the world around demands that we recognize and acknowledge that testifying to how one becomes disabled not always positions disability as "accidental" but highlights how it was created through violent design. As Erevelles explains, this line of argumentation is difficult to make within disability studies, a "context where disability is theorized as a possibility rather than a limit, because this begs the more controversial question: How is disability celebrated if its very existence is inextricably linked to the violence of social/economic conditions of capitalism?"[20] Jasbir Puar underscores this argument when she describes a New York City disability pride parade on the same day and just blocks away from a Black Lives Matter march against deathly and disabling police violence (mostly against disabled Black people).[21] I maintain that it is possible and necessary to hold, perhaps uneasily and with difficulty, both truths.

Indeed, the rising field of Black disability studies is dedicated to the work of holding the multiple, shifting truths of Black experiences, representations, and theorizations of the bodymindspirit.[22] Black disability studies as a methodology also reckons with the impact of violence on Black bodymindspirits, and demonstrates that ableism harms all Black people, regardless of (dis)ability.[23] Moreover, those in the field of Black disability studies, such as Sami Schalk, Moya Bailey, and Izetta Mobley, have explained why disability studies scholars need to consider illness and disease, such as schizophrenia, hypertension, diabetes, and heart disease, and the racist (sometimes slow) violence that creates and contributes to their disproportionate presence among Black people, as disability justice issues.[24] Moreover, Black disability studies recognizes the long history of Black people, particularly Black women, writing about and organizing around issues central to disability justice.[25] The work of scholars like Christopher M. Bell, Therí A. Pickens, Sami Schalk, Timothy Lyle, Anna Mollow, Moya Bailey, Nirmala Erevelles, Dennis Tyler Jr., Michelle Jarman, Delia Steverson, and myself, to name a few, are creating new paradigms that allow scholars, borrowing the words of Black feminist hip hop and pleasure theorist Joan Morgan, to "fuck with the grays" of Blackness and disability.[26]

Refusing to Be Made Whole draws on Black disability studies methodologies not only to identify and analyze disability discourse in contemporary Black women's writing but also to centralize that writing in the Black disability studies archive.[27] Specifically, I employ methods and analyze my archive from a Black Feminist Disability framework. Black feminist disability studies, as Moya Bailey and Izetta Mobley outline, approaches race, gender, class, sexuality, and disability through an intersectional lens to "better understand the realities for those multiply marginalized within society"[28] through recognizing that ableism—what they call a "eugenics impulse"—undergirds misogynoir.[29] Bailey and Mobley direct scholars to Black feminist writing as examples of texts that approach race, gender, and disability through an intersectional lens, which Bailey and Mobley do to theorize and model a Black feminist disability studies methodology. Therefore, along with Bailey and Mobley, I turn to Black women's health activism as a location of what Schalk calls Black disability politics.[30] I extend their work on contemporary Black women's health movements to argue that as the Black Arts Movement served as a cultural articulation of Black nationalist and Black Power politics, Black women's literature from the 1970s through the 1990s served as a literary and cultural arm to Black women's health activism. Although not without contention, movements for Black liberation and civil rights have always been accompanied by Black cultural articulations of racial politics. The New Negro

Movement was inspired by the Great Migration of Black folk to northern cities to escape dehumanization, poverty, and violence in the South. The lynching plays of Georgia Douglass Johnson and Alice Dunbar-Nelson delved into the ethical binds and psychic strain southern Black people navigated at the constant threat of lynching, which Ida B. Wells journalistically exposed and organized to combat. Richard Wright and Ralph Ellison dared people to recognize and humanely bear witness to Black male interiority under the strain of racism, and both actively bolstered the Black psychiatric health movement by working with the Lafargue Clinic in Harlem. The Black Arts Movement is commonly positioned as—to use Black Arts theorist Larry Neal's description—"the sister of the Black Power concept." Black women's health activism increased as Black women took their wellness into their own hands in the 1990s, and Black women's theorizing of the bodymindspirit in the writing of the previous decade was central to this work.

Self-help movements that worked to educate and empower Black women to ensure their wellness exploded in popularity in the 1990s. Building on the work of reproductive justice activism, cancer awareness, and, increasingly, HIV/AIDs awareness, Black women began to talk seriously about the impact misogynoir had on their bodymindspirits. Organizations like the National Black Women's Health Project organized and hosted local focus groups and conferences, as well as produced a publication dedicated to Black women's holistic health. They covered a range of issues from addiction to cancer and, as Sami Schalk points out, addressed the wellness of Black women's body, mind, and spirit.[31] Books such as Evelyn C. White's *The Black Women's Health Book: Speaking for Ourselves* (1990) and Linda Villarosa's *Body & Soul: The Black Women's Guide to Physical Health and Emotional Well-Being* (1994) provided an outlet for Black women to testify to their experiences with illness, injury, disease, dis-ease, and disability. Essays by allopathic and homeopathic practitioners educated women about the care of their bodymindspirits. In addition to more traditional essays on health and wellness, these self-help books often included excerpts or passages from the essays, life-writing, and, even, poetry and fiction by Black women writers. For instance, *The Black Women's Health Book* includes several of Lucille Clifton's poems, an excerpt from Alice Walker's essay "Beauty: When the Other Dancer is the Self," and a selection from Toni Morrison's *Beloved*, to name a few. June Jordan wrote the foreword to *Body & Soul*. bell hooks's self-help book, *Sisters of the Yam: Black Women and Self-Recovery*, is titled after and draws on Toni Cade Bambara's *The Salt Eaters*. These health activists recognized Black women's writing as a repository of healing knowledge. In fact, many Black women writers were active in various health movements and explicitly used their writing to further their activism. In *A Joyous Revolt: Toni Cade Bambara, Writer and Activist*, Linda Janet Holmes writes about Toni Cade Bambara's reproductive justice work with local birth centers and clinics. N'tozake Shange and Bebe Moore Campbell raised awareness about mental illness among Black women. In fact, Campbell wrote her novel *72-Hour Hold* as a literary text meant to destigmatize mental illness among Black folks, emphasize the necessity of seeking mental health care, and caution Black people about the obstacles they may face navigating the mental healthcare system. Pearl Cleage not only thematically addressed Black women and HIV/AIDs in her novels and plays, but she was also an on-the-ground HIV/AIDs activist.[32] In *Refusing to Be Made Whole*, I not only explicitly articulate this body of creative writing as informative of and as an extension of contemporary Black women's health activism, but I also recognize their work as an archive of cripistemologies.

Coined by Lisa Duggan but fleshed out in conversations among crip scholars at the periphery of formalized academic spaces, cripistemology questions "what we think we know about disability, and how we know around and through it." Whereas under neoliberalism, knowledge about disability is controlled by market forces that target what Merri Lisa Johnson and Robert McRuer call the debility dollar, or the money spent on impairments, cripistemologies are the ways of knowing about and through disability not controlled by the market or coopted by the state. While largely developed by and among white disability studies scholars, cripistemology is a concept that is inspired by Black southern folk culture. Johnson and McRuer open their introductory article in a special issue on cripistemologies with "Southerisms" quoted from Randall Kenan's 1989 novel *A Visitation of Spirits*. The quoted Southernisms, such as "it's always something," captures crip knowledge that "it does not always get better" while serving as a metaphor for cripistemology's origins in the "backwoods" of academic theory. Though used metaphorically, these Black folk Southernisms are, in and of themselves, snatches of Black cripistemologies. Like Kenan's novel, Black women's contemporary literature serves as an archive of this wisdom. In their care-filled representations of Black life, they preserve Black folks' disability knowledge, and as they use their essay, life writing, and fiction to theorize the Black bodymindspirit and relations of power, they produce their own.

So far, I have argued that Black women's writing necessitates—demands even—interpretive strategies that read bodymindspirits through a holistic lens that considers both the violence that marks them as well as the many ways Black women continue on living and fighting despite and through them. This is not only true for engaging thematic foci but also for formal and aesthetic practices. Like Bailey and Mobley, I identify Black women's health activism as invested in disability justice issues. Moreover, I take seriously and take up Black feminist scholars who implore us to consider the importance and centrality of spirituality in Black women's lives. As Brittney Cooper asserts, "If academic Black feminism hopes to be impactful to broad swaths of black women, particularly those outside of the academy, then it must forthrightly begin to attend to questions of the spiritual and the sacred."[33] I contend that attention to spirituality is imperative to an intersectional reading of the bodymindspirit in Black women's writing. I argue that Black women turn to Africanist spiritual paradigms to understand their violently (re)made bodymindspirits. Thus, *Refusing to Be Made Whole* is the first monograph of which I am aware to take up both Black feminist disability studies, and spirituality in Black women's writing.

Bodymindspirit: Africanist Spirituality in Reimagining Disability and Healing

In *Refusing to Be Made Whole*, I argue that one must attend to the Spirit and spirituality when examining Black women's representations and theories of the body. More specifically, contemporary Black women writers evoke, invoke, and remix Africanist spiritual cosmologies to theorize the bodymindspirit, illness and disability, and healing and wholeness. In this book, *Africanist* spiritual thought, belief, and practices describe the Africanness of the syncretized spiritualities presented in contemporary Black women's writing. Africanist suggests a relationship or kinship to African origins without making claims about Africa or Africans.[34] My use of Africanist spirituality also differs from, even as it incorporates, African Derived Religions (ADRs), religions and spiritual practices that were retained and transported during the transatlantic slave trade and evolved through syncretization with Indigenous American beliefs and Christianity in the Americas and the Caribbean. People throughout the African diaspora practice the numerous ADRs, like Obeah, Vodou, Lucumi, Espiritismo, La Regla de Ocha, Candomble, conjure, and others.[35] Though most Black women writers were very conscientious of the many distinctions among ADRs, they usually presented a spiritual paradigm that is an amalgamation of multiple ADRs and other spiritual traditions, including paganism, New Age thought, American Indigenous spiritual beliefs, and African American folk magic like conjure. For instance, Toni Cade Bambara blends and borrows from conjure, mysticism, nature reverence, and metaphysics to craft and conceive the spiritual system(s) practiced in *The Salt Eaters*.[36] Therefore, I identify the spirituality in Black women's writing as Africanist to allow for the creative license Black women take in their written portrayals of these spiritual systems and to respect how Africanist spiritual practices have had to adapt in the US context. As Kameelah L. Martin clarifies in regards to Vodou and Voodoo in *Envisioning Black Feminist Voodoo Aesthetics* (2016), American Voodoo differs from Haitian Vodou because "Protestant intolerance" in the Americas resulted in a "[. . .] process of syncretization . . . leaving the organized practice of African religions more watered down." This distinction, for Martin, ". . . symbolizes the cultural erosion the religion has suffered on American soil."[37] In other words, as a (Protestant) settler colony, white, Indigenous, and Black folks were in a proximity that increased white surveillance of Black populations, forcing enslaved Black folks to use more covert means of hiding their traditional African beliefs and practices. While many practices were retained, they were so hidden by the cover of Christian beliefs as to have conscious awareness of their presence erased.[38] By using Africanist, I attempt to capture the African influence on these spiritual ideas and practices while acknowledging how Black women's will to self-define shapes their understanding of these practices as well as the necessary transformations they have had to undergo in an American context.

In Black women's writing, Africanist spiritual systems are especially important because they house, transmit, and therefore connect Black people in the US to African history and culture, knowledge Black people have been vehemently denied. Africanist spirituality allowed the revolutionary and militant generation of post-1970s writers to preserve the primacy of Spirit in their lives without internalizing narratives meant to reify racial oppression. Africanist spirituality particularly connected Black women writers to legacies of folk healing traditions that centered, uplifted, and empowered Black women, such as Black women herbalists and midwives. As Judylyn S. Ryan affirms, "Spirituality . . . is the foundation on which the Black woman artist constructs her vision of empowerment."[39] For instance, Alice Walker's early interventions of race into feminist theory, Womanism, is now largely associated with Black feminist theological theories and praxis. Throughout *In Search of Our Mothers' Gardens,* Walker invokes, nurtures, welcomes, celebrates, and seeks solace in the Spirit. Indeed, a womanist "Loves the Spirit."[40] Scholars of spirituality and Black women's literature such as Akasha Gloria Hull, Houston A. Baker, Gloria Wade-Gayles, Elizabeth J. West, Georgene Montgomery, Judylyn Ryan, and Kameelah L. Martin all identify Africanist spirituality as central to Black women's literary tradition. In this tradition, Africanist spirituality is presented as a wellspring of self-and-communal knowledge. It is a way of knowing and being in the world. It is a source of power and empowerment.

In contemporary Black women's writing, Africanist spirituality is key to understanding their representations of disability and healing. Central to these is an Africanist understanding of the self as the interrelation of body, mind, and spirit. In Africanist cosmologies, there is no separation of the three. What affects one affects all. While disability studies scholars like Margaret Price and Sami Schalk have made important interventions in the relatedness of the body and mind, the bodymind,[41] this figuration is inadequate to interpret illness, physical difference, and wellness in Black women's writing because it fails to account for the spirit. Therefore, I use the term *bodymindspirit* to capture the interrelatedness of all three aspects of identity. I draw on M. Jacqui Alexander's assertion that "[since] body is not body alone but rather one element in the triad of mind, body, and spirit, what we need to understand is how such embodiment provides the moorings for a subjectivity that knits together these very elements."[42] I join a small collection of activist and academic writers like Alexander and Chicana literature scholar Christina Garcia Lopez, who use the word bodymindspirit to discuss the three as entangled in Black and other women of color's subject formation.[43]

The Africanist understanding of the interconnectedness of bodymindspirit shapes Black women writer's understanding of illness, injury, and disability, as well as wellness and healing. Moreover, Africanist paradigms of the bodymindspirit also view the individual bodymindspirit as connected with those in the entire community. Consequently, sickness in the body is also understood as sickness in the mind and soul. Furthermore, the sickness may be *in* the body, but not *of* the body. Instead, the origin of dis-ease in the bodymindspirit is likely an effect of dis-ease in the community, or a combination of personal and interpersonal discord. Within this paradigm, the sharp divisions between body and mind, individual and society, material and spiritual are absent. In Black women's writing, for instance, illness and injury affect body, mind, and spirit. Moreover, conditions of the bodymindspirit are usually caused by interpersonal conflict or, and especially, as a consequence of misogynoir: communal sources of dis-ease are usually tied to social injustices like state violence, environmental racism, gender violence. When one or more elements of the bodymindspirit are neglected or injured and harmed by social injustices, they cause physical, psychic, and spiritual discord in Black women's lives and their surrounding communities. In coming to understand the source of dis-ease, Africanist spiritual healing practitioners not only ask "*How* it happened but also *why*."[44] As such, Black women writers reject as inadequate traditional biomedical health care because it fails to address the entire bodymindspirit and both the individual and community. In fact, it is often a hostile and dangerous space to Black bodymindspirits as a location of systemic and institutionalized racism. Instead, Black women writers represent collaborations between Africanist healing practices, such as herbal remedies, midwifery, rootwork, conjure, laying on of hands, and mysticism of real, mythologized, deified, and imagined powerful Black women, and, at times, when appropriate, biomedicine. For instance, in *The Salt Eaters*, Velma's psychiatric distress is as much a part of her neurodivergency as it is a result of misogynoir and discord in the Black community. Velma's dis-ease is not only felt in her bodymindspirit but also throughout the Black and person of color community in which she is connected. It literally shakes the earth. Her distress is related to changes to the natural environment, as if a storm were coming. This storm, as well as Velma's distress, is also connected to an approaching cosmic shift. Black doctors, prayer warriors, and a midwife, psychic, rootworker, and conjure woman must work together to heal the multiple and dynamic sources of Velma's dis-ease. Just as the community comes together for Velma's healing, as she heals, Velma is, in turn, responsible for healing the community. In the words of Velma's godmother, Sophie, "And did you think your life is yours alone to do with as you please? That I, your folks, your family, and all who care for you have no say-so in the matter? Whop!"[45]

Black women writers not only draw on Africanist spirituality to understand and diagnose illness and dis-ease, but they also use it to understand and define healing, wellness, and wholeness. In Black women's writing, healing is a process, a journey that cares for, (re)balances, and sutures body, mind, and spirit. Although disability studies scholars have been suspicious of the discourse of healing for its relationship to medicalized concepts of cure, attention to race requires, as Michelle Jarman argues, "a more nuanced engagement between disability and healing."[46] For instance, the goal of healing in Africanist spirituality is not necessarily being cured as the absence of disability. For one, as scholars of African-derived and African American folk religions observe, "differently shaped bodies, sometimes deemed a 'deformity' in Western eyes, might instead be considered spiritually meaningful."[47] In some Africanist spiritual systems, disability does not always signal deficiency. This argument is supported by the presence of disabled deities, ancestors, and spirits in various African-derived religions. For instance, the *lwa* Eshu, a trickster, is said to have one leg, and Audre Lorde identifies with the one-breasted goddess Seboulisa. Furthermore, the presence of disabled deities destabilizes the concept of ability in humans within these spiritual systems because there is a close connection between the bodies of people and the physical characteristics of spirits. When a spirit chooses a practitioner, they often possess, or "mount," that practitioner, and that person takes on the characteristics, including gender and disabilities, of the deity. As Omise'eke Tinsley notes, deities not only "activate" the soul but also the body, "[so] now regardless of skin color, age, genitalia, or ability, when the servitors enter into trance, their body *is* temporarily that of the lwa (Vodou deities)."[48] Able-bodied people can, momentarily, take on the disabilities of the Orishas. We see this in Nalo Hopkinson's *Brown Girl in the Ring* when the protagonist's grandmother goes from having two legs to taking on the differently limbed embodiment of the Orisha Osain. Within African cosmologies, Gender nor ability are static. Moreover, Africanist spirituality troubles the Western concept of health as a (moralized) attribute, one that can be lost but should be attained again. Instead, as Stephanie Y. Mitchem proposes, "In African American communities, 'wellness' may be a better descriptive term to use with discussing the aims of families and individuals in healing processes as opposed to the term 'health.' Wellness implies a temporary condition rather than a possession.... 'Wellness' references activity and goals rather than a finished product that is a commodity."[49] Healing is and emphasizes practice and process without expectation of a return to "health" and able-bodiedness. The bodymindspirit is always in flux, in the process of becoming. Black women writers turn to Africanist spiritual cosmologies' flexibility to imagine healing and wholeness as inclusive of disability. If, as Sami Schalk argues, Black women change the rules of reality,[50] then Africanist spiritual practices and beliefs are the brick and mortar, the building materials that make up these new worlds.

That Black women in a largely US context craft Africanist spiritual systems influenced by African-derived religions that allow them to embrace disability in their work does not mean they reflect contemporary views of disability across the African continent. There are many cultures on the continent, and many of these cultures circulate ableist, harmful views of disability and often use spirituality to justify such views, especially in the postcolonial era.[51] Indeed, many scholars link violence against disabilities to religion.[52] For instance, a popular precolonial origin myth for disabilities is that the Orisha Obatala, drunken on palm wine, created disabled people. While this is commonly viewed as a mistake, he is the patron of disabled people who takes special care of them. Rather than see this as a cause to disdain disabilities, as Mary Nyangweso argues, "... the purpose of the story alludes to the reality of imperfection in this world and how imperfections are sometimes expressed in physical disabilities. The moral teaching in the narrative is about the acceptance of imperfections since God is on the side of all."[53] Precolonial Indigenous African religions "inherently glorified and/or approved disability."[54] Contemporary treatment of disabled people does not represent the value of disabled people in Indigenous African spirituality.

Although scholars of Christian theology and disability have started to strive for an inclusive, liberatory theology of disability,[55] Africanist spiritual paradigms of disability differ from the (Christian) religious models of disability. The religious model understood the presence of disability as a comment on one's morality; it is a punishment for sin, a marker that one has separated oneself from the divine. As Henry Stiker argues, disability demarked the limits of the sacred from the profane, with disability squarely in the realm of the profane, as an issue of man, not of God.[56] Early in the Judaic tradition, the ill and diseased were ostracized and cast out of the community, particularly from holy spaces, as with lepers.[57] With the advent of Christianity and the example of Jesus, healing focused on curing the body as evidence of God's power and grace. While the Enlightenment shifted explanations of disability away from religion to science, the religious model of disability and its focus on the individual's body as aberrant and wrong and in need of healing as the absence of disability persists and moreover set the foundation for the medical model.[58] Alternatively, the religious model has also positioned disability as a blessing. While this facet of the religious model of disability has the potential to move toward a liberatory theology of disability, it falls short in that it aligns disability with suffering.[59] Although some early Christian writers express spiritual ecstasy in what others have read as madness, these writers are denied spiritual authority because of their supposed madness and/or gender. In other words, they are not considered representative of the church. Rather, in the religious model, disability is a blessing because it is through physical suffering that one becomes spiritually refined or pure. An off branch of this logic is the infantilization of disabled people as inherently good and godly because of their supposed eternal childlike state. Though they may be physically limited and suffering on earth, they are promised able-embodiment in the kingdom of Heaven.

Whereas other scholars of Black women's writing interpret dis-ease and spiritual healing metaphorically, as we see in Gay Wilentz's *Healing Narratives* and Donna Weir-Soley's *Eroticism, Spirituality, and Resistance in Black Women's Writing*,[60] in *Refusing to Be Made Whole*, I read illness, disease, dis-ease, and disability as well as healing as both metaphor and material. Moreover, I am interested in African spirituality not only as a literary trope and device, but also relevant to the private lives of the Black women writers. Disability studies scholarship has tended to critique the use of disabled characters as tropes, metaphors, and literary devices. Disability presented as such has tended to represent disabled characters as stereotypical, flat, and dispensable. Disability in these works fail to represent the lived reality and concerns of disabled people. Disability in Black women's writing has been critiqued on these grounds.

However, as Sami Schalk argues in *Bodyminds Reimagined*, "disability can take on both metaphorical and material meaning in a text." Additionally, "[reading] for both the metaphorical and material significance of disability in a text allows us to trace the ways discourses of (dis)ability, race, and gender do not merely intersect at the site of multiply marginalized people, but also how these systems collude or work in place of one another."[61] Building on this, I contend that in the worlds of the various texts by Black women writers, disability and spiritual realities are both metaphor and material.

That said, a quick note on genre. It could be said that *Refusing to Be Made Whole* is a book that analyzes Black speculative fiction. The ghosts, *loa*, orisha, and magic in most of the books I discuss seem to invite readings of them as fantasy or magical realism. Kinitra Brooks argues that Black women write across genres such as horror, science-fiction, etc., what she terms fluid fiction, and Sami Schalk and Therí Pickens have both published books that approach Black women's speculative fiction from a Black disability studies frame.[62] This book is indebted to their work. I, however, choose not to position these writings as speculative fiction largely because the African-derived spiritualities represent cosmologies, ontologies, and epistemologies that, although present a different reality than what is generally accepted as plausible or possible, are nevertheless a reality and within the realm of possibility for the cultures out of which Black women write, the worldview of their readership, as well as some of the Black writers themselves. As Toni Morrison explains, "My own use of enchantment simply comes because that's the way the world was for me and the black people I knew."[63] While Black women writers may use Africanist cosmologies as a literary trope and political metaphor, and though they may take much creative license and liberty in their representations of these spiritual systems, to consider the world of the Spirit as speculative in Black women's essay, life-writing, or fiction would be, for me, to dismiss—and diss—Black people's discredited knowledge. This does not mean that some of the novels here cannot be considered speculative fiction; I just refrain from doing so here.

Moreover, this choice acknowledges that for Black women writers, like Toni Cade Bambara, to name just one, there is, indeed, a world of the Spirit that interacts with and shapes the world of the flesh. Scholars avoid talking about Black women's and other women of color's spiritual beliefs and practices because, as AnaLouise Keating notes of Gloria Anzaldúa's spiritual activism, academia is an antispiritual space. Academics are spirit-phobic (this, of course, excludes the covert-ish institutionalization of Western [white] Christianity).[64] I argue that academia's spirit-phobia is rooted in a sanist commitment to reason and rationality that is fundamentally anti-Black.[65] Black women writers were cognizant and wary of how sanism could be used to discredit and/or further marginalize them. In Akasha Gloria Hull's *Soul Talk: The New Spirituality of African American Women* (2001), many of the writers she interviews, like Lucille Clifton, state that they feared attributions of mental disability—being called crazy—because they believed in spirits, ghosts, signs, premonitions, and the like.[66] These women recognized that the label "crazy" has been mobilized against Black people, particularly Black political and aesthetic revolutionaries, to present Black folk as violent, untrustworthy, and socially abject.[67] This is particularly troublesome in a climate where Black women are presented as always already mad—mad as both irrational and deviantly angry.[68] However, not taking Black women's spirituality seriously limits our understanding of Black women writers' works and politics. As Hull argues, Black women writers are deeply invested in the spiritual and its political efficacy.[69] Connection to the spiritual invigorated and inspired Black women's political mobilization. In analyzing Black women's fiction, life-writing, and essay, I hope to underscore the political and practical impetus and implications of Africanist spiritual paradigms of embodiment have for their imagined audience, which, as Valerie Lee compellingly argues, includes readers and the writers themselves.

Indeed, writers like Toni Cade Bambara, June Jordan, and Audre Lorde all recount moments where they (re)turn to their writing for healing. While I try to avoid reading literary works biographically, I do want to join Lee in emphasizing the centrality of writing as a healing event for Black women. In Africanist spiritual cosmologies, words have power, life force. *Nommo*. Black women writers, as M. Jacqui Alexander contends, ". . . share the belief in the power of spoken medicine, the power of utterance, the literal understanding of Ashé, which means 'so be it.'"[70] Black women writers usher *nommo* to transform the act of reading their writing into what Lee calls healing events. Black women writers are "sistah conjurers." As Lee outlines, a "sistah-conjurer" is someone who "uses storytelling as a curative domain." For sistah conjurers, "conjuring up stories [is] necessary for their psychic survival;" therefore, these writers "[spin] a story as a healing event."[71] This is both related to and distinct from theories of narrative healing as understood within the medical humanities. For these academics, narratives are used to understand patient perspectives of their illness to make treatment plans that take cultural perspectives into account. Sistah conjurers "live in conjure" and "speak a 'conjure discourse.'"[72] Black women writers do not translate the beliefs and cultures of Black folks to white medical institutions to help develop biomedical treatment, though, as Ann Folwell Stanford's work demonstrates, this work can certainly help to improve biomedicine.

As sistah conjurers, Black women writers speak healing and wellness into their readers' lives and their own.

Dissembling Narrative Wholeness: Disability and Black Women's Writing Aesthetic

In *Refusing to Be Made Whole*, I not only argue that Black women writers turn to Africanist spiritual knowledge to understand and represent becoming disabled, healing, and wholeness, but disability also informs the aesthetic practices that have come to characterize Black women's writing. The novel, as literary disability studies scholar Lennard J. Davis contends, is a genre that reifies normalcy—bodily and generic.[73] However, this assessment doesn't account for how the intersections of race, gender, and disability impact one's writing aesthetic. The novel as reproducing normalcy is a white aesthetic practice. As Karla F.C. Holloway argues, "The search for wholeness characterizes the critical enterprise within Western cultures. It represents a sensibility that privileges the recovery of an individual (and independent) text over its fragmented textual dimensions."[74] Black women's writing, however, "dissembles" this quest for wholeness.[75] Whereas Western, white fiction mobilizes the novel in service of ableist normalizing processes through its insistence on linearity, progress toward conflict resolution, and a return to a mythical stasis or wholeness, Black women's writing refuses to be made whole.

Instead of wholeness, Black women's writing aesthetic seeks to embrace Otherness and fragmentation. In "Speaking in Tongues" (1989), for instance, Mae Gwendolyn Henderson argues that "[w]hat is at once characteristic and suggestive about black women's writing is its interlocutory, or dialogic, character, reflecting not only a relationship with the 'other (s),' but an internal dialogue with the plural aspects of self that constitute the matrix of black female subjectivity. . . . What distinguishes black women's writing, then, is the privileging (rather than repressing) of 'the other in ourselves.'"[76] Moreover, Black women writers do not try to present the self-as-Other as a cohesive identity. As Elizabeth Alexander argues of Audre Lorde, Lorde does not create a whole self but instead allows the fragmentary aspects of her identity to remain together in tension. It is out of this fragmented, embodied identity that Lorde writes. Lorde "choose[s] corporeal language to articulate what she could not previously put into words."[77] Consequently, Alexander contends, "The African-American woman's body in Lorde's work—specifically, her own body—becomes a map of lived experience and a way of printing suffering as well as joy upon the flesh."[78] Black, female subjectivity—both suffering and joy—are inscribed on the flesh and articulated in Black women's writing through the flesh. This writing understands enfleshed identity as "fundamentally collaged" and "overlapping and discernibly dialogic."[79] The fragmented bodymindspirit, in Black women's writing, impacts the form and aesthetic—the shape—of Black women's narrative.[80]

The shape of Black women's writing, embodied aesthetics, results in a novel aesthetic that, as Gayl Jones, a prolific novelist herself, contends, "revise[s] (or rewrite[s]) genre, characterization, style, theme, structure, viewpoint, values." Black women's novels are comfortable with "[paradox] and ambivalence." Black women's writing may "support or challenge your sense of logic or rationality;" however, "depending on who you are," you may experience Black women's novels as "full of contradictions."[81] Analyzing Octavia E. Butler's oeuvre, Therí A. Pickens explicitly links disability as informative of Black women's writing. Specifically, Pickens argues that the aesthetic practice of penning "open-ended conclusions that frustrate the narrative cohesion associated with the novel form, intricate depictions of power that potentially alienate the able-bodied reader, and contained literary chaos that upends the idea of ontological fixity" reflect Black women's engagements with the intersections of race, class, gender, and disability in their work.[82] In *Refusing to Be Made Whole*, I identify moments in Black women's writing that reflect these outlined aesthetic practices, as well as draw attention to additional ones. In Black women's writing, the interconnections of disability and Africanist spirituality in Black literature and culture result in aesthetic and formal elements that disable narrative.

As such, I identify contemporary Black women's writing and, specifically, the elements of Black culture that they incorporate into their aesthetic, such as root work, as Black cultural locations of disability. Black cultural locations of disability is a concept that merges two seemingly conflicting theories of disability in the cultural imagination and lives of disabled people. Disability Studies scholars Sharon Snyder and David T. Mitchell theorize cultural locations of disability as spaces where disabled people are siloed, such as nursing homes, psychiatric institutions, and rehabilitation centers, that produce an overabundance of writing about disabled people that shapes our cultural understanding of disability. Although disabled people can come together in community in these spaces, they have no control over their narrative as the archive of disability knowledge emerges most often through medicalized documents about disabled people for the consumption of the able-bodied populace. Disability culture, on the other hand, wrests representational power away from the able-bodied hegemony and is instead wielded by the self-forged communities of disabled folk who create disability art and culture that liberates disability from ableist narratives of tragedy and suffering and celebrates disability as a political and cultural identity. Examples of disability culture are the Society for Disability Studies's Annual Convention Dance or the productions created by crip performing arts troupe Sins Invalid. The enmeshed yet uneasy history of Blackness and disability results in Black cultural spaces best understood as constantly shifting and vacillating between these two poles. Black cultural locations of disability speak to the aesthetic practices informed by Black folks' often violently shaped disabled bodymindspirits. Black folk culture created in Black communities of the Jim Crow South, such as blues music and quilting, or even the Black women's health activism that fills the absences, gaps, and silences on Black women's wellness, are Black cultural locations of disability. Contemporary Black women write of, and out of, these spaces on the margins of society to archive and contribute to this rich archive of Black cripistemologies.

Chapter Breakdown

In each chapter, I address a prominent critical discourse within Black feminist literary studies through the intersecting lens of Africanist spirituality, race, gender, class, and disability. In each chapter, I examine a mix of Black women's essays, life writing, and fiction for how race, gender, disability, class, and sexuality emerge as both thematic and aesthetic concerns. Specifically, I refresh conversations about representation, community, motherhood, and sexuality by approaching them through a Black feminist disability studies framework. Black women authors as diverse in style as Gayl Jones is to Alice Walker present violent misogynoir as debilitating to Black women's bodymindspirits. Although these characters seek to start the healing process, healing and wholeness as the absence of disability is not the result or the goal. Drawing on Africanist spirituality, Black women writers reimagine wellness. What results is a text that dissembles narrative wholeness.

In the first chapter, I take on questions of testifying and bearing witness in Black women's writing. In this chapter, I argue that Black women's will to self-define is in tension with the political imperative to bear witness to Black life. Through addressing issues of disabling histories, self-representation, and mental disability in Gayl Jones's *Corregidora* and *Eva's Man*, I identify how Black folk cultures provide the means for Black women to hold both imperatives—testifying and bearing witness—in tension. By reading Black blues culture as a Black cultural location of disability, which draws on theories of disability culture and cultural locations of disability, I contend that Jones incorporates mental disability and the disability aesthetics of blues culture to produce what I consider a disabled text. In *Corrigedora*, Ursa Corregidora draws on her experience of becoming disabled by ongoing histories of racialized gender violence to empower her blues song as an alternative means of bearing witness to history while also testifying to her own truth. Whereas *Corregidora*'s concern is the blues singer, *Eva's Man* focuses on the blues listener. By modeling blues listening, Eva Medina Canada demonstrates ways of bearing witness to those whose bodymindspirits fail or refuse to testify in normative modes. Jones's disabled novels raise questions and conflicts about the limits of representation and who represents whom, revealing the limits of Black feminism's engagement with questions of representation.

In Chapter 2, "Black Community, Crip Communities of Care," I identify the conflict between testifying and self-definition and bearing witness as reflective of larger issues of gender and Black community. Specifically, I take up contemporary Black women's critique of hypermasculinity in Black nationalist discourse on the Black community. Turning to Alice Walker's *Meridian* and Toni Morrison's *Paradise*, I argue that heterosexist masculinity robs Black nationalist understandings of community of care. This lack of care results in disabling violence against Black women's bodymindspirit experience with illness. Healing, for both the individual and the community, begins as Black women reimagine the community through care work and interdependence as understood in Africanist and Indigenous American spiritual thought.

In Cripping Motherhood, I analyze motherhood and disability in Sarah E. Wright's *This Child's Gonna Live* (1969), Octavia Butler's *Parable of the Sower* (1993) and *Parable of the Talents* (1998), and Sapphire's *Push* (1996) to argue that motherhood empowers disability identity and the reverse. Building on Patricia Hill Collins's and bell hooks's theories of Black motherhood, I also reveal that ableism alongside racism and sexism inform controlling images about Black motherhood and collude to present barriers to Black mothering. Although the Black church disempowers Black motherhood in *This Child's Gonna Live*, the Africanist and cripistemology of Earthseed in *Parable of the Sower* and *Parable of the Talents* plants the seed for world liberation. Therefore, while Black mothers don't always achieve maternal agency, disabled motherhood, as a healing practice and epistemology, is empowering. Wright, Butler, and Sapphire portray disabled mothers who nurture and fight for the survival of their children and community.

In my fourth chapter, I approach Alice Walker's *By the Light of My Father's Smile* through Audre Lorde's essay "The Uses of the Erotic: The Erotic as Power," which I position as a queercrip theory of the Spirit. In so doing, I address the problematics of Black women's sexuality, mainly how sexual violence and respectability have limited Black women's sexual agency and thwarted Black women's sexual subjectivity. Black women writers, however, turn to Africanist spirituality to shift the conversation around Black women's sexuality to not only focus on violence but also include pleasure. Through *By the Light*, I demonstrate that Black women's writing, the erotic and the divine, are often violently severed in ways detrimental to Black women's wellbeing. Healing in these works involves a return to Africanist spiritual beliefs that respect and honor the erotic as an affective and spiritual onto-epistemology.

I conclude *Refusing to Be Made Whole* through a meditation on Black crip survival in the face and fact of Black death. In this final chapter, I ask what gets erased and rendered invisible in the overwhelming focus on deathly violence against Black bodymindspirits. I argue we lose Black queercrip survival. We miss moments in Black cultural production that represent and embrace Black aliveness, no matter how brief. Moreover, I illustrate how Black women use Africanist cosmological understandings of life continuing from the material world into the spiritual. This is not to suggest that there is no need to contest deathly violence against Black life. Instead, this is to celebrate Black livingness and detail how Black women consider the fight for Black aliveness even in the face of physical death. Drawing on Afrofuturism and crip technoscience, I argue that Black women's writing and theory serve as a crip technoscience of the Spirit, a queercrip spiritual technology, that enables writers like Toni Cade Bambara and Audre Lorde, who, when faced with their own mortality, had to redefine what futurity looked like for Black women, including themselves, and redefine winning in the war against debilitating and lethal anti-Blackness.

Chapter 1

If I am Crazy, Can I Be of Sound Mind?

Representation, Disability, and Black Women's Novel Aesthetic

One of the most common themes taken up in contemporary Black women's writing and the concomitant body of literary criticism is representation.[1] As Cheryl Wall asserts, Black women's writing has been "preoccupied" with questions of representation, and questions and debates over representation have characterized the canon of African American literary criticism from its inception.[2] In her foundational book *Black Feminist Thought*, Patricia Hill Collins argues that Black women have relied on collective self-definition to counter-hegemonic "controlling images" that circulate about them, such as the Mammy, Jezebel, and Sapphire stereotypes.[3] Often, Black women have been tasked with or have felt pressure to positively represent the race as corrections to these and other racial stereotypes used to justify marginalization, surveillance, and control of Black life and violence against Black bodies. For many others, this has meant representing Black women and Black people as the intricate and multifarious beings that they are. In other words, Black women reject the narratives created and widely circulated by and for others to instead define and share how they view and understand themselves, how they experience life, and who they aspire to be. As Collins asserts, "U.S. Black women intellectuals have long explored this private, hidden space of Black women's consciousness, the 'inside' ideas that allow Black women to cope with and, in many cases, transcend the confines of intersecting oppressions of race, class, gender, and sexuality."[4]

This will to self-define characterizes Black women's writing even as it at times conflicts with bearing witness and testifying to collective experiences of racial subjugation.[5] As part of the cultural work of Black movements for civil rights, writers have borne witness to the injuries and injustices wrought by anti-Black racism. For contemporary Black women writers, however, this also involves testifying on how anti-Black racism and white supremacy inflame heterosexist violence. Black, mostly male, creators and critics, however, castigated these cultural producers, from N'tozake Shange to Toni Morrison, for theorizing and speaking on the long-repressed variegated truths of their experience of sharing community with men who cope with racism through heterosexist violence. Yet, as Ann duCille so incisively reminds us: Black male novelists had already begun to lay bare these secrets, but without the vitriolic backlash. "Phallic" or "masculinist" interpretive strategies, as duCille identifies them, metaphorize and thus render invisible the gender violence portrayed in Black men's writing.[6] Many of these same critics failed to reprimand other Black male writers who penned violent characters or comment on the portrayal of gratuitous violence against women. Richard Wright's Bigger Thomas rapes and murders Bessie, his Black girlfriend, and Ralph Ellison's Jim Trueblood rapes his daughter Mattie Lou—both without commentary. Some celebrated Eldridge Cleaver's gall as he exclaimed, "I became a rapist. To refine my technique and modus operandi, I started out by practicing on black girls in the ghetto . . . and when I considered myself smooth enough, I crossed the tracks and sought out white prey."[7] Yet Black women have been venomously accused of airing Black folks' dirty laundry.

Further complicating the matter of representation and self-definition has been sanism or discrimination against those deemed crazy or mentally ill. Western society demands rationality and Reason as a prerequisite to credibly articulating one's experience and subjectivity, yet women of all races, Black people of all genders, and queer folks of all races and genders have all been renounced as lacking rationality and/or Reason or outright being reduced to a mental illness. Thus, positioning Black people as crazy, mentally unsound or unfit, or as paranoid, and the like, has been a strategic mode of casting doubt on Black testimonies of injustice and expressions of pain. The fact that the very modality of social change that Black folks engage in is pathologized in a sanist society has exerted pressure on many Black activists, intellectuals, and scholars to distance Black people from labels of mental inferiority even as they address the deleterious effects racism has on the Black psyche. Others have leaned into Black madness as a pathological consequence of anti-Black racism that suggests the veracity of hegemonic representations of Black deviance as they seek to compassionately explain it.

Both affirming Black women's experiences of the world and improving their mental health have been a foci of Black women's health activism. Writers from Bebe Moore Campbell to N'tozake Shange have advocated through their prose and activism for greater access to mental health resources while trying to destigmatize the use of mental health care. Black women writers have also noted the harms perpetuated by the psychiatric industrial complex. In addition to addressing Black people's experiences with mental health care, Black women writers have theorized the inherent ableism embedded with sexism and racism used to silence or discredit Black women's testimony, disparage Black women's control over their subjectivity, and justify injuring Black women's bodymindspirits. For instance, their writing reveals the sanism inherent in the controlling images of the Mammy, Jezebel, and Sapphire. As I will discuss in chapter three, the Mammy is often represented as slow-witted. The Jezebel is figured as incapable of making reasonable decisions about her sexuality,[8] and the Sapphire is irrationally angry and aggressive. These figures are deviant according to white, heterosexist norms in part because of their supposed inability to perform and maintain proper affective states. This is exemplified, for instance, when Eva Medina Canada from Gayl Jones's *Eva's Man* recognizes that she is treated as sexually disposable and irreparably crazy because people use the Jezebel figure as shorthand for her personality.

Indeed, Gayl Jones is among those Black women writers who comments on the psychiatric industrial complex and is interested in exploring the psychological consequences of racism. As Cassey Clabough has highlighted, Jones's early fiction particularly takes on Black madness as a theme. In this chapter, I discuss how Jones embraces madness as an onto-epistemological standpoint for the will to self-define and challenges readers to divest from able-mindedness and rationality and create multiple, accessible ways of showing up and bearing witness to Black life.

Published at the tail-end of the Black Arts Movement, Gayl Jones's *Corregidora* and, to a greater extent, *Eva's Man* appeared to defy injunctions to represent the race positively and challenge debasing stereotypical representations of Black women. Indeed, in a *New York Times* review, June Jordan reproached *Eva's Man* for spreading "sinister misinformation about women—about women, in general, about black women in particular, and especially about young black girls forced to deal with the sexual, molesting violations of their minds and bodies by their fathers, their mothers' boyfriends, their cousins and uncles."[9] I argue that the critical responses to Jones's work, as well as the writing itself, reveal a tension between the will to self-define and the pressure to sympathetically and generously represent and bear witness to Black life. Complicating this conflict is how Black affect and thought are regularly dismissed as irrational—a point underscored by the two "mad" protagonists of Jones's novels. In other words, able-mindedness through the demonstration of rational thought is considered a prerequisite for self-representation. Those deemed mentally disabled or mad have their experiences invalidated and voided. The mad can be and are spoken for and are objects of discourse, but they can never be the creator or subject of their own self-fashioning. This is especially the case with *Eva's Man*, which garners a shorter reading precisely because I want to avoid the traditional sanist methods used to examine the work (and also because it's such a damn difficult text to write about—perhaps intentionally so). These two early novels explore the limits of representing the race and history, embrace madness as an onto-epistemological standpoint for the will to self-define, and challenge readers to divest from able-mindedness and rationality and create multiple accessible ways of showing up and bearing witness to Black life.

I first flesh this out through returning to readings of history, trauma, melancholy, and witnessing in *Corregidora*. By reading for disability as well as reading through disability, I demonstrate how we can not only read the protagonist as a disabled character but also read the novel as a disabled text. I identify the African American vernacular tradition of the blues as a cultural location of disability that offers a chance for healing despite the lack of a cure. I then go on to analyze madness, representation, and witnessing in *Eva's Man*. In this short section, this note, really, I extend my discussion of disabled texts, arguing that *Eva's Man* is a disabled novel that has been subject to sanist analysis of its main character and content. Although many critics dismiss the generative potential of Eva Medina Canada and/or *Eva's Man* (the pressure to be generative is ableist itself), I contend that Eva provides a model of blues listening, a modality of witnessing that does not demand reason, sanity, or even articulation from its subject.

What did I do to Be so Black and Blue: The Disabled Blues Novel in Gayl Jones's Corregidora

Corregidora is a story of historical and personal injury and healing told from the first-person perspective of Ursa Corregidora, a Kentuckian blues singer during the mid-twentieth century. Ursa's story begins after Mutt Thomas, her first husband, accosts her in a jealous, drunken rage, causing her to fall down cement steps, miscarry, and undergo an emergency hysterectomy. Throughout the novel, Ursa struggles to feel whole, particularly within a matrilineal context where "making generations" has been key to cultural remembering.

Ursa's great-grandmother and grandmother refuse to allow officials to burn away their stories of sexual subjugation and torment at the hands of Simon Corregidora, a Brazilian slaver and brothel owner, with other official documentation of slavery in Brazil. Thus, they birth (girl) children who bear witness to their history of subjugation and abuse and whose very bodies are an archive of slavery's violence. However, Ursa can no longer reproduce children as witnesses to this history; moreover, Great Gram's and Gram's stories vicariously traumatize Ursa. As a consequence, Ursa experiences physically, emotionally, and spiritually debilitating symptoms. Although she is infertile and finds intimacy and communication difficult, Ursa nevertheless forges a new mode of bearing witness to her family's history that also allows her to voice the truth of her own experiences and fashion a subjectivity of her own design. While there is no indication or suggestion that Ursa is cured, the novel does suggest she experiences a period of healing by reconciling other people's expectations of her with who she was and is becoming. She redefines what wholeness means to her. History may mark Ursa's bodymindspirit, but navigating an altered way of being in the world challenges Ursa to imagine creative, nonreproductive paths of reconciling with histories of violence that break rather than reproduce the cycle of trauma.

It is generally accepted that *Corregidora* is a blues novel concerned with memory, history, and trauma.[10] *Corregidora* has inspired a body of creative and critical interpretations of how Black women writers and Jones, in particular, tackles issues of historical trauma writ on the body and mind.[11] That many *Corregidora* scholars approach the novel through psychoanalysis as a theoretical frame suggests that they recognize how Ursa's traumatic experience wreaks havoc on her mental state.[12] Casey Clabough's research on Jones's body of work quite adeptly notes that Jones used her early fiction to explore her interest in "abnormal psychology and mental illness" and how those interests "often intersect with her references to the history of slavery in the Americas."[13] By approaching these themes through a Black feminist disability perspective, I demonstrate that Ursa's psychic trauma is not merely a metaphor for violent histories but how those pasts materially impact Black people's experience of their bodymindspirit.[14] I connect Ursa's journey toward self-determination and the barriers she meets in doing so as a mentally disabled person with the continued effects of slavery's afterlives have on the wellbeing of Black folk.[15] I understand Ursa's healing process and redefinition of wholeness, particularly within and through the blues, as indicative of how disability aesthetics underpin the formation of Black literary and cultural products in service of facilitating healing experiences informed by Africanist paradigms of wellness.

Birthing Hysteria: Trauma as Disability and Mad Witnessing

Contemporary Black women's writing underscores that disability is cultural, social, and political; it's fluid and contextual. In *Corregidora*, for example, Ursa is physically and psychically injured and scarred by patriarchal violence. For Ursa, Mutt's act of domestic abuse results in a loss of physical capacity and a change in psychic wellness: after her emergency hysterectomy, she can no longer have children, which contributes to and intensifies trauma-induced moments of impaired cognitive and affective functioning. Ursa's injuries are disabling within a culture that exalts reason and affective restraint and values women for their sexuality and ability to reproduce. For Ursa, the latter is particularly salient in the wake of violent cultural and familial histories that result in compulsory childbearing. In other words, Ursa occupies familial and cultural milieus that expect her bodymindspirit to think and perform in a way it no longer can; within this context, Ursa experiences her injuries as disabling. And, while not always true for people who undergo changes in how their bodymindspirit looks or works, Ursa initially experiences disability as distressing. Post hysterectomy, Ursa feels an acute sense of loss and struggles to feel whole. Ursa narrates, "I lay on my back, feeling as if something more than the womb had been taken out."[16] Ursa not only registers her missing organ, but she also senses a more intangible loss, a spiritual loss. At first, Ursa's feelings of emptiness seem to conform to the "figuration of feminine identity as an absence."[17] While this is an understandable reaction to miscarriage and a violent, sudden change in her body, nevertheless, as a textual device, it inadvertently also aligns disability with absence. Yet, *Corregidora* seems to suggest that Ursa's feeling of loss is less rooted in the wounded body and more in what is expected of certain bodies. She expects her value as a potential romantic partner to diminish because she can no longer perform social and cultural scripts for gender norms. She becomes acutely aware of those scripts as she realizes the new framework for her life. For instance, as she tries to plan her immediate postrecovery future, she feels incongruent with this more normative sequence of expectations to return to work, start a new relationship, etc. Within this schema, everyone else is able to perform accordingly except her. Her disability renders her queer, outside of heteronormative temporalities.[18] Ursa's concern that her life is "already marked out" presages how feminist crip studies scholar Alison Kafer introduces her monograph *Feminist, Queer, Crip*: ". . . people have been telling my future for years. . . . my wheelchair, burn scars, and gnarled hands apparently tell them all they need to know. My future is written on my body."[19] Ursa, like Kafer, understands that the disabled body is perceived as a text where one's past, present, and future are predetermined and legibly inscribed. Disability not only "demands a story,"[20] but it prescribes one as well.

Ursa is boxed into rapidly shifting and conflicting narratives about what Black womanhood ought and will mean for her. While all of these narratives announce themselves as self-evident on and through her disabled Black body, Ursa's attempt to place herself within them, to find a place for herself in them, reveals these narratives as both constructed yet materially consequential and as symbolically overdetermined yet empty of representations that ring personally true. Impairment is not a problem of the body to be cured or a problem of plot to be re/solved. Rather, it reveals the plots themselves as "markers so loaded with mythical prepossession that there is no easy way for the agents buried beneath them to come clean."[21]

Yet *Corrigedora* suggests that even if one could "come clean" of the "names by which [they] are called in the public place,"[22] they'd still have to deal with the fleshy reality of the body. Jones's novel seems to insist that Ursa's Black body has a materiality that cannot be evaded. Ursa's elders bank on the persistence and tangibility of enfleshment to stand up against the void created by historical effacement and silence that controlling images come to occupy. Great Gram and Gram tell Ursa that after slavery in Brazil ended, officials "*burned all the slavery papers so it would be like they never had it.*"[23] To resist their violent erasure from history, Great Gram and Gram exhort Ursa to make generations as an alternative archive, one ingrained in the spirit and psyche and preserved in the flesh. Birthing children not only carries on the family lineage but also creates and preserves a body of evidence, pun intended, against a debased society that has attempted to expunge the mar of slavery from the historical archive.

It is Ursa's physical body that speaks to history's wrongs, particularly her long hair. The beauty politics around Black women's hair is quite fraught. Hair that is dark-colored, tightly coiled ("nappy"), and grows out and up instead of down is detested for its distance from the light, straight, and drooping hair that signifies white femininity.[24] Ursa's lighter skin, but particularly her long hair is the materialized trace of Simon's perfidy. Ursa's long hair testifies to "Corregidora's evil" in her.[25] When Ursa is born "baldheaded," Irene believes that Great Gram and Gram hated her despite Ursa's "[white] skin."[26] Hair "like rivers" even more than skin color, for Great Gram and Gram is the physical evidence against Brazilian slavery.[27] Great Gram's and Gram's desire that Corregidora women have long hair speaks to an Africanist spiritual understanding of hair. Hair, like water (rivers), holds memory. Hairstyles, in some West African tribes, locate one in history and culture. One's family, status, gender, spiritual character, and more can be read in the hair.[28] Long hair locates Gram, Irene, and Ursa within a lineage of enslaved mulatto concubines: it hints at the white master as a parent and marks one's potential for sexual slavery as a mulatta.[29] While longer hair within the hierarchical matrixes of white supremacy is valued for its proximity to whiteness, the Corregidora women's emphasis on long hair inverts this logic. They still value long hair for its proximity to whiteness; however, they reconfigure whiteness as "evil" rather than beauty. Great Gram, Gram, and Irene concretize slavery's violence by drawing attention to the visible registers of their mulatta identity, how Simon's brutal sexual assaults to their flesh irrevocably changed the appearance of future generations' bodies. "Great Gram was the coffee-bean woman but the rest of [them] . . ." are not.[30] This rupture in phenotypical presentation is a violent inscription of their (enslaved) Black womanhood. What was meant to be a materialization of their legal and discursive thingafication, however, becomes, for the Corregidora women, the ineradicable and enduring evidence the enslavers wished to destroy. The stories held within the burned documents can be destroyed, but the solidification of discursive difference through and on violated Black bodies cannot. While the Brazilian officials may have burned slavery's paper trail, the Corregidora women's flesh remembers.

This embodied record that the Corregidora women have so carefully gestated and preserved is threatened when Mutt's actions destroy Ursa's ability to continue making generations. The corporeal archive of Simon Corregidora's violence is lost with Ursa's womb. Whereas Great Gram experienced a fundamental embodied transformation into her status as a sex slave when she gives birth to a mulatta, Ursa experiences a similar transformation when her womb is removed, which is made visible by her surgery scar. This transformation in her body radically shifts Ursa's understanding of herself. "Great Gram was the coffee-bean woman . . . But I am different now. . . . I have everything they had, except the generations."[31] Ursa's change in her ability to reproduce both, for her, belies the narrative she "always thought" about herself, that she was different from them, while simultaneously making her different. She is a body of evidence, but she can no longer produce future evidential bodies. Ursa's post-hysterectomy body is not only disabled when held up to the expectations her family has for Corregidora women's bodies, but her inability to meet their charges also disables her family's work of embodied historiography.

And yet, even as the text insists on the materiality of the body, Black being in *Corregidora* is not reduced to the body. Ursa is bodymindspirit. For Great Gram and Gram, the psyche, like the body, is a material component that can also be molded into evidence. Ursa isn't just evidence in the flesh; Great Gram and Gram ensure that historical memory is imprinted on her mind and spirit, too. According to them, "*they can't burn conscious . . . And that's what makes the evidence. And that's what makes the verdict.*"³² It is not enough to have these bodies of evidence. They must have the mind and spirit to go with it. Great Gram and Gram impart this consciousness by bearing witness to Simon's brutality and pass this knowledge to each new generation of Corregidora girls. As Ursa tells Tad, "My great-grandmama told my grandmama the part she lived through that my grandmama didn't live through and my grandmama told my mama what they both lived through and my mama told me what they all lived through and we were suppose to pass it down like that from generation to generation so we'd never forget."³³ Great Gram and Gram rely on the Black oral tradition and the cultural and spiritual work it performs in crafting communal subjectivity to preserve what was so wantonly and easily destroyed in the written word. Specifically, they inhabit the role of Griots, communal storytellers and historians, that are responsible for transmitting a people's genealogical and historical knowledge.³⁴ Griots are essential to cultivating communal identity.³⁵ Great Gram and Gram turn to an Africanist mode of historical documentation to create "consciousness."

Bearing witness to historical injury is a political act. As Kalí Tal argues in her now foundational work on critical trauma studies, "Bearing witness is an aggressive act. It is born out of a refusal to bow to outside pressure to revise or to repress experience . . ."³⁶ Great Gram and Gram refuse to submit to the violent acts of historical erasure perpetuated by the Brazilian government. They refuse to let go of the resentment and rage they feel for Simon Corregidora, and they want each generation to take on and hold that anger until the time comes to hold Simon and the institutions that enabled and supported him accountable. As Tal continues, bearing witness is "a decision to embrace conflict rather than conformity, to endure a lifetime of anger and pain rather than to submit to the seductive pull of revision and repression."³⁷ However, willingness to experience prolonged periods of anger and emotional pain is pathologized in medicalized understandings and expectations of healing. Critical readers of *Corregidora* have recognized Great Gram's and Gram's and particularly Ursa's emotional pain as a symptom of trauma incurred from Simon's sexual violence and, for Ursa, Mutt's domestic violence. Joanne Lipson Freed, Elizabeth Swanson Goldberg, Jennifer Griffiths, and Stephanie Li, to name a few, have acknowledged Great Gram's and Gram's attempt to resist historical effacement, yet they evaluate this choice within the medicalized rubric that conceptualizes and idealizes healing as a cure. Thus, this mode of reading understands *Corregidora* as a novel about healing where Great Gram, Gram, and, to some extent, Irene are pathologized for refusing to heal while Ursa is understood to either achieve healing or fall short in the process. Despite the sociopolitical violence that causes psychic injury, ongoing and unresolved and unhealed trauma is a personal failure—one that Great Gram and Gram repeat and reproduce generation after generation.

Trauma as disability in *Corregidora* is repetitious and recalcitrant. This novel not only underscores the pervicaciousness of the traumatized bodymindspirit but also disability's unruliness. The disabled bodymindspirit refuses to conform to views of disability as isolated and individualized and recovery as linear and healing as absolute. In *Corregidora*, trauma, as disability studies and trauma theorist Angela Carter argues, is "*a way of feeling, being, moving, and knowing the world.*"[38] Carter aptly points out that trauma is not only held in the bodymindspirit but is also socially constructed. Trauma only exists against the backdrop of a population presumed to be and/or constructed as untraumatized and the assumption that one has had access to a "good life" before one experiences trauma.[39] Moreover, a Black feminist disability studies perspective challenges us to consider understanding trauma as "an affective embodiment that disrupts the ability to perform the hegemonic standards of person."[40] Black people have been categorically excised from personhood. Even their attempt to demonstrate and perform personhood fails to result in conferred humanity. Indeed, Black folk have had to navigate the fraught terrain of always having their affective life dismissed as a failure to perform personhood, as evidence that they lack subjectivity.

Ableism has been the mechanism by which Black bodies were/are legally and socially constructed as in/un/not human, a state of discursive non-being that left them materially vulnerable to physical, mental, and spiritual injury.[41] Ursa aptly describes this recursive process when she names the bodymindspirit instability, the trauma, Great Gram and Gram experience as hysteria. While reflecting on their experience of sexual violence and incest, Ursa wonders, "How many generations? Days that were pages of hysteria. Their survival depended on suppressed hysteria."[42] Hysteria comes from the Greek word for womb, *hystera*. The hysteria that Great Gram and Gram experience is indeed a sociocultural debility of the womb. On the one hand, the law of *Partus sequitur ventrem* transfigured specific African identities into Blackness, then conceptualized Blackness as a physical, intellectual, and social disability, as congenital—transferred from mother to child.[43] On the other hand, Blackness marked people from birth as a slave, making them vulnerable to any and every manner of wounding. For the Corregidora women, wounding occurs as sexualized injury: Great Gram and then Gram, by the condition of their Blackness, were subjected to sexual violence that quite likely injured their bodies and undoubtedly wounded their minds and spirits. However, enslavers commonly practiced prohibiting their human property from expressing emotional and spiritual pain. It was outlawed for enslaved persons to strike out against white people. Even more insidiously, the enslaved were often directed to perform joy and jollity as they experienced great suffering. Saidiya Hartman so poignantly explains that forcing displays of pleasure "[obscures] violence and [conflates] it with pleasure."[44] These dynamics are in place when Great Gram risks rape to verbally defend a young boy Simon sends a mob with dogs after. As Simon rapes Great Gram, she imagines that each penetrative thrust she endures is another footstep towards freedom for the boy. This scene is a literal rendering of Hartman's argument: Simon mistakes Great Gram's cries of violation and guilt for cries of pleasure from his performance. Simon conflates enacting sexualized violence with giving pleasure. Misreading Great Gram's cries of emotional and spiritual pain as cries of pleasure erases her suffering. In Great Gram's testimony, she reveals slavery's eroticism of violence: the boy was found floating in the water; and although she never sees it happen, she is sure that Simon rejoiced at the boy's death. It is into this traumatizing violence that Great Gram is condemned to deliver her children. Great Gram's womb, for instance, produces yet another Black body (Gram) for Simon "to submit to his genital fantasies."[45] Even after Black wombs ceased to (re)produce enslaved people, Great Gram had to endure the pain that she could not protect her daughter from this injurious violence, as Christina Sharpe so brilliantly brings into focus.[46] Moreover, Great Gram's womb birthed children to which she had no legal claim; for all of Great Gram's and Gram's repetitive conscious-making of slavery's abuses, they refuse to speak on the children they were not allowed to keep, the boys that Corregidora sold off.[47] Great Gram's and Gram's "days that were pages of hysteria," are days spent in psychic distress that they could not afford to succumb to or express for their own survival, yet later refused to contain. Disability is discursively created through laws but these laws also debilitate. They lead to psychic harm that is experienced as disabling.

Even more, Great Gram's and Gram's hysteria is rendered invisible. How could they experience childhood sexual trauma when, according to the laws and systems of their time, they were never children and have no subjectivity to traumatize? They were flesh. Reduced to the "signs of [their] sex" yet aggrandized as "magic." What is a traumatic trigger in the face of ongoing violence and abuse? Who, besides Ursa, recognizes Great Gram's and Gram's psychic distress? How effective is treatment when the source of trauma is systemic and continuous, and their expression of psychic pain is illegible? Great Gram's and Gram's testimony, without the historical legal archive to substantiate their claims, would be dismissed as untrue. Even Ursa, as a child, reacts with incredulity at the depths of Simon Corregidora's and his wife's cruelty. Great Gram's and Gram's testimony would be, to use Anna Mollow's terminology, hysteric*ized* or "treated as . . . 'hysterical' symptoms rather than legitimate diseases."[48]

The tumultuous psychic landscapes Black people were consigned to navigate while enslaved were also hystericized and were used as further evidence of their absent subjectivity. For instance, members of the white plantation class justified enslavement by arguing that Black Africans and American-born Black people lacked the affective range to experience sorrow. This inability to grieve and mourn disqualified them as humans. Here, we see the contradictions of sanism when used to buttress sexism and racism: emotionality and rational thought are mutually exclusive. The liberal human was constructed as affectively dynamic but yet not so besieged by emotion as to not be capable of exhibiting and exercising Reason.[49] Black property not only failed to experience and express sorrow and grief, emotions thought to convey sentience, but they were also empty of higher orders of thought. Enslaved Black people were deemed incapable of coherently and logically articulating subjectivity—they were absent of mindedness. Lacked consciousness. Even today, people with mental disabilities are routinely constructed as vacuous. Their supposed unbridled emotion, deviant behavior, experiences of realities deemed fanciful, and/or nonnormative modes of communication evince this.[50] Mentally disabled people, therefore, lack the mindedness to credibly articulate a subjectivity and testify to their lived experiences. Great Gram and Gram not only reject that madness is the absence of the mindedness to feel emotional pain and express their own subjectivity, but they also declare they have the power to create consciousness, and memory and anger are the foundations of the conscious Great Gram and Gram attempt to form in their daughters. The repeated words of their stories of sexual exploitation not only concretize memory, but they also serve as kindling for wrath, "As if it were only the words that kept [their] anger."[51] As they hold on to rage and pain, they not only experience "days that were pages of hysteria" but they also nurture melancholia. Great Gram's and Gram's determination to maintain a hysteric and melancholic state exemplifies the use of madness as political resistance.

Éva Tettenborn draws attention to how characters in the African American literary tradition embrace melancholy, a pathologized psychic state, to bear witness to loss historically unaccounted for or witnessed only by participants in racialized violence. According to Tettenborn, these mentally disabled characters "must be read as subjects engaged in acts of political resistance to dominant versions of memory and historiography."[52] These characters both "claim" disability even as they use it to hold violent systems accountable for debilitating them.[53] In other words, disability is not just an embodied state or relationship between bodymindspirits and social environments and attitudes. It is, as La Marr Jurelle Bruce asserts, a practice.[54] It is something one can do.

Great Gram's and Gram's madness is a method of retaining hate that reminds them who is responsible for their suffering. Theirs is less about reconciliation and incorporation into the polity and more about accountability and marring the systems *and* the individuals who enact harm. Their method of reckoning refuses the erasure that incorporation into the nation-state would enact. By testifying, they resist disappearance.[55] This is not to perpetuate harmful views that experiences of mental disability and psychic distress are faked, self-induced, or imaginary. As I will elaborate in my reading of Ursa's experiences of trauma, mental distress is real and can be experienced as painfully debilitating. I do wish to point out, however, that in *Corregidora* mental disability is politicized. Through Great Gram and Gram, *Corregidora* historicizes what many conceive as a private, wholly subjective experience. Mental disability is no longer a chemical or behavioral problem; it is an appropriate response to continuing histories of sociopolitical wrongdoing. Laying claim to hysteria and melancholia is refusing to participate in their own phenomenological and historical erasure by overcoming a past that is not yet past, a past, to use the words of Jones's Eva Medina Canada, that "is still as hard on [them] as the present."[56] Moreover, Great Gram's and Gram's employment of melancholia is embodied: they reproduce their identification with the lost objects of girlhood, family, freedom, and recognition generationally through their reproductive imperative. They create an archive of flesh and memory that cannot be erased.

Living with Trauma

If "bearing witness is an aggressive act," "the act of witnessing . . . is . . . a dangerous one."[57] Listening to Great Gram's and Gram's pain contributes to life-long experiences of mental and spiritual instability for Ursa. Ursa not only bears witness to her Great Gram's and Gram's histories of injustice until she internalizes their memories and they fold into her own, but she also experiences the effects of holding these memories as disabling, so much so that they drastically shape Ursa's ability to self-define and speak truth to light to her own experiences. Here, we see the tension between feeling responsible for bearing witness to the communities' harms and testifying to one's own experiences. This is the balance that Ursa must continue to find. And she must do so by working with, not overcoming, her disabled bodymindspirit.

Second-hand or not, living with trauma interferes with Ursa's day-to-day physical and cognitive functioning and poses barriers to achieving her desires, such as romantic and sexual intimacy. For example, Great Gram begins sharing memories of being raped by both Simon Corregidora and his wife when Ursa is just five years old. Ursa is so profoundly affected by this and Great Gram's and Gram's other recollections that Simon starts to haunt Ursa's dreams. She has night terrors about him sexually assaulting her that lasts into adulthood, though she has never met him. Later, after her hysterectomy, she begins to have nightmares about Mutt. These night terrors are so intrusive that they make it difficult for her to rest.

Simon not only frequents Ursa's nightmares, but he also maintains a stronghold over her erotic life in much the same way he dictated the other Corregidora women's. Although he regularly rented out their bodies for his patrons to use sexually, Simon forbade—with the threat of death—Great Gram and Gram to have intimate and sexual relationships with other men of their choosing, particularly Black men. Simon made it violently clear that he didn't "wont nothing black fucking with [his] pussy"[58] by roughly grabbing their genitals while asserting his ownership of them or subjecting them to clientele more likely to transmit disease. Great Gram and, presumably, Gram viscerally learn that nontransactional intimacy, particularly with Black men, is dangerous, a message that was passed on to Irene. Irene finds intimacy so frightening that she cannot lay claim to her feelings of desire and pleasure with Ursa's father, Martin. Irene displaces her sexual arousal for her body's own maternal imperative, and she shares that she experiences nothing when she has sex with Martin. She remains silent as Martin expresses his romantic interest. Ursa has experiences much like her mother's and foremothers'. Like Irene, Ursa also struggles with emotional and physical intimacy that disrupts her ability to sustain romantic and sexual connections. Part of the pre-hysterectomy conflict between Ursa and Mutt results, in part, from Ursa's difficulty with emotional vulnerability. Even after her hysterectomy, for instance, Ursa's new beau, Tadpole McCormick, unsuccessfully tries to develop a loving and emotionally intimate relationship with her. Their affair begins when he assumes responsibility for Ursa's postsurgical care and his willingness to witness Ursa's experiences with traumatizing violence. Ursa, like her mother Irene, responds to Tad's declarations of love with silence and although she agrees to marry him, she never fully reciprocates his affection. The scene following Tad's proposal suggests, in part, why. Ursa dreams about discussing her hysterectomy with Mutt and revealing she was pregnant at the time but miscarried. Great Gram's and/or Gram's voice interjects this flashback with snippets of her/their sexual exploitation, of Simon and his customers "feeling up in [her] pussy."[59] For Ursa, partner intimacy, sex, and even marriage conjure complex personal and familial traumas. Here, the trauma of sexual violence obstructs intimacy. It is both a history that continues to resonate in their present—Mutt, too, claims ownership over Ursa's vagina in language that echoes Simon's—and it is a compulsive thought, a cognitive disruption that severs Ursa's connection to Tad and prevents her from being present in that moment with him. Bearing witness obstructs Ursa's ability to reckon with her personal trauma and lay claim to her own intimate relationships.

Ursa also struggles to find pleasure in sexual intimacy. For Ursa, sex is inextricably tied to reproduction, which Tad adeptly recognizes as "a slave-breeder's way of thinking."[60] Whereas Irene, Ursa's mother, misinterprets sexual desire with viscerally experienced baby fever and fears and abstains from sex, Ursa has sex, albeit often fear-inducing and unfulfilling, and, after her hysterectomy, accompanied by a profound sense of loss. Moreover, Ursa worries that her broken, absent womb has also damaged other parts of her, that, as adolescent Jeffy ventriloquizing her mother asserts, it "Mess up their minds and then fuck up their pussy."[61] Whether or not the hysterectomy physiologically alters Ursa's body, she does often find it difficult or impossible to have vaginal intercourse. Though orgasm can be very difficult to achieve through vaginal penetration alone, even pleasurable clitoral stimulation is immediately followed by physical and psychic pain and anxiety for Ursa. The spiritual trauma that Ursa inherits mentally and physically tightens her "up like a fist."[62] Sex is triggering. For instance, after a difficult sexual encounter with Tadpole, Ursa has a flashback or nightmare. Once again, she is confronted by Mutt, discussing the womb she now lacks. In this flashback, she explicitly parallels Simon Corregidora's violence with Mutt's. For Great Gram, Gram, Irene, and, especially, Ursa, disabling trauma is a fraught experience. Great Gram and Gram practice melancholia to evidence a subjectivity that others claimed they lacked and to archive a history that others tried to erase; however, their refusal to let go of the past not only preserves the memory but also repeats the harm. For Ursa, the consequences of bearing witness to another's trauma results in a dis/abled bodymindspirit experienced as limiting and painful—a bodymindspirit that has, as Ursa poetically remarks, "Barbed wire where a womb should be" and breast that curdles milk.[63]

The Disabled Blues Novel: Self-Representation and Healing

Corregidora not only examines disabling trauma thematically but also captures and attempts to present the phenomenological experience of the traumatized bodymindspirit formally. Aesthetically, *Corregidora* is a non-normative novel. It fails to construct a narrative as a linear unfolding of events that reach a denouement and satisfying conclusion. Like much of

Black women's writing, time is not chronological, and the conclusion is open-ended. The ending offers no easy answers. The story refuses narrative wholeness. As mentioned at the onset of this section, *Corregidora* is told from the first-person point of view focalized through Ursa. The text of *Corregidora* is Ursa's speech, recollections, and thoughts. Considering Ursa's experience with debilitating trauma, critics like Elizabeth Goldberg attribute these narrative characteristics as textually reflecting Ursa's trauma.[64] Claudia Tate attributes the nonnormative characteristics to *Corregidora*'s fit within the genre of the blues novel.[65] I argue that the two are inextricable. Blues culture is intimately intertwined with histories of disability, from the influence of mad bluesmen on developing the genre and the highly celebrated blind bluesmen of the early to mid-twentieth century to its emphasis on affective states associated with feeling blue, such as depression.[66] Moreover, as La Marr Jurelle Bruce so perceptively notes, and I quote at length

> During the height of its popularity in the mid-twentieth century, blues music potentially functioned as a codified and conscious system of black sublimation, transforming black rage, lust, and despair into palatable metaphors and catchy tunes. Paradoxically, blues music may entail quite the opposite effect insofar as it does not disappear rage, lust, and despair; rather, it retains these affects as the disposition of the singer and listener. Indeed, blues songs sometimes *cheer* black lust, *threaten* black violence, *promise* to 'shoot'—thus *exclaiming* black madness.[67]

The simultaneous yet paradoxical psychic function of allowing the blues singer to both sublimate socially unsanctioned emotion and desire while also discursively exclaiming it makes the blues an apt method of mad witnessing and self-definition. Moreover, this sublimation and exclamation is not just captured in the plot, characterization, and dialogue of the story, such as Great Gram's and Gram's repressed hysteria and purposeful melancholy or Ursa's conscious reflections on the physical and psychic consequences of violence that leads to debilitating trauma, but it is also enacted in the very embodiment of the text. *Corregidora* is Ursa's blues song that speaks truth to life of trauma through a traumatized bodymindspirit. This relationship between the blues and trauma results in what Michael Bérubé would call a disabled narrative. *Corregidora* is not only about impairment but is also impaired.

Throughout *Corregidora*, there are moments where sentences, characterization, and narrative fail in their role as such. Many of these instances can be attributed to trauma as expressed through formal elements of the blues. For instance, Gayl Jones uses aposiopesis several times throughout the novel—not just during dialogue but also in Ursa's exposition. Thinking about the "consequences of fucking," for example, Ursa considers how slavery made Black women "hard." She thinks about her and Mutt's relationship and who is at fault for her seeming brokenness. She decides to herself, "Naw, that n----r's to blame. What's bothering me? Great Gram, because I can't make generations. I remember everything you told me, Great Gram and Gram too and."[68] The sentence abruptly ends without continuing into the second clause warranted by the coordinating conjunction "and." Moreover, it is punctuated by a period, although the sentence remains incomplete. Donia Allen identifies this, and similar uses of aposiopesis, as blues breaks. Allen argues that the break signals Ursa's doubt concerning Mutt's culpability in losing her womb (Allen forcefully maintains that was an accident) and a way to demarcate the transition from one voice to another, in this case from Ursa's to Great Gram's in the page break and flashback that follows.[69] I also add that this is an experience of trauma captured in the composition of the text. Although the narrative switches perspectives, this perspective is provided through Ursa's memory. The aposiopesis textually enacts the cognitive rupture in Ursa's thought and sense of time and place as she has this flashback. It's as if we are in Ursa's bodymindspirit and viscerally experience the cognitive (dis)functions as she does. While textual disruptions and flashbacks are not uncommon novel tropes, particularly in postmodern literature, this one is explicitly linked to mental disability via trauma and embedded in the form of the writing itself. The impairments of the text are produced as and when Ursa experiences impairment of the bodymindspirit.

The textually embodied manifestation of Ursa's trauma also results in a breakdown of distinctions between characters. For example, Ursa often confuses or conflates Mutt and Tadpole with Old Man Corregidora as flashbacks cause her to forget with whom she is in conversation and as personal and collective trauma bleed one into the other in her dreams. During one dream sequence, for instance, Mutt comes to her, yet she tells him, "I don't know you." Considering she also dreams of Simon, it is initially unclear to whom she is speaking until Mutt replies: "What do you mean you don't know me? I was in your hole before he even knew you had one," and Ursa responds "At least I still got one, ain't I? You didn't take that away from me."[70] We know this is Mutt because of the reference to their sexual relationship and Ursa's hysterectomy, though Ursa also has dreams where Simon claims to have had sex with her, too. Similarly, the voices and memories of Great Gram, Gram, Irene, and, to some extent, Ursa's meld together. It is unclear to the reader and even to Ursa herself exactly whose experiences she is recollecting. The consciousness Great Gram and Gram try to create in Irene and Ursa overwhelms and represses their individual consciousnesses. The textual rendering of Ursa recollecting dialogue often fails to distinguish speakers. Dialogue isn't always set aside in quotation marks; new speakers aren't always introduced and/or indicated by a new line; and, even when it is, Jones's ability to capture the natural, messy flow of conversation as experienced through Ursa's psychic instability muddles which quoted lines belong to which characters. This is further exacerbated by Jones's ability to capture the rhythm of blues music in speech. Ursa's way of thinking is shaped by trauma, but it also echoes the sound, flow, and poetry of the blues. Much like characterization in blues music, Ursa's cognition transforms her man—which is often shifting, changing, and returning—to the any-man of blues songs.

Though Ursa's traumatized bodymindspirit is often associated with loss and lack, the change in how her body and mind function also creates the possibility for transition, transformation, and healing, largely through her relationship with the blues as a cultural location of disability. As I've noted, disability history is interwoven in blues music and culture. I contend that we should consider the blues a Black cultural location of disability. As stated in the introduction, here, I merge two seemingly divergent conceptions of disability in the cultural imagination. On the one hand, Sharon Snyder and David T. Mitchell theorize cultural locations of disability as institutional spaces set aside for disabled people, where the able-bodied staff compose an archive of materials that shape our cultural understanding of disability.[71] On the other hand, disability culture is the production of celebrated community and art by and for disabled people.[72] The enmeshed yet uneasy history of Blackness and disability results in Black spaces best understood as constantly shifting and vacillating among these material, imagined, and creative spaces. Blues culture has simultaneously been a creative space where Black disabled bodymindspirits have been siloed even as these creators feel pressured to repress their specific experiences of nonnormative bodymindspirits and it has been a milieu for and mode of inhabiting, being, and experiencing the world.[73]

Consequently, within the location of Black disability blues culture, loss and lack are filled with potential. For instance, as a blues singer, traumatizing experience enhances rather than takes away value from Ursa's art. After surviving Mutt's physically, psychologically, and spiritually violent assault that results in a miscarriage and sterility, Ursa's voice also becomes impaired. Although Ursa knows that the hysterectomy operation has little to nothing to do with her vocal cords, her singing voice changes and she worries if she is still talented.[74] Her then friend, Cat, responds, "Your voice sounds a little strained, that's all. But if I hadn't heard you before, I wouldn't notice anything. I'd still be moved. Maybe even moved more, because it sounds like you been through something. Before it was beautiful too, but you sound like you been through more now."[75] The damage to Ursa's vocal cords reflects the life-experience she has now acquired, life experience that lends embodied experiential authority to her role as griot cum blueswoman.[76] Cat even assures Ursa that her transition is in line with other female blues singers like Ma Rainy who had incredible mainstream success. Other characters also note Ursa's improved talent once her voice becomes strained. After the hostile demise of her relationship with Tadpole, Max, the owner of the Spider, Ursa's new full-time singing gig, tells her, "You got a hard kind of voice," and there is "something powerful about you."[77] Rather than end her career, her strained voice bolsters her talent. It is the hardness of Ursa's newly impaired voice that brings patrons to listen to her at the Spider.

It is no coincidence that disability improves Ursa's talent as a blueswoman. Musicologist and singer Laurie Stras's examination of disability and popular music aptly speaks to why. In "The Organ of the Soul: Voice, Damage, and Affect," Stras contends that damaged vocal organs may be considered a disabling impairment within the world of classical music, but within popular music genres, they are "positively enabling." In fact, they facilitate audience "empathy and identification"—and perhaps even mutual healing—by the injured organ's perceived ability to convey personal experience. As Stras significantly notes, "hearing damage in a voice . . . connects the listener inescapably with the body of the performer, and the emotion in the performance is communicated as a testimony of personal experience rather than as an expression or invocation of the idea of emotion."[78] The sound created by injured vocal cords is especially popular in the blues tradition. As Stras notes, "Damaged voices abound in the blues canon; indeed the very sound of the blues singer has been defined by voices in which physical suffering is almost palpable."[79] Ursa's suffering is physically inscribed not only in her long hair and lighter complexion and her hysterectomy scar, but it is also writ into her vocal cords. Ursa's testimony is not just in the song, it *is* the song. The interplay of physical, psychic, and spiritual injury boosts Ursa's talent. She has a career that lasts over two decades.

Becoming disabled compels Ursa towards self-definition. Like Great Gram and Gram, Ursa has no authoritative documentary legal evidence to make her case. And, now infertile, she can no longer make generations whose bodies bear witness to ongoing histories of sexualized racist violence instead. She cannot, like Irene, evade her own stories, and the text never suggests there is another, more socially sanctioned public venue for her to present their case. Besides, the intersections of class, gender, and dis/ability bar her from those platforms anyway: she is a working-class Black woman from Kentucky whose way of talking reflects her location and traumatized brain. Yet Ursa still tells her story. She turns to the blues, a Black spiritual, artistic form, to testify and, perhaps, find healing, reprieve, and redress. As L.H. Stallings reminds us, Jones crafts her narrative spaces according to cosmological realities other than Western white European epistemologies of being.[80] Specifically, I am interested in the blues's connection to conjure. As Yvonne P. Chireau explains, "Conjure and religion [are] intrinsic to the origins of the blues."[81] Conjure is an Africanist healing and harming practice, and the conjurer is both a historical figure and a figure in Black cultural production. Kameelah L. Martin explains, "The conjurer served as the spiritual advisor and doctor during the centuries of chattel slavery in the Americas and has since advanced into a type of hero recalled in the folktales, personal narratives, fiction, and visual representations of the African diaspora."[82] Conjure, like the blues, is a space and practice that has drawn in Black people of varying bodymindspirits who mold the craft. The practitioners of conjure have been pathologized as deviant for their differing bodymindspirits and differing, non-Western cosmologies. As such, much like blues culture, conjure is a Black cultural location of disability.

Ursa uses her conjure blues to heal and harm. In a dreamscape where Ursa is defending her career singing the blues to her mother, who believes the blues to be "devil's music," Ursa implores Irene, "Then let me give witness the only way I can. I'll make a fetus out of grounds of coffee to rub inside my eyes. When it's time to give witness, I'll make a fetus out of grounds of coffee. I'll stain their hands."[83] Here, Ursa offers her blues song as an alternative to the generations she can no longer bear. In this blues song, Ursa turns the multiple extractions and extortions of forced labor from enslaved Africans into the body of evidence. This new body of evidence is one to which she will be an embodied witness, but it will also physically mark those responsible for the harm—not just the victims of harm. This and other blues songs are what Kameelah Martin would call a conjuring moment, instances where Ursa performs as a conjure woman and blues woman. As a folk tradition that incorporates and builds on other Black folk traditions, the blues often incorporates conjure narratives. Blues songs often speak of interpersonal conflict resolved (or exacerbated) by a trip to the conjure wo/man. In *Corregidora*, however, Ursa, the blues singer, *is* the conjure woman. As typical with conjure, her blues is supposed to both harm those who have historically harmed her and her family as it bears witness to and heals her family's pain.

Ursa's blues songs situate her at a crossroads, which in conjure culture is a powerful place to be. The crossroads is where magic happens, where change occurs. Her willingness and ability to have nonreproductive sex (she performs fellatio on her ex-husband, Mutt) at the novel's end suggests this change, a change akin to healing. Gayl Jones, however, complicates and redefines healing. For Ursa, there is no return to a pretraumatized state in part because there has never been a time where she has existed as not traumatized. Instead, healing, for Ursa, appears to mirror Angela Carter's understanding of her trauma. Carter speculates,

> When I began to understand trauma as a way of feeling, being, moving, and knowing the world, I no longer felt pressured to "overcome" something that seemed to be a part of who I was. All of a sudden, I was able to find something like composure during my "breakdowns" because I started to think about myself as fluid, changing, flowing, rather than something solid that was broken and in need of fixing. I began to find a kind of calmness during my "flashbacks" because I began to imagine myself floating through space and time. These flashbacks were not something to forcefully interrupt but instead moments let [sic] play out with compassion.[84]

We see this at the end of *Corregidora*. Ursa meets Mutt again after twenty-two years. When he declares (not asks) that he wants her back, she is clear that she still hates him. Not as strongly as before, but still. She knows that she does not want him back, but she remains quiet. She returns to the hotel where they used to live, and she is clear that she does want to have sex with him. She gets on her knees and begins to perform fellatio. While "sucking" it for Mutt, Ursa begins to reflect once again on her Great Gram's life. It seems that she has another flashback, but she is allowed to process this flashback, integrate it into her present, and therefore, it isn't experienced as jarring—for Ursa or textually. There is no break, simply a flow into dialogue. As with Carter's experience, this is a moment of Ursa as "fluid, changing, and flowing" between herself, Mutt, Great Gram, and Simon. Ursa feels confused about her boundaries and borders, but this confusion is not distressing. Their sexual encounter isn't distressing, either. Rather than reflect on what her womb can't do in this moment, she swallows Mutt's cum and searches for understanding from her foremothers' and her past. Healing and wholeness, therefore, speak to one's ability to conciliate one's frustrated expectations of the bodymind and imagine and choose other pathways that may offer spiritual peace. For Ursa, healing and wholeness are the ability to come to terms with history and the body without overcoming the body.

Jones's vision of healing is as ambiguous as the body as social text and material being is itself. Indeed, characteristic of Black women's disability writing aesthetic, the novel ends ambiguously and open-ended:[85] Ursa's act of fellatio is parallel to a similar act her great gram performed on Simon Corregidora. She does something sexual, or not sexless, a moment of "pleasure and excruciating pain." But rather than end with Mutt's murderous wrath and Ursa absconding away like Great Gram, Mutt speaks his desire for psychic safety. Ursa states her limited ability to fulfill that request, and they embrace. Thus, Ursa's act revisits and revises the first—she does not (possibly) castrate Mutt. Instead, they embrace. The blues, as a narrative performance, is also a healing event, and the ending is the blues tradition of repetition with, what will perhaps, and what we hope will be, difference.

Explicating the relationship between the blues and disability, conjure and healing illuminates the complex thematic concerns and aesthetic practices in Jones's novel. Disability heightens and illuminates how bearing witness affrays the will to self-define in *Corregidora*. Ursa's change in function materializes Ursa's dis-ease with Great Gram's, Gram's, and Irene's reproductive injunction, their demand that Corregidora women make generations of embodied evidence to resist archival erasure and witness to slavery's violence. When Ursa can no longer perform as the Black female body is expected, she is then compelled into self-definition and chooses self-creation through her blues music. Yet even this is touched by disability: Ursa's cognitive function is altered by distressing trauma. In a turn that subverts ableist logic, Ursa's impaired vocal cords make her voice apt for the blues, and her traumatized mind leads to innovative narrative form. While the blues cannot promise restoration, it can offer reconciliation of body, mind, and spirit, of witnessing and self-definition, of broken relations. The blues offers the opportunity to do things again—to do them otherwise.

Despite Ursa's trauma, she is nevertheless able to articulate her experience and delineate her subjectivity in ways that are legible. While Ursa is far from the pinnacle of respectability, Ursa fits, by and large, within normative frames of communication and behavior. She can compellingly testify to the truths of her life because she possesses rhetoricity. But what about those who lack rhetoricity? What about those who do not have the ability to communicate in normative and/or legible modes? What about the people whose experiences of reality deviate greatly from our own or what we socially view as possible? While it is common to at best speak on their behalf but more likely ignore their existence altogether, Jones's second novel demands and exemplifies another path. In the next section of this chapter, I discuss how Jones represents a character whose actions and mental disability present more of a challenge of understanding and compassion.

Madness, Representation, and Interpretation in *Eva's Man*

While Jones focuses on the healing possibilities of the blues singer and song in *Corregidora*, it is the blues listener that proves instructive in Gayl Jones's 1976 second novel, *Eva's Man*. In *Eva's Man*, the central voice and figure, Eva Medina Canada, is incarcerated in a psychiatric prison after she poisons and attempts to castrate a new lover. When arrested, Eva offers no explanation or justification for her brutal actions. She instead remains silent. When Eva does start to speak to others about her life and what happened with the man, Davis Carter, we learn that she met him in a blues bar, agreed to go with him to his hotel room, and spent the subsequent several days with him. During that time, he may—or may not—have held her against her will. He may—or may not—have raped her. She may—or may not—have been afraid of him. We also learn that Eva has experienced sexual abuse or been subjected to predatory men her entire life. Eva's testimony, along with the stories she shares of other people that weave the fabric of her life, is the text of this novel.[86] Though focalized through Eva, like *Corregidora*, the narrative is polyvocal. Eva both testifies and bears witness. However, whatever we believe we know about Eva and the people she encounters are cast into doubt as Eva appropriates, conflates, and revises conversations, experiences, and events during her tellings and retellings. Moreover, Eva confuses details. She lies and misremembers. She stops sentences short and sits in silence. She does not distinguish—or indicate distinctions—among dream, fantasy, and reality. For these reasons, characters in the story, as well as reviewers and literary scholars alike, label Eva insane, or mad. Like *Corregidora*, *Eva's Man* is rendered through the first-person voice of a Black woman coming to terms with violent and traumatizing histories, including her own actions, but *Eva's Man* is a considerably more difficult text to critically engage. Although Ursa's trauma-inflected blues song results in repetition, moments of unclear character distinctions, and eruptions of flashbacks that at times make the story arc confusing to follow, *Corregidora* is a mostly coherent narrative. *Eva's Man* lacks this coherency. Eva not only commits a ghastly crime that taxes the sympathy and affronts the respectability of most readers, but Eva's nonnormative communication style, for many, renders her testimony unreliable and incomprehensible. Eva's actions are not only grotesque and abject, but so, it seems, is Eva herself. June Jordan decries that "Eva Medina . . . is nobody I have ever known."[87] *Eva's Man* and the critical engagements with the novel raise complex and uncomfortable questions about (self-)representation and bearing witness, such as *whose* narratives hold social, political, and critical value and *how* do we witness and relate to and with the experiences and self-fashioning of people who can't, don't, or won't use normative modes of communication?

How and what exactly *Eva's Man* and Eva herself communicate has been a source of divisive critical readings. Critical analysis of Jones's book straddles between reading Eva as agentive or Eva as bound and beholden to the narratives, myths, and stereotypes attributed to her; Eva as fighting patriarchy or Eva as capitulating to it; Eva's silence as resistance or Eva's silence as defeat. Initial reviews of *Eva's Man* lambasted the novel for its crass presentation of Black sexuality that seemed to rehash the vilest stereotypes about Black men and women. Jones's contemporaries rejected Jones's grotesque representation of the Black female body characterized by the book's repetitive rendering of abject bodily functions like eating, pissing, menstruating, farting, and cumming. They particularly lamented Eva's and Elvira's sexual desire, viewing both as hypersexual and Elvira as aggressive and "predatory." Men, like Addison Gayle, marked Jones as the newest addition of Black women writers out to get Black men. Gayle even goes so far as to attack Jones herself, decrying, "if Gayl Jones believes that Black men are what she says they are, she ought to get a white man."[88] Gayle's comment, in particular, reveals the tension between self-determination and bearing witness: the desire for varied, realistic portrayals of Black life versus the demand to produce positive counter-hegemonic representations of Black people. Ironically, Gayle responds to Jones's supposed failure to do the latter by resorting to the very same—he evokes harmful, hateful stereotypes about Black women's sexuality, specifically the trope of Black women as treacherous Jezebels in sexual—if not political—collusion with white men. His critique of Jones's novel seamlessly transitions to a critique of Jones herself.

In fact, more than one male critic of Jones's novel has erased the distinction between Jones and Eva as an ad hominem assessment of the book. For instance, Bernard Bell, in his brief biography of Jones's life that precedes his critical summary of her work, solicitously shares the details of her and her husband's experience with psychic distress and state violence. While I am reticent to provide the details of Jones's experience for fear of reproducing the voyeuristic tone and tenor of the reporting of the event, I choose to do so because the mobilization of these events to discredit Jones's work exemplifies precisely what's at stake in the argument of this chapter. In 1998, after the successful publication of *The Healing*, Jones's first book in twenty years, she and her husband got into an altercation with the local police that ended in Jones's husband's suicide and her incarceration in a psychiatric hospital for suicide watch. The newspaper report provides a catalog of events and actions that, for me, gestures towards the direct experience of snarled histories of medical racism and state violence and surveillance. Reporter Rick Bragg speculates that Jones has perhaps become "something much like a character in her books."[89] Bell, who cites Bragg, nearly definitively makes that conclusion. Bell transitions into his critique of Jones's oeuvre by stating, "Like the blues women in her highly successful early novels, Jones has lived a life of quiet desperation, volcanic desire, male domination, and deep distrust of white Americans."[90] This is quite an assertion, considering that Jones is renownedly private. Moreover, Jones has stated in multiple interviews that her work is not autobiographical. Nevertheless, subtly, sanism mixes with misogynoir to lubricate the slippage between Jones and Eva in Bell's assessment.

That a brilliant storyteller, educator, and literary critic can be so glibly likened to a character that most consider barely articulate quite poignantly demonstrates that madness is contestatory and contested. To ask—which is to suggest the possibility—if one can be crazy yet of sound mind is to expose the sane/mad binary as lubricious and, more importantly, to reject that the (severely) mentally and cognitively disabled lack mindedness, which often stands as a synonym for subjectivity. While people are often frustrated with the impenetrability of the mad mind, it goes unnoticed that the imposed criteria of madness are unctuous and, therefore, even more elusive to pinpoint—with far greater consequences. It's not simply that attributions of mental disability are routinely used to disqualify the *ethos* of a speaking subject. It's that madness easily becomes grounds for eradicating the voice and subjectivity of another altogether. This erasure creates a vacuum—a black hole to use Catherine Prendergast's phrasing and evoke Evelyn C. Hammond's pivotal essay on Black women's sexuality[91]—that is often filled by narratives other people create, people who are granted license to articulate the mentally disabled person's experience by the authority of their presumed, comparably able mind alone. The ostensibly able-minded not only feel capable of speaking for the mentally disabled, but it appears they feel a compulsive desire to do so. If "disability's very unknowability . . . consolidates the need to tell a story about it" and disability "inaugurates the act of interpretation,"[92] mental disability generates an urgent desire for the able-minded to both interpret the utterances and very being of the mentally disabled and tell their story against and over mad folks' self-expression. Eva Medina Canada vehemently resists and rejects both and compels other ways of witnessing and exercising relationality. Compared to *Corregidora*, it does seem like *Eva's Man* is "the blues that lost control,"[93] but *Eva's Man* isn't a blues novel about the blues singer and song; it's a blues novel instructive on blues *listening*.

Who Speaks for Whom?
—Rhetorical Disability and Black Madness

The mentally disabled are stripped of representational power. It is not that they are unable to produce discourse, although that is sometimes the case, but that the discourse they produce lacks authoritative weight. Those who inhabit or experience reality differently from others are wholly dismissed as unreliable. When people do listen to the mad, their discourse is taken, as Catherine Prendergast astutely notes, as a barometer of their in/sanity.[94]

In Eva's case, the gruesome nature of her crime turns requests for her testimony into a desire for a verbal freakshow where her madness is put on display for the entertainment of the sane. For instance, true crime aficionados, journalists, law enforcement, and psychiatrists all want Eva to tell her story—or any story. Eva tells us:

> I tell them so much I don't even get it straight any more. I tell them things that don't even have to do with what I did, but they say they want to hear that too. They want to hear about what happened between my mother and father as well as what happened between me and that man. One of them came in here and even wanted to know about my grandmother and grandfather. I know when I'm not getting things straight, and I tell them I'm not getting this straight, but they say that's all right, to go ahead talking. Sometimes they think I'm lying to them, though. I tell them it ain't me lying, it's memory lying. I don't believe that, because the past is still as hard on me as the present, but I tell them that anyway. They say they're helping me. I'm forty-three years old, and I ain't seen none of their help yet.[95]

In this précis of the narrative to come, Eva displays a self-consciousness often denied to the mad or mentally disabled. She knows when she is misremembering the details of her life and claims to be forthright about the limits of her recollection. Her audience doesn't care, and so she keeps going. There also seems to be a divide and distinction between misremembering and lying—one of which Eva is aware. Misremembering is aligned with understandable, if not natural, cognitive failure, while lying is an unacceptable moral failure. Eva, however, destabilizes the division. She blames her faulty memory for errors in her recollection, although she is quite cognizant of the psychic and material ongoing consequences of the past on her life (she has been incarcerated in a psychiatric institution for five years). While scholars often point out Eva lies because she admits that she doesn't believe that her memory lies but continues to tell spectators that anyway, it seems to me that in the same spirit as others who interpret her and her actions, she is settling for the easy answer. She is forgoing deeper reflection on her relationship to the past and memory. And why not? Despite accusations of lying, there is little public and medical investment in Eva's truth. Those who wish to "keep it living" aren't interested in justice for Davis or helping Eva heal. Eva jeers that she has yet to benefit from anyone's supposed assistance. That these people consume Eva's stories with disregard for her truth—whatever that may be in the moment—bespeaks a divestment from bearing witness in the name of true care.

While Eva, as a storyteller, may indeed be playing a game with her voyeuristic audience, they, too, are playing a game of sorts with her as well. They request her testimony not to bear witness but to test their ability to break Eva's silence and confirm their own evaluations of her psychic state. In addition to Eva's seeming babble, Eva's nonnormative communication is marked by silence many find incomprehensible. Eva doesn't speak to explain her actions to detectives or in court. Eva often doesn't speak to her assigned psychiatrist. Eva also goes quiet during conversations with others; she doesn't even speak to correct their false assumptions about her. Indeed, nearly everyone in the story believes that they know Eva and what she wants and needs. They've summed her up: Eva's (mad) Black womanhood tells them all they need to know. *Eva's Man* isn't a "whydunit"—everyone has already predetermined her motive. Characters draw on stereotypes about poor Black women to assess Eva and her crime. The novel starts with how newspapers use visual cues to signify Eva's Black womanness as untamed and savage by presenting her with her hair "uncombed" and "looking like a wild woman."[96] Early on, it is also clear people understand Eva through narratives of Black women as hypersexual. Eva's cellmate informs her that people think of her as a whore. Most men, including Davis, believe Eva is a prostitute, and when she rejects their propositions, they berate her with epithets that she is a "cold ass," "evil ole bitch." Those in the criminal justice system paint her as a disgruntled lover, claiming she killed Davis after discovering he was married. The psychiatrist, as well as most literary scholars, believe that Davis comes to represent all the men in Eva's life. But this evaluation isn't in service of psychic and spiritual healing; it's him trying to pierce the mystery of Eva's madness, joking and "proud of himself" that he "got *something* out of [Eva]" when she breaks her silence with "who."[97]

Even Davis feigns interest in learning about Eva, asking her several times why she refuses to talk to him and tell him about herself. However, like the spectators, detectives, lawyers, and doctors to come, Davis, too, has little interest in bearing witness to Eva's life. When Eva does share anecdotes with Davis, he curtails her expression of emotional intimacy with sexist remarks about women's scents or menstruation, or he attempts to have sex with Eva. Each time Eva suggests that they may be engaging in an authentic romantic connection—often by noting his displays of care for her menstruating body or remarking to him when they perform roles associated with marriage—Davis also forecloses and rejects that possibility. Davis claims to want to know who Eva is and where she is from, yet appears to have no intentions of reciprocity.

Eva's Man complicates the politics of representation and the will to self-define. It complicates the act of testimony and bearing witness. Throughout *Eva's Man*, not only is Eva's subjectivity presumed to be visible and self-evident by her (mad) Black womanhood, but characters also expect access to Eva's interiority. Before Eva's diagnosis of insanity, she has no interior subjecthood because her inner life is presumed to be public. Elvira even jokingly renames Eva's pubic hair—hair that is typically thought to be hidden away by clothes and undergarments, hair thought to be private—to "public hair." As Kevin Quashie eloquently asserts, "The determination to see blackness only through a social public lens . . . is racist."[98] To do so assumes that Black people have no inner life, which is an assumption that is deeply entwined with sanism. In Eva's case, Blackness and madness intersect to reaffirm the suppositions of the other: Eva has no inner life to which outsiders are not privy because she is Black. She has no inner life to excavate because she is mad. Representation, bearing witness, and testimony lose oppositional thrust in a world that expects politicized self-disclosure from Black people and that dismisses the discourse of the mad.

The Interpolated You and the Blues Listener

Eva insists on her right to protect her inner life. She regularly practices what Quashie calls quiet. According to Quashie:

> The idea of quiet is compelling because the term is not fancy—it is an everyday word—but it is also conceptual. Quiet is often used interchangeably with silence or stillness, but the notion of quiet in the pages that follow is neither motionless nor without sound. Quiet, instead, is a metaphor for the full range of one's inner life—one's desires, ambitions, hungers, vulnerabilities, fears. The inner life is not apolitical or without social value, but neither is it determined entirely by publicness. In fact, the interior—dynamic and ravishing—is a stay

against the dominance of the social world; it has its own sovereignty. It is hard to see, even harder to describe, but no less potent in its ineffability. Quiet.[99]

By reading both Eva's silence and elisions as "quiet," I avoid arguing for or against Eva's self-imposed silence (and, by association, madness) as either subversive or obsequious. And yet, there is a seditious element to Eva's ardent demands for quiet against ongoing attempts to deprive her of it. For instance, in a moment of psychic distress brought on by the psychiatrist's incessant interrogation and inability to understand as Eva talks to him about Davis, Eva blurts, "Don't explain me. Don't you explain me. Don't you explain me."[100] Eva's bellows, which are soon silenced with forced medication, resonate from the examination room of the psychiatric prison to the psychic space occupied by the reader. In fact, *Eva's Man* situates the reader in the same position as the psychiatrist, particularly literary critics, many of whom come to the same interpretive conclusions. Thus, the novel exposes the reach of intimate violation: the psychiatrist's inquisitive probing is as harmful as the dirty popsicle stick Freddy Smoot uses to sexually assault her, which is as invading as our literary diagnosis of Eva's madness. All of these are nonconsensual penetrative acts. They are assertions of power.

How, then, does one bear witness while respecting the sovereignty of another person's quiet? Particularly, how does one listen when a person uses nonnormative communication, including silence? *Eva's Man* is quite instructional in this practice. Although the novel provides scathing critiques of the failure to bear witness, it also offers insightful and illuminating examples of how to behold another. Ironically (or perhaps not) it is Eva who is quite perceptive and adept at witnessing. For instance, it is Eva who notices and notes the violence encapsulated by circulating images of Davis's dead, mutilated body. She shares, "It bothered me at first when I found out they'd used his picture in there, one showing what I did."[101] While some Black people choose to circulate images of horrific violence enacted upon loved ones to display the brutality of oppressive systems, such as Mamie Till's choice to show pictures of her beaten, bloated son's body in his casket, this tactic, as many Black intellectuals have pointed out, fails to elicit widespread sympathy or even justice. Instead, mass circulation of the violence wrought against Black bodies contributes to the already normalized Black body in pain. Images and now videos of Black injury and death circulate the news and social media in an irreverence unthinkable for white bodies. For all of Eva's madness, she is sound enough to be aghast by this

Reasonable violence. A couple of paragraphs later, however, Eva offers a story that is quite instructive.

Eva reflects on the time during her trial when Davis's wife came to visit her. Eva explains, "I didn't want to see her because I didn't know how I was going to feel," but Eva carries on with the visit regardless. Eva recalls,

> She was a skinny, run-down-looking woman in a black hat. For some reason, I had expected her to be a big, handsome-looking woman. She didn't say anything. She just stood there outside the cell and stared at me, and I stared back. The only thing I kept wondering is how did he treat her. Because it looked like he made her worse than he made me. I mean, if she was as bad-off on the inside as she looked on the outside. She must've stood there for close to fifteen minutes, and then left. She didn't have anything at all in her eyes—not hate not nothing. Or whatever she did have, I couldn't see it. When she left, I wondered what she saw in mine.[102]

Eva sits with Davis's wife in silence. She doesn't force her to speak. She doesn't claim to know what this woman feels or desires. However, Eva recognizes and admits that she made baseless assumptions about how this woman would look. Eva approaches the encounter with empathetic curiosity, wondering about Davis's wife's experiences while also recognizing Eva's own limited ability to fully know this other person. Eva doesn't conflate their experiences. Though the woman's vacant eyes suggest, perhaps, her own madness, Eva identifies with rather than withdraws connection from her. Whatever ideas Eva has about the woman's brokenness are expressed with a healthy dose of doubt: Eva suggests that there are fundamental limitations about what she can see and know about this person. Eva acknowledges Davis's wife's subjectivity as someone with an inner life all her own. They stare at each other in mutual quiet.

In this encounter, there is mutual becoming and affirmation of their subjectivity. Staring, as Rosemarie Garland-Thomson explains, is not the same as the gaze, which is inherently oppressive. In their stare, meaning is made. Their mutual subjectivity is forged: "... what begins as simple staring, a visual groping toward a new and stimulating sight, has the potential to enact something akin to what psychologist D.W. Winnicott (1965) calls the holding function. To be held in the visual regard of another enables humans to flourish and forge a steady sense of self. Being seen by another person is a key to our psychological well-being, then, as well as our civil recognition."[103] It is not enough to simply stand witness to one another. One must behold another. Importantly, to behold doesn't require normative communication. Indeed, it requires a divestment from the able-mindedness that prizes the self-certainty of Reason.

Conclusion

Representation matters. And yet, Black women have also felt silenced by the weight of positively representing the race in ways that demand they erase or ignore their experiences with oppression by those who hold more privilege by way of their gender, ability, sexuality, citizenship, religion, etc. But as Audre Lorde affirms, "I have come to believe over and over again that what is most important to me must be spoken, made verbal and shared, even at the risk of having it bruised or misunderstood."[104] What is captured in this powerful line, and what I have discussed in this chapter, is the risk of not just being misunderstood but rendered misunderstood through accusations of craziness. In a world that values reason but measures reason through adherence to hegemonic discourse, it is all too easy to dismiss the experiences of oppression by the most marginalized—perhaps because we don't understand them—as unreasonable, unbelievable, crazy-making. This is a distressing irony, considering how debilitating white heterosexist supremacy is to the mind. The solution is not a deeper investment in able-mindedness but perhaps a divestment from it. As Toni Morrison theorizes in *Sula*, one can be "crazy," but that does not mean that one doesn't have "sense or, even more important . . . no power."[105] Clarity and coherence of speech and thought are nice but not required for empathetically bearing witness. Blues listening doesn't require understanding the/each other. Indeed, it questions and challenges the feasibility of understanding altogether. Blues listening recognizes that we need not fully understand each other to agree that one has the right to exist in safety and dignity.

In this chapter, I have taken up the theme of the will to self-define along with the issues of bearing witness to highlight how sanism upends these journeys within the public sphere. Black women's writing, such as Gayl Jones's *Corregidora* and *Eva's Man*, demands that we are attuned to how ableism operates to deny people their subjectivity and cast doubt on their experiences of debilitating prejudice. Healing is not achieving able-mindedness, although peace of mind is aspirational- but coming to peace with one's mind in all its permutations. In the next chapter, I dig deeper into the conflict between testifying and bearing witness, particularly in the political and cultural formulation of Black community.

Chapter 2

Black Community, Crip Communities of Care

> There must have been a time when an artist could be genuinely representative of the tribe and in it; when an artist could have a tribal or racial sensibility and an individual expression of it. There were spaces and places in which a single person could enter and behave as an individual within the context of the community.
> —TONI MORRISON, "ROOTEDNESS: THE ANCESTOR AS FOUNDATION"

In the previous chapter, I discussed the tension between bearing witness and the will to self-define as a prominent theme in Black women's writing. In this chapter, I locate this tension as emergent from the larger conflict of misogynoir and ableism in community activist work. In other words, in this chapter, I discuss crip community as thematically central in Black women's writing, and the discourse produced about it. Within the contemporaneous feminist movement and movements for Black liberation, particularly the Black Nationalist movements of the 1960s[1] the primary focus of this chapter, Black women often found themselves and their concerns invisibilized, minimized, or outright dismissed and criticized as divisive. For instance, Don L. Lee praises Mari Evans's assertion of herself as a "black woman." The strength of her assertion, for him, lies not in the specificity of her multiple identities but rather in his reading of her Black womanness as "generically and historically black." Evans's ideal woman Black nationalist was not "fragmented, hysterical," didn't have "sexual problems with her mate," and "doesn't feel caught up in 'liberated womanhood' complex/bag—which is to say she is not out to define herself (that is, from the position of weakness, as 'the others' do)." Black women who wrote nuanced representations of Black life that privileged their perspectives and experiences were often considered man-bashing and dismissed as "hysterical" and "fragmented," as if those were pathological. And yet they persisted. Black women wrote stories that embraced fragmentation and presented flawed people involved in conflict and contradiction, such as disabling and debilitating battery, sexual assault, and exploitation, as well as spiritual, emotional, and physical abandonment and uneven commitment to liberation work within the domestic sphere and larger political community. They represented heteropatriarchy as psychically and physically harmful and injurious to both women *and* men in the Black community and envisioned empowered, bold, audacious, and fallible, brokenbeautiful[2] women protagonists and personas who reject and/or upend patriarchal dominance.

Many Black men framed these narratives as an attack on men and the Black community as a whole. Black aesthetic theorist Mel Watkins, for example, accused Black women writers of breaking an "almost universally accepted covenant among black writers" to present positive counter-representations of Black people. Contradictorily, Watkins criticizes Black women writers for their move away from a "subtle invocation of art" to a "blunt demonstration of politics and propaganda."[3] These women authors were not only treacherous to the Black community when they discussed heterosexism, but they also compromised artistic integrity.

Despite the challenges ableism and sexism posed for them, and despite sexist charges of racial heresy, to use the words of Black feminist literary scholar Ann duCille, Black women writers remained committed to and embraced their work for and connection to Black community. Their unflinching representations of the beauty and the pains of Black life were indeed part of these authors' healing practices, bearing witness to uncomfortable truths not only served for personal healing but also communal, with communal healing necessary for personal healing. Communal interdependence and care work are necessary for individual and collective liberation and survival.

This understanding of conflict, care, and community reflects an Africanist worldview and understanding of unwellness and wellness. In Africanist spiritual systems, illness, injury, and disease are not individualized experiences but rather relational and communal, reflecting the spiritual belief that the individual is in relation to and unified with one's community. Healing, or returning to wellness, is not the sole responsibility of a single person but that of the community. At times, that means the individual must heal her relationship with the community, and other times, it means the healing process must involve members of the larger community. Moreover, healers are often members of the community rather than separated from it by institutional and infrastructural gatekeeping, as one sees with hospitals and doctors' offices. Illness and disease are occurrences that not only happen at the level of the individual but also that of the community: as Stephanie Y. Mitchem explains, "a community can be deemed ill."[4] Whereas the biomedical discourse of epidemics (or even illnesses considered endemic to a community) focuses on communicable diseases that impair the physical health of many individual people within close geographic proximity, communal unwellness as understood within Africanist spiritual paradigms can be physical, as well as spiritual, and the community experiences this unwellness collectively, in unity. Black women writers such as Alice Walker and Toni Morrison position Black community as central to experiences of illness, injury, and disease. Within their writing, the unwell individual within the community becomes a metaphor for the harms enacted against marginalized individuals within the community—i.e., discord within the community—as well as harms enacted against the community by larger social and political forces. Simultaneously, these women's works bear witness to the actual debilitating harm that disproportionately impacts Black communities by the mechanisms of social and political domination under critique through the metaphorical Black body. The communal experience of unwellness, in these writers' narratives, is integral to Black (racial) communal identity. Moreover, they present Black cripistimologies of communal caregiving as political work.

Black women writers often represent Black community as shaped and cultured through a shared historical experience of debilitating racial marking and strengthened by a shared commitment to interdependence and care. Stephen Knadler, for example, argues that there is overwhelming evidence that disability affected entire communities of African Americans in the late nineteenth and early twentieth centuries. While white supremacists used this information as proof of African Americans' racial degeneracy and inferiority,[5] Black race leaders like Booker T. Washington and W. E. B. Du Bois cited pervasive illness and impairment in the Black community as evidence of US racial injustice. Problematically, as Knadler argues, they also attempted to veil disability. These men mobilize disability to critique racist oppression while attempting to divorce disability from Blackness, which disability studies scholars, like Douglas C. Baynton, disparage because it fails to deny "that disability is an adequate justification for social and political inequality," and "thus, while disabled people can be considered one of the minority groups historically assigned inferior status and subjected to discrimination, disability has functioned for all such groups as a sign of and justification for inferiority."[6] In other words, these minority groups reproduce ableist ideology by trying to distance themselves from disability to secure racial and gender equality. This assertion does not take into consideration Black women activists' differing roles in and approaches toward the movement for racial and gender equity. For instance, as Stephen Knadler also notes, "While key race men such as Booker T. Washington fashioned public narratives that veiled disability even while addressing medical disparities in the community, African American women were often the primary agents of black public health work outreach."[7] Whether that activism has emerged as rootwork and midwifery on antebellum plantations, or "laywomen's" campaigns to educate newly emancipated poor Black folk about the connection among epidemics, health, and hygiene, or Black women's fights for reproductive justice, or even our contemporary period of activist commitments and communities centered on issues such as HIV/AIDs, breast cancer, and mental illness, Black women have historically centered health activism as inextricable and central to racial uplift and liberation. These activists have known quite intimately that their personal wellness depended upon communal wellness because they viewed themselves as integrated within their communities. Granny midwives offered their healing services from within the very plantations they, too, were forced to work on; the club women guided poorer Black women through the stereotypes of sexual depravity that also threatened their unmolested wellness; civil rights leaders cried out against medicalized racism against Black women from the depths of barrened, appendectomied wombs; Black women artist-activists campaign, distribute resources, and form healing circles around HIV/AIDs, mental disability, and cancer that touches the lives closest to them and snuffs away their own lives. When understood through a Black feminist disability studies lens, particularly one attuned to Black spiritual beliefs, it is clear that Black women have centered disability as a political issue in their community activist work without distancing themselves from the disabled Black community.

Interestingly enough, disability and community are not frequently joined in the popular imagination and discourse. Disability is often considered a personal and private problem and can, therefore, be experienced as isolating. Additionally, disabled people have, historically, been isolated: they've been cordoned away in backrooms and asylums. Consequently, as feminist disability studies scholar Rosemarie Garland-Thomson observes, one rarely sees representations of disabled people in community. When disabled people are considered as a group, it's typically through the ableist discourse that constitutes written medical research and records or through ableist cultural fantasies of patients in homes or care facilities that come to represent disabled people shoved and/or crammed together in various sites of incarceration such as psychiatric institutions and nursing homes or siloed institutional spaces like special education classrooms. Moreover, able-bodied doctors, nurses, teachers, parents, and policymakers speak for disabled people in these congregated spaces. Even these instances of representing groups of disabled people fail to imagine them as having a collective social, cultural, and political voice. The idea that disability is a singular, tragic experience is so pervasive, as Garland-Thomson so pluckily notes, "the concept of a disability community in which one might *thrive* seems counterintuitive."[8] To counter the notion that disability is an isolated, tragic experience, Garland-Thomson analyzes "feisty narratives" of disability community in the movie *Murderball* (coming harrowingly close to celebrating toxic masculinity), Simi Linton's disability memoir *My Body Politic*, and the Society of Disability Studies' (SDS) annual convention dance. Within these spaces, particularly the SDS dance, disability identity is sexy, sensual, and sexual, creative and joyous. Representing disabled people thriving in community among each other is powerful and necessary work. It destabilizes the assumption that disabled people lack a collective social, cultural, and political consciousness.[9] As Margaret Rose Torrell contends, "The construction of a disability community in the disability narrative is a potent act of resymbolization: the emphasis on communities of disabled people as interactive, supportive, and engaged in enjoyable activities counters conventional thinking about disability as an isolated, lonely state."[10] The assumption that disability is a private and personal issue and that disabled people are isolated, however, does not reflect the complex experiences of Black disabled people in community, such as those Knadler and Smith discuss. These arguments do not consider how entire communities are materially marked because of and to establish them as marginalized from the normate. They fail to account for how both healing and disability are fundamental to strategies toward and envisions of Black liberation.

In what follows, I discuss community, disability, healing, and political activism in Alice Walker's and Toni Morrison's writing. Marginalization, pathologization, abject poverty, illness, injury, and impairment, and criminalization are imposed conditions—that are often racialized and gendered[11]—that must be challenged. The abolitionist, anticapitalistic, antinationalist, and anti-individualist epistemologies that develop from those conditions, however, can and should be valued and retained. For Walker and Morrison, it is possible to challenge oppressive conditions while still appreciating survival paradigms emergent from those conditions as necessary for collective liberation and thriving. Walker's and Morrison's political critiques demand that we hold multiple truths in uneasy tension. Both Walker and Morrison recognize the importance of community in liberation work, but they also recognize collectivity is fraught—especially when ableist, patriarchal, capitalist, heterosexist ideologies remain uncontested. A liberatory community cannot be achieved through a single-axis politic. Collective liberation must attend to multiple axes of oppression—or be intersectional—and requires individual healing with the help of the community to serve the community. It requires communal care.

There is, as I discussed in the introduction, a difference between disabled (and otherwise oppressed) people hoarded together in institutional spaces and spoken for and about (cultural locations of disability) and disabled people in community who strive for shared identity and vie, through activism, art, and care, for collective justice (disability culture). However, as I contend in the introduction and the previous chapter, much Black cultural production emerges in a space betwixt the two or a space where the two are enmeshed— what I call Black cultural locations of disability. Black cultural locations of disability are sites where Black disabled people are often cornered and contained but nevertheless build communal culture and identity—like the Black communities in Walker's and Morrison's essays, life-writing, and fiction. While previously, I discussed the blues and conjure as Black cultural locations of disability that Black women writers thematically and formally incorporate into their work, in this chapter, I first turn to Alice Walker's second novel, *Meridian* (1976), and then to Toni Morrison's first novel after earning the Nobel Peace Prize in Literature, *Paradise* (1999), to discuss how Black cultural locations of disability shape Black women writers' understanding of community and racial identity. In *Meridian* and *Paradise*, Walker and Morrison reveal how the injuries of heterosexism and racism, as evidenced by beaten, maimed, injured, diseased, and sick Black bodymindspirits, forge a communal identity through interdependence and mutual caregiving as crip solidarity.

I pay particular attention to Walker's *Meridian* and Morrison's *Paradise* to demonstrate how Black women provide a nuanced history of Black civil rights activism, especially the Black nationalist movements of the 1970s, that celebrates these movements' successes while attempting to learn from their failures. Each novel reveals how investment in white American myths of rugged individualism and desires for heteropatriarchal supremacy, both deeply ableist ideals, combined with internalized ableist misogynoir injures community and thwarts liberation. Both Walker and Morrison craft brokenbeautiful protagonists whose experiences of becoming debilitated individuals within fractured communities are a heuristic exploration of models of healing and liberation. Both protagonists draw on Africanist spirituality to heal personal injuries but also reconfigure the value of the disabled body within community as well as imagine other strategies of Black liberation.

Southern Cripistemologies in Alice Walker's In *Search of Our Mothers' Gardens*

Alice Walker's *In Search of Our Mothers' Gardens* (1983) is a collection of her speeches, reviews, and essays written between 1966–1982. Herein, Walker draws on her life growing up poor in the deep South and her activist work, as well as the experiences of her foremothers, to contextualize the lived experiences of Black southern women, theorize the effects of sexism and racism on these women, specifically, and identify their survival in the face of oppressive forces. *In Search of Our Mothers' Gardens* is most noted for Walker's early articulation of Black feminist intersectional theory, *womanism*. Walker opens her collection with the following definition of womanism:

> womanist
>
> 1. *FROM WOMANISH.* (Opp. of "girlish," i.e., frivolous, irresponsible, not serious.) A black feminist or feminist of color. From the black folk expression of mothers to female children, "You acting womanish," i.e., like a woman. Usually referring to outrageous, audacious, courageous or *willful* behavior. Wanting to know more and in greater depth than is considered "good" for one. Interested in grown-up doings. Acting grown up. Being grown up. Interchangeable with another black folk expression: "You trying to be grown." Responsible. In charge. *Serious.*
>
> 2. *Also*: A woman who loves other women, sexually and/or nonsexually. Appreciates and prefers women's culture, women's emotional flexibility (values tears as natural counterbalance of laughter), and women's strength. Sometimes loves individual men, sexually and/or nonsexually. Committed to survival and wholeness of entire people, male *and* female. Not a separatist, except periodically, for health. Traditionally universalist, as in: "Mama, why are we brown, pink, and yellow, and our cousins are white, beige, and black?" Ans.: "Well, you know the colored race is just like a flower garden, with every color flower represented." Traditionally capable, as in: "Mama, I'm walking to Canada and I'm taking you and a bunch of other slaves with me." Reply: "It wouldn't be the first time."
>
> 3. Loves music. Loves dance. Loves the moon. *Loves* the Spirit. Loves love and food and roundness. Loves struggle. *Loves* the Folk. Loves herself. *Regardless.*
>
> 4. Womanist is to feminist as purple to lavender.

Walker's definition of womanist treasures Black girlhood, particularly those behaviors most selected for suppression, such as audaciousness. It recognizes the political and dialectal knowledge-making between Black girls and Black women, and it recognizes that southern Black vernacular and folk culture are central to their liberation theories and dreams. It draws from Black girls' and women's knowledge, their common sense or folk knowledge. It is an explicit intervention in feminist and Black civil rights liberation thought. It's queer. It's sensual. It's embodied. It's deeply spiritual. It demands unwavering love of self. Womanism establishes how Walker approaches the topics in her collection and names the theory she derives from her contemplation and written exploration of those experiences, many of which are of illness, injury, and impairment. As such, womanism is a *cripistemology*.

Named by Lisa Duggan, cripistemology eludes definition; rather, it questions "what we think we know about disability, and how we know around and through it."[12] Cripistemology is a concept that draws, in part, from Black southern folk culture, Black feminist theory and activism, and "the backwoods" of queer theory and disability studies.[13] Within neoliberalism, disability identity and disability studies have gone mainstream.[14] Merri Lisa Johnson and Robert McRuer explain this phenomenon quite well in their introduction to "Cripistemologies," the 2014 special issue of the *Journal of Literary and Cultural Disability Studies*. Under the neoliberal state, disability subjectivity is determined through official processes, such as medical diagnoses, that confer the power to identify disabled subjects to medical practitioners and the state, who then determine which bodies and minds are legibly disabled and, therefore, which disabled people have access to resources. *Disability knowledge*, then, is not produced by disabled people but rather by market forces targeting the *debility dollar* or the money spent on impairments. Disability knowledge differs from cripistemologies in that market forces encourage people to identify as sick or ill or disabled and, therefore, if they identify as potential consumers of biotechnologies and pharmaceutical products.[15] Cripistemology, on the other hand, is the "crip creativity" that "can never be [completely] closeted" or snuffed out by these constellations of crises ignited under neoliberalism.[16]

Indeed, *In Search of Our Mothers' Gardens* archives Black women's "crip creativity" under the strain of abject poverty, curtailed or absent reproductive agency, disempowered motherhood, and heterosexist abuse. Walker identifies how Black southern women, "creatures so abused and mutilated in body, so dimmed and confused by pain, that they considered themselves unworthy even of hope," forged outlets for their personal creativity and strategies for communal survival.[17] These life-sustaining ways of knowing and navigating the world are the "backwoods" insights about the failures of the state, the self-destructive mechanisms of racism, the "intense," "deep," if, perhaps, "*unconscious*,"[18] spirituality gleaned from crip epistemologies unable to be coopted by the market forces, forging what Johnson and McRuer call the "crip economy."[19] For instance, Walker, much like Stephen Knadler does in his book, retrieves histories of how systemic and institutionalized racism debilitated swaths of southern Black folks while the poverty that often accompanied racism left these communities absent of avenues of treatment. In her essay "The Black Writer and the Southern Experience," for instance, Walker laments the loss of Black crip community. She reflects, "And because we never believed we were poor and therefore worthless, we could depend on one another without shame. And always there were the Burial Societies, the Sick-and-Shut-in Societies, that sprang up out of spontaneous need."[20] Here, Walker draws an implicit connection between racism and poverty with debilitating conditions of slow death. In the deprivation of state-provided safety nets, southern Black folks turned to each other. In this model of Black disability community, poverty and interdependence are divorced from shame, which supports communities of caregiving. In this passage, Walker theorizes the conditions needed for successful interdependence, the difference between interdependence and charity: dignity. The connected experiences of racialization, poverty, and debility not only provide a sense of unity-in-action but the experience of disability itself involves a crip mode of knowing and being that Walker finds valuable: for Walker, as she explains in her essay "One Child of One's Own," "Illness has always been of enormous benefit to me. It might even be said that I have learned little from anything that did not in some way make me sick."[21]

Community, Commitment, and Care in *Meridian*

In *Meridian*, Alice Walker provides a critical portrait of the civil rights and cultural and revolutionary Black nationalist movements as experienced by a poor, southern teen wife and mother.[22] Meridian Hill is rescued from the suffocating life of single parenthood after she volunteers for an SNCC-*esque* civil rights organization, scores high on an IQ test, and is offered a scholarship to an elite southern women's college. She makes the daunting choice to place her son up for adoption to take advantage of the rare opportunity to earn her high school and college degrees. Meridian's choices, while liberating, are personally and communally fraught. For one, it strains her relationship with her mother, who disapproves of what she believes is shirking one's maternal obligations. College and the various civil rights organizations she joins become a source of discord as Meridian soon realizes that her past and personal values are at odds with her middle-class peers'. Misogynoir is pervasive and has consequences to Meridian's mental and physical well-being. Meridian has traumatic flashbacks and develops symptoms that cause skin discoloration, alopecia, emaciation, muscle tics, loss of consciousness, vaginismus, and episodic blindness. Although Meridian's illness is produced by trauma and is debilitating, Meridian doesn't always experience her symptoms as distressing, particularly because she draws on Africanist-Indigenous beliefs about illness and wellness to understand her relationship to her body and its connection to others. Moreover, Meridian moves to a small Georgia village where she eventually finds community among poor, southern disabled Black people for whom she advocates and who, in turn, care for her. *Meridian* presents community as capable of both harming and healing.

Classism, sexism, anti-Blackness, and ableism—from without and within Black communities—create communal dis-ease as well as personal illness and injury, and Meridian's broken Black female bodymindspirit has been understood to represent the political and psychic harms of these oppressive forces. While Meridian's sick body has been interpreted as a metaphor for the cultural and political harms Black people have sustained under racism and Black women due to misogynoir, it has hardly compelled material readings of illness and debility.[23] Reading Meridian's body as also reflective of actual bodies, however, draws our attention to the embodied, lived—and ongoing—consequences of injustice. We come to see how becoming disabled has been a marker of becoming Black. Moreover, debility, in the text, is at the core of how poor Black southerners are racialized, and this shared experience of racialized debilitation becomes a point of southern Black identity. Much like the Black women health workers who did not distance themselves from disabled Black people, Walker's representation of Black southerners preserves and values the communities of Black folk debilitated even in the wake of slavery. It doesn't supplant them with the able-bodied revolutionary leader. Ableism, sexism, racism, and classism harm the Black community by relegating them to second-class citizens and instilling Eurocentric ideologies and ideals that create psychic and spiritual discord in the self and the community, and it strips bodymindspirits of wellness. Healing, then, is a task for both the individual and the community. One cannot heal without the other; both must heal for each other. Healing in *Meridian* is directed toward the ideological and political sphere. It is within the disabled Black communities that Walker expresses her "[nostalgia] for the solidarity and sharing a modest existence can sometimes bring,"[24] where we see models of how healing as liberation could be achieved. Liberation comes not just through voting or closer proximity to whiteness—though equality and equity are important goals. Liberation comes from mutual caregiving. This mutual caregiving offers alternative modes of activism that don't necessitate the erasure of difference.

Failed Communal Belonging in *Meridian*

Meridian locates heterosexist ideals as injurious to Black women as a whole and Black women's liberation work specifically because of the narrow role delimited to Black women within those spheres. Despite the radical vision of an economically independent and culturally self-determined Black community that Black Nationalism promised and promoted, it suffered a gross cessation of imagination in its vision of Black women's place in the movement. Specifically, Black Nationalism imagined motherhood as the only suitable role for Black women. Black women were reduced to wombs that could birth more liberation warriors, which merely appropriated the reproductive function assigned to Black women during chattel slavery in the Americas. Both racial philosophies posit that Black women's transubstantiate dark(er) skin into ontological Blackness.[25] Consequently, Black Nationalism failed to imagine Black female ontology as different from the racist reproductive function established during slavery. Indeed, this varies little from the racist rhetoric circulated by white society and institutions, such as the conclusions made in Daniel Patrick Moynihan's 1965 report "The Negro Family: The Case for National Action," now infamously known as The Moynihan Report. Far too many men in liberation movements agreed with deeply racist and sexist conclusions that Black women, particularly Black mothers, the supposed Black matriarch, were pathologically emasculating. The rampant un-and-under employment, subpar wages, dilapidated infrastructure in Black communities, and alarming health disparities faced by the Black community could be traced to overly domineering Black mothers. However, subservience and obsequence to Black men also fail to guarantee Black women respect because domestic labor and mother work is derided as women's work. Black women were expected to reproduce the Black liberation army to free the community—and perform the necessary administrative work of movement making—but that labor is unappreciated and rationalizes subordinating women within the community.

Through Meridian's vexed relationship with motherhood, Walker illustrates how heterosexism within Black spaces debilitates Black women and creates communal discord and unwellness.[26] In *Meridian*, Black motherhood is all at once reified, maligned, isolating, and unifying. It is empowering even if, more often than not, it is an entrapping, stultifying, and suffocating experience. For instance, Meridian's fellow activist and lover, Truman Held, who represents the idealized masculine Black nationalist, responds to Meridian's reproducing body with violent ambivalence. He finds Meridian's Black (nonvirginal) maternal body sexually aversive and disposable when white female bodies are sexually available. But when he is no longer useful or interesting to white women, he finds Meridian's Black body regenerative—of his ego and his Blackness. Only then does Meridian become, in Truman's eyes, a beautiful "African woman" with whom he is in love. At this realization, he urges Meridian to "*Have* my beautiful black babies."[27] The usually pacifist Meridian thrashes Truman with her backpack. Meridian's rage is not feminist indignation at Truman's sexism, is not anger at his understanding of Black Nationalist womanhood as motherhood. She is incandescent at Truman's empty performativity of Black unity. Truman's request that Meridian mother the movement is not an appeal toward collectivity or community but is utterly self-serving and selfish. Meridian is moved to rage at the violence of Truman's Black nationalist *indifference*: up until this point, he has ignored and dismissed Meridian's declarations of love and commitment in favor of sexual frolicking with the white women volunteers. When he is finished with the volunteers, he then has sex with Meridian, recklessly sows his seeds of future revolutionaries in her womb, and then he disappears. Meridian becomes pregnant only to realize he has started dating yet another white exchange student, so she chooses to have an abortion that she keeps secret in light of Truman's affective (and racial) betrayal. If Meridian's maternal body is the material and metaphorical progenitor of the movement's future, Truman's irresponsible, inconsistent, and flippant dis/regard for her physical body speaks to his actual ambivalence toward the imagined nationalist community. Meridian's Black maternal body holds rhetorical and theoretical value in Truman's Black nationalist vision, but he resists affective connection to Black women—he immediately dodges Meridian's youthful declarations of love—and he never feels compelled to offer protection, support, or care. The aesthetics of Black unity, as signified through the image of Black love, fails to ensure actual communal or interpersonal practices of Black love.

Indeed, several men Walker presents as Black Nationalists fail to offer authentic care. The visual signification of marrying a Black woman stands in for care, often amid violence against Black women. For instance, Black nationalist leader of yesteryear, Mr. Raymonds, marries a dark-skinned Black woman to compensate for his light complexion, and he lectures Meridian on the danger of sexual assault white men pose to Black women, yet he sexually molests and attempts to rape Meridian when she goes to work in his office. Meridian tolerates his assaults because he is physically weak and mildly impotent, which seems to improve Meridian's ability to resist his abuse, and, most importantly, he gives Meridian supplies and food she needs.[28] The Black nationalist focus on racial oppression renders Meridian's experience of intra-racial sexual violence not invisible but unimportant—frivolous. Meridian, with an armful of groceries, runs into Truman, who then asks what provisions Meridian has received from Mr. Raymonds today. Truman comments on Mr. Raymonds's paternal generosity before jokingly suggesting that Mr. Raymonds is less philanthropic and more sugar daddy. Truman jokes, "Does he ever . . . hobble you around his desk?" Although Meridian verbally responds with a quick "Nope," the narrator interjects with, "But of course that was not true."[29] The dialogue and exposition suggest that it is well-known and perhaps even taken for granted that Mr. Raymonds is sexually exploitative—at best. However, Truman then goes on to complain about his experience of racial microaggressions, such as being called "boy" and being made to perform demeaning menial labor working for wealthy, southern white people at a country club. He finishes his rant, "You women sure are lucky not to have to be up against'em all the time."[30] In Truman's estimation, only Black men experience racism, only Black women experience sexual violence, and the latter is inconsequential if committed by a Black man. Consequently, liberation work fails to strive for a political platform and communal ethos that makes Black women safe. The rhetoric of unity is belied by what Black queer studies scholar Erica R. Edwards identifies as the violence of charisma, particularly "the epistemological violence of structuring knowledge of black political subjectivity and movement within a gendered hierarchy of political value that grants uninterrogated power to normative masculinity."[31] This uninterrogated masculine power allows for the rhetorical and visual illusion of racial unity as it obscures the experienced failure and brokenness of community as writ on the Black female body.

Black women pay the physical cost for Black men's empty performance of community care and political collectivity. Black women have and continue to provide the physically, mentally, and spiritually taxing labor of day-to-day movement work: canvassing, calling, mailing, cooking, planning, filing, and typing—on top of careers, family care, and daily violence. Women kept Black nationalist organizations afloat, and yet issues important to them were depoliticized. Seongho Yoon compellingly argues that the sexist hierarchy of labor celebrated what Edwards would call the charisma of nationally recognized Black male leaders, a hierarchy that subordinated the grassroots leadership Black women contributed through their work to sustain the daily operations of local organizations.³² As many women activists remonstrate in Toni Cade Bambara's groundbreaking 1970 anthology, *The Black Woman*, this labor is not only minimalized and taken for granted, but the excess of it also leads to debilitating burnout. Bambara centers her first novel, *The Salt Eaters* (1987), around the psychically devastating effects this labor has on one Black woman activist.³³ Disability so pronouncedly proliferates Black women's literary tradition, particularly post-Black Power and Black Arts Movement, because Black women build on the salvageable tenets of Black Power consciousness and mainstream feminism to consider deeply the impact of "double jeopardy" on the bodymindspirit, to forge creative, sustainable solutions to both counter the deleterious effects of this violence, and to make spiritual peace with the bodyminds they inhabit. Speaking out and drawing attention to the discord—great and small—as felt in and on the bodymindspirit was the first step.

Misogynoir within Black communities not only perpetuates interpersonal and social hierarchies that devalue and dismiss Black women's concerns and make being within their communities unsafe, but it also wreaks havoc on Black women's physical bodies. Illness, injury, and impairment are not only an opportune metaphor to express the harm Black women experience because of sexism but also reflect the embodied, lived consequences of that harm. Sexist violence disables and debilitates. Yet this injury as a product of sexist violence is easily obscured through ableist narratives that view the female body as inherently fragile and weak. In other words, misogynoir disables yet creates structures that silence women disabled by it. Meridian's most intense symptoms—depression, flashbacks, night terrors, headaches, blurring vision, hair loss, and weight loss—develop after she places Eddie Jr. up for adoption, as she silently endures institutionalized sexism at her college and racial violence during activism. Meridian doesn't share her experience with other characters. She never testifies about the abuse she encounters. Instead, the third-person limited narrator provides seemingly unbiased and detached accounts of Meridian's and the other characters, interactions in both chronological time and memory. Structurally, the narrative juxtaposes Meridian's experiences with illness and other causal events in her life; etiology is established through parataxis. And, all too often, Meridian's mysterious symptoms are linked to violent encounters with men.

While the entire novel is a series of flashbacks patched together, a "crazy quilt," the technique of suggesting etiology, particularly sexual abuse as debilitating, through parataxis begins in the chapter "English Walnuts." This chapter assays Meridian's early experiences with her sexuality and sex. In so doing, the the chapter documents how the culture of silence among Black women leaves Black girls vulnerable to predation and disempowers their sexual agency.[34] Meridian, as a young girl, is devoid of sexual agency because her mother has carefully cultivated ignorance about sex.[35] Meridian begins to experience sexual abuse as a prepubescent child as older men take advantage of her youthful naivete and age-appropriate curiosity about gendered physical differences and sex, which has been made all the more mysterious and, therefore, intriguing by the silence and sense of taboo around it. Readers learn that Meridian's first sexual encounters begin when she is just twelve when a local funeral parlor owner, George Daxter, exploits Meridian's curiosity and sweet tooth to sexually molest her. This continues until shortly after she marries her teenage husband. In addition to Daxter, Meridian also encounters Daxter's unnamed assistant, whom she "allows" to chase her around. "The Assistant" pressures Meridian to have sex with him, admonishing that "[experience] is the best, the *only*, teacher," and yet he "was very clever and so never actually forced her beyond a certain point."[36] Moreover, none of these men, nor Meridian's teenage husband, consider Meridian as a sexually desiring subject. We see this, for instance, when the narrator explains that, "Besides, Eddie did not seriously expect more than 'interest' from her" about sex.[37] For all the agency the narrator claims on Meridian's behalf by explaining Meridian's complex experiences of curiosity, fleeting pleasure, and complicity, the power imbalances underscored by Meridian's naivete (Daxter lures her in with candy) and ignorance demonstrate the abusive, predatory, and violent nature of the exchanges.[38]

Most compellingly, they are linked to the strain in Meridian and Eddie's marital sexual intimacy: Meridian has involuntary *physical* reactions during sex that make penetration difficult to impossible. When having sex—or, rather, laying down for sex—Meridian's legs lock, her body stiffens, and her sexual desire dissipates. While the narrator never announces these physical responses as a result of sexual exploitation, the body of the text presents the connection. In one particular encounter in "The English Walnuts," Meridian's physical response is underscored as the scene ends with the narrator explaining that "[Meridian's] response to Eddie's lovemaking [isn't] as uncomplicated as [Eddie] appeared to think."[39] This sentence is immediately followed by a paragraph break that then starts the different, seemingly unrelated story of Meridian's experience with Daxter and The Assistant. This is an example of the formal play attributed to *Meridian*. There are similar moments throughout the novel. For instance, in the chapter I discuss above, "The Conquering Prince," after Truman jokes about Mr. Raymonds seeking sexual favors from Meridian, the moment before she dismisses him with a curt "Nope," Meridian's eye muscle spasms. From there, although this time without the paragraph break, the narrative shifts from the encounter with Truman to a reflection on Meridian's relationship with Mr. Raymonds. Here, the text more explicitly links Meridian's illness and impairments to intra-communal sexist violence by juxtaposing dialogue, Mr. Raymonds's diatribe about how Black women need to be protected from white men, a form of racialized sexual violence acknowledged and validated in the Black liberation organizations, circles, and leaders Meridian encounters, with narrated action, description of Mr. Raymonds sexually harassing Meridian. These men foreclose serious discussion of these abuses, and Meridian never discloses them. Instead, *Meridian* juxtaposes the rhetoric and the actions of charismatic leaders like Mr. Raymonds and Truman, who use the discourse of community and care but whose actions enact harm against Black women. Injury is signaled by slight yet textually significant moments of changes in bodily function. In a culture of silence and disregard towards intra-communal violence, both Meridian's body and the textual body testify. However, like triggered, trauma-related impairments, these embodied testimonies erupt unpredictably and disrupt the chronological plot of the story. Walker's exploration of the embodied impact of oppressive violence structures the "crazy quilt" form of her novel. Debility dissembles the wholeness of Walker's narrative.

And yet there is aesthetic, theoretical, and material space for broken, non-whole bodies of words and flesh. Disability in Walker's and other Black women's writing is not only linked to oppression and dispossession, but it is also a source of aesthetic innovation and a natural, valuable form of bodymindspirit diversity. For instance, as I have been slowly establishing, disabled embodiment inspires Walker's "crazy quilt." One, the culture of quilt-making and elaborate gardening in the southern Black community in which Walker grew up can be considered what I call a Black cultural location of disability. This is evident not only in the direct reference to madness in naming her aesthetic "crazy" but also evident in the histories and folk culture Walker retrieves, attempts to capture, and celebrates with her writing. Walker describes her mother's gardening, as well as other Art Black women have created, like quilting, cooking, and singing, as a coping mechanism against the madness that threatens to consume her as a creative Black woman conscripted by sexism, racism, and poverty. As we learn through the disabled character Maggie in Walker's often anthologized short story, "Everyday Use," quilt-making, like gardening, is not only artistic and creative but also practical. Yes, one can frame and display a beautiful, handstitched quilt, but it is better used to keep warm, to supplant elemental exposure in poor living conditions because of a divestment of resources as racial dispossession. Additionally, Walker signals that for Black women, these activities stemmed "a numb and bleeding madness." These cultural activities are a pragmatic form of creative expression to keep figurative madness at bay. While Walker uses "madness" metaphorically in this cited passage, in her other essays and stories, gardening, quilting, cooking, and singing self-sooth against over-stimulation, anxiety, depression, and—La Marr Jurelle Bruce has aptly noted—exclamation (murder of self and/or others).[40] In other words, these activities are all also ways of *stimming*—self-stimulating and often repetitive actions used to alleviate the overwhelming and potentially incapacitating symptoms of some mental and neurological disabilities. Black women's folk Art can be read as the creative product of disability. Walker's mother's gardens, Mama's quilts in "Everyday Use," and my nana's macaroni and cheese and fried chicken lie somewhere in between cultural locations of disability that confine and the disability culture that liberates. As Gayl Jones draws inspiration for formal innovation from the blues as a Black cultural location of disability, Walker draws on Black women's quilting. What results is *Meridian*, a novel that frustrates and upends normative modes of storytelling through a disability writing aesthetic. Like Walker's mother's gardens, a disability aesthetic enables a creative response to the embodied consequences of oppressive histories.

Meridian also makes space for broken, nonnormative bodymindspirits. While many characters in the novel are driven mad by the strain and heartache of racial violence—Meridian included—others seem to be naturally predisposed to madness. For instance, the chapter "Indians and Ecstasy" explores Black-Indigenous relations through the matter of land ownership. Here, the narrative uses parataxis to position madness as pleasurable spiritual euphoria. Meridian's parents inherit a sacred Indigenous American burial ground—the Sacred Serpent—as part of their family's land. This land, at least as far back as Meridian's great-grandmother, her father's grandmother, Feather Mae, is linked to madness and euphoria. Feather Mae is rumored to have "some slight and harmless madness"[41] and, as a youth, she would visit the coil of the Sacred Serpent and "[step] into another world."[42] The "spiritual intoxication" she experiences compels her to renounce organized religion, most immediately the Black Baptist Church, in favor of her own brand of paganism: "near the end of her life she loved walking nude about her yard and worshipped only the sun."[43] Meridian comes to understand that her father experiences a similar spiritual euphoria in the coil of the Sacred Serpent, and she, too, goes to experience the snake's coil. What begins as a slight, stinging pain then turns into what Meridian describes as a literal out-of-body experience. Meridian and her father come to learn that they share this spiritual connection to the land, the dead, the living, and being; however, this also comes with the realization that they, too, "[share] the peculiar madness of her great-grandmother."[44] Although Feather Mae's life is not sketched out enough to determine if she has always experienced "some slight and harmless madness," that Meridian and her father also share this madness suggests not only an understanding of diverse minds but also that neurodiversity may be pleasurable. I am not arguing that madness cannot be experienced as distressing. Many people in the material world outside of Walker's novel, as well as the characters within it, experience mental distress. Walker, too, writes of how poverty, sexism, and racism constrain Black women to the point of phenomenal madness.[45] What I am arguing is that Walker imagines the experience of madness along a spectrum that also considers experiencing reality nonnormatively as a source of euphoria. What could be an unsettling and alarmingly new, unbelievable experience of reality is, for Feather Mae, Meridian's father, and Meridian, experienced as ecstasy.

Walker draws on Indigenous American practices to challenge the ableist presumption that mental disability must always be experienced as debilitating. Many Indigenous American tribes have induced altered psychic states for bodymindspirit healing, particularly feelings of psychic and spiritual dis-ease. While states of altered consciousness have been affected using ceremonial drumming, dancing, and, less often, ingesting plants such as Peyote, Walker connects Feather Mae's and Meridian's altered states of consciousness to their connection with the land as sacred. Walker's emphasis on the Sacred Serpent as a burial ground where the remnants of Indigenous people nourish their food suggests that this sacred land is a point of ancestral connection. As Barbara Alice Mann shares from Indigenous wisdom, "for the first five feet down, Mother Earth is made of the Ancestors."[46] As is often reported from those who participate in ceremonial healing through consciousness-altering spiritual practice, Meridian and her father return from the coil of the Sacred Serpent feeling "renewed," "intoxicated," and "ecstatic." These ceremonies have proven so successful that researchers have taken great interest in their efficacy in treating mental illnesses and use them as a cultural element to more traditional Western mental health therapies and treatment regimens for Native populations. Rather than focusing on curing or treating mental illness, Walker focuses on how these spiritual states heal ancestral alienation yet arouse madness.

Tellingly, Feather Mae discarded religions that failed to root their theology in present, physical experiences of ecstasy. Here, Walker joins Black nationalist critiques of Western Christianity as forced upon and then embraced by Black people. Black nationalism took issue with the theology of previous generations because nationalists believed the Black church encouraged Black people to accept the long-suffering of racism on earth in favor of the peace and pleasure that awaited them in heaven. Although they offered a condescending and reductive understanding of Black Christian spiritual practices,

Black Nationalists quite aptly identified how white enslavers imposed Christianity on Black Africans to both justify white supremacy and dominance and make enslaved Black people compliant. Black Nationalists recognized that in addition to these goals, the imposition of Christianity on Black people also served to strip them of their traditional spiritual beliefs. Thus, Black cultural nationalism exhorted Black people to rediscover their ancestral spiritual practices. While Walker is similarly critical of Christianity, she also refuses to adopt non-Western spiritual practices uncritically. Instead, like many of her contemporaries, she crafts a syncretic spiritual paradigm that borrows from and revises multiple Black and Indigenous American and, in Walker's case, explicitly pagan beliefs and practices. These Africanist spiritual systems differ from Christianity in that disability is not automatically presumed to be in need of healing. Although Christian religious models have understood disability as a blessing, they understand disability as such within the belief that it is through physical suffering that one becomes spiritually refined or pure. Walker offers a spiritual model based on interconnectivity and the immediacy of physical pleasure. Feather Mae and her descendants embrace their experience of mild madness not because they suffer from mental alterity but because they experience ecstasy in it. Moreover, Walker does not silo pleasure to one facet of being; rather, it is felt in the entirety of one's bodymindspirit. Walker's spirituality echoes Audre Lorde's Africanist spirituality as theorized in "Uses of the Erotic: The Erotic as Power."[47] Moreover, Walker draws on the Africanist and Indigenous spiritual belief that wellness is "harmony within oneself, with others, and with one's surroundings."[48] Feather Mae, Meridian's father, and Meridian all experience physical and spiritual pleasure that seems to stem from or is enabled by their mental difference. This rejects Enlightenment understandings of the body, mind, and spirit as distinct. In Walker's spiritual cosmology, they are all interconnected, and what affects one affects them all.[49] Wellness *and* disability in Walker's novel are a source of connection—with one's bodymindspirit, with the land, and with history. While the possibility of being mad gives Meridian and her father pause—they at times "brooded" over the implications of it—Meridian is particularly awe-struck that their shared madness becomes a "tangible... connection to the past."[50] Disability is a source of generational continuity.

Disability Community, Communities of Care

Black nationalist ideology promised to provide a sense of racial unity and community through racial consciousness, but its investments in patriarchy resulted in marginalizing the very people whose labor sustained these organizations—Black women. Moreover, the focus on race served to obscure intra-communal violence. While Black women criticized these elements of the movement for how they inhibited community building, they did not divest from the concept of community altogether. Black women activist-writers rejected the rugged individualism that serves as the center point of white supremacist capitalist society, but they also rejected the rhetoric of a racial community that assumed homogeneity and privileged men. The latter simply reproduced the former. Both ideologies are absent of care.

Care and caregiving are undervalued aspects of everyday life. Because individualism and independence are prized in the US, those who more visibly rely on care services are often looked down upon and infantilized. Seeking help far too often accompanies a loss of dignity. People who need care are widely understood as a burdensome drain on valuable resources. Moreover, asking for care, especially from state agencies, makes one vulnerable to abuse, surveillance, policing, and loss of freedom and agency through institutionalization. Moreover, care work is problematically gendered. It's diminished because it's considered women's work. Care work is also racialized. Poor women of color are most often assigned caregiving labor such as domestic work, home health aides, and childcare with little appreciation, much abuse, and little compensation. *Meridian*, critiques the exploitation of women's caregiving through its critique of motherhood. When women are assigned care work to the exclusion of other choices, and when that care work is done in isolation, it is a source of slow soul murder.

Yet care and caregiving are essential to survival. In the midst of economic divestment and the absence of a social failsafe, Walker describes communities marked by interdependence and care. Caregiving, in Walker's (re)vision, is communal and has the power to lessen or erase the stigma and shame of poverty. Caregiving, as a disability justice praxis, seeks to transform care into what writer, artist, and disability justice activist Leah Lakshmi Piepzna-Samarasinha describes as "a collective responsibility that's maybe even deeply joyful." Care, according to Piepzna-Samarasinha, is "about our attempts to get what we need to love and live, interdependently, in the world and in our homes . . . where [disabled people] are in control, joyful, building community, loved, giving, and receiving, that doesn't burn anyone out or abuse or underpay anyone in the process."[51] Care work is a love praxis. And, as bell hooks so soulfully and carefully theorizes, "To truly love we must learn to mix various ingredients—care, affection, recognition, respect, commitment, and trust, as well as honest and open communication. . . . we cannot claim to love if we are hurtful and abusive. Love and abuse cannot coexist."[52] Care is the practice of love. Whereas the masculinist ideologies of Black nationalist community allowed and enabled violence and abuse, Walker imagines communities connected by an embodied shared past and strengthened by caregiving as a love praxis.

In Walker's novel, Meridian feels ostracized from people and communities that lack care. For instance, the Black nationalist community in which Meridian finds herself ignores sexual violence against girls and women. Saxon College circumscribes their Black female students to rigid prescriptions of Black ladyhood and shames those who fail or refuse to comply. These are all failures of care for the Black bodymindspirit. Indeed, the moments where the community fails to tend to the sick, disabled, or diseased bodymindspirit are the moments that the text most vehemently criticizes the absence of care in Black communities. For instance, although various characters and the narrator mock Saxon throughout the novel, it is when the president of the college refuses to allow Meridian and other students to bury Wile Chile, a young girl abandoned and dis/abled because she never learned the language and societal norms around hygiene and manners, that the text excoriates the institution. Meridian's friend Anne-Marion calls the president a "flaky bastard" and "dishrag" for "crackers."[53] The president refuses to risk his proximity to white power and economic privilege by aligning Saxon with Black disrespectability as symbolized by Wild Chile's undisciplined, unmanageable, unredeemable, and therefore disposable disabled bodymindspirit. This failure of care compels the Saxon students to stage the first riot in the college's history. In *Meridian*, white supremacy and capitalism are interwoven with an ableist, medical model approach to disability that centers on cure. Wild Chile refused to be cured through socialization into Black middle-class values and so remained disposable even after death. The Saxon upper administrators and local leaders deny her burial in the local cemetery.

Meridian, too, is rendered disposable for recalcitrant illness. For instance, after Meridian has a particularly long flare-up of symptoms that keep her in bed, Anne-Marion concludes that "she could not endure a friendship that required such caring vigilance. . . . [she] could not continue to care about a person she could not save."[54] She ends their friendship. While Meridian's illness, for Anne-Marion, certainly signifies Meridian's sensitivity to social injustice, chronic illness itself requires an ethos of caregiving and interdependence that Anne-Marion rejects, particularly if said condition cannot or will not be solved through cure. Tellingly, despite Anne-Marion's revolutionary nationalist politics, she is deeply invested in capitalism. The narrator explains,

Anne-Marion did not know if she would be a success as a capitalist, while Meridian did not think she could enjoy owning things others could not have. Anne-Marion wanted blacks to have the same opportunity to make as much money as the richest white people. But Meridian wanted the destruction of the rich as a class and the eradication of all personal economic preserves.⁵⁵

Capitalism's investment in individualism and exceptionalism feeds into curative logic and results in an ableist refusal of care.

While Meridian fails to discover care in formal Black civil rights organizations, she does discover belonging along with and through care among the poor Black folks throughout the South. In the novel, Meridian eventually moves to Chicokema, a small Georgia-Alabama village, to advocate for the poor. There, Meridian finds belonging among others who are similarly ill. The narrator observes that though "[Meridian] was frail and sickly-looking ... among the impoverished, badly nourished black villagers ... she did not look out of place. In fact, she looked as if she belonged."⁵⁶ Meridian not only looks like them, but she also shares a similar outlook that has been shaped by chronic illness. The narrator continues,

> [like] them, she could summon whatever energy a task that had to be performed required, and like them, this ability seemed to her something her ancestors had passed on from the days of slavery when there had been no such thing as a sick slave, only a 'malingering' one. Like the luckless small farmers around her who tended their crops 'around the weather' ... she lived 'around' her illness. Like them, it seemed pointless to her to complain.⁵⁷

Just as shared trauma creates comradery, so community emerges around disability. Meridian and the people of Chicokema are joined by "the interrelations of identity, history, and the body."⁵⁸ The debilitated body indicates a shared or similar history of racial injustice. Similar experiences with chronic illness provide them a sense of shared history with their common enslaved ancestors and a shared understanding of illness, labor, and life. For instance, she tells Truman, "Of course I'm sick,'" and then continues that the Chicokema poor "have a saying for people who fall down as I do: If a person is hit hard enough, even if she stands, she falls. Isn't that perceptive?"⁵⁹ The folks of Chicokema recognize how oppression disables. Yet, their approach to illness is not one that focuses on or privileges "cure"—indeed, they are much too poor to afford medical treatment—but one that necessarily integrates illness into daily life activities. And, just as feminist disability studies scholar Susan Wendell argues, chronic illness and pain do not preclude action but rather demand that one learns how to manage and work around it.[60] This is not the same as the "overcoming" narratives that disability studies scholars denounce for their ableism and unreasonable demands. It is a "perceptive" and pragmatic approach to bodies and socio-economic conditions with roots in enslavement, knowledge garnered through experience with disability and borne out of crisis—a cripistemology.[61] Disability, therefore, is not only a tangible source of generational and historical continuity but also a source of communal Black disability consciousness.

Central to this disability-informed paradigm of labor is an emphasis on interdependence and mutual caregiving. Meridian shifts her activist practice to demonstrations of care. For instance, Meridian stands down a tank for the rights of poor, mostly Black, children to have equal access to see a mummified woman. While she and the adults know that the exhibit is fake and its owner profits from patriarchal violence, the poor residents appreciate her willingness to suffer for rights, no matter how trivial, the civil rights movement failed to secure.[62] While Lauren Cardon positions Meridian as Chicokema's "leader" for her activism,[63] I argue that the relationship is symbiotic. When Meridian collapses into paralysis from her efforts, the men in town gently carry her across their shoulders to the home they provide, and they "[bring] boxes and boxes of food," "even . . . a cow."[64] The villagers care for Meridian just as much, or more than, she cares for them. The focus on caregiving challenges myths of independence and individualism that have been used to pathologize disability. Not only is the disabled body often not able to perpetuate the illusion of independence and thereby privilege the individual, but it often completely shatters the myth of independence by reminding society of the body's vulnerability. While some disability studies scholar-activists have inadvertently reproduced the focus on individuality in their emphasis on access and independent living, scholars like Rosemarie Garland-Thomson challenge the value placed on independence altogether. Meridian may be "always alone," but her commitment to mutual care and activism will also always position her within the community.

In her early autobiographical essay and fiction, Walker poignantly critiques the absence of care in Black nationalist communities. Communal identity, as imagined by much Black nationalist discourse, failed to consider the political and social concerns of Black folks who were not heterosexual cis Black men. Indeed, the Black nationalist community cloaked the harm engendered in patriarchy. Black women, like Walker, criticized this version of collective liberation. In her writing, Walker instead mines southern Black culture for a model of liberation structured around interdependence and mutual caregiving. Because of ongoing histories of injurious and debilitating racialization, this southern Black communal ethos is informed by shared experience of the disabled bodymindspirit as understood through Africanist and Indigenous spiritual cosmologies that offer alternative understandings of brokenness, healing, and wholeness. In Walker's writing, we get southern, Black cripistemologies—crip ways of knowing—that move toward embodied practices of togetherness and communal care.

In the next section, I will continue this conversation about community and care in Toni Morrison's *Paradise*. As in my analysis of Walker, I identify how Morrison posits the misogyny of nationalist ideology as disabling. I will discuss how these injured women who are most marginalized by patriarchy find crip community together, especially as they work together to heal. In this section, however, I devote more attention to how Morrison theorizes healing and wholeness through an anti-ableist Africanist spiritual frame.

Powerful Disabled Women Empowering Disabled Communities in Toni Morrison's Fiction

As with Alice Walker's *Meridian*, Toni Morrison's 1997 novel *Paradise* also troubles Black nationalist understandings of communal liberation. Set between the late 1800s and 1975 in the fictional Exoduster town of Ruby, formally called Haven, *Paradise* follows Ruby's undoing as its leaders adopt ideologies reflective of the heterosexist discourse in Black nationalism. Militant exclusionary practices and heteropatriarchy eventually lead the male leaders to attempt mass murder against a group of five women who live in an abandoned Catholic school for "Indian Children." Through each chapter, each named for a different woman associated with the convent and/or citizen of Ruby, Morrison takes us in and out of time and place to explore the growing tensions in Ruby and the heartaches that drive each woman to the Convent where they will eventually begin the task of healing. In so doing, Morrison presents two ideas of community—one violently masculinist and the other women-centered and in the process of becoming.

Like Walker, Morrison critiques how heterosexism in Black communities transformed the discourse of racial solidarity into gender solidarity in ways that enable harm. Morrison particularly takes on negative stereotypes attributed to Black women and, rather than reject them, she revalues them. Like Alice Walker's Meridian, a disabled character who refuses to let dominant concepts of proper womanhood and motherhood dictate her actions, Toni

Morrison represents disabled characters who also shun societal prescriptions for womanhood. Disability identity empowers these women to subvert oppressive ideologies and carve out spaces where others, also marginalized for their inability or refusal to meet the demands of the dominant society, can find refuge and communal belonging. Whereas much Black nationalist discourse envisioned communal liberation around either cultural or financial self-determination, Morrison imagines liberation as the mutual desire to heal from the effects of oppression and then go out in the world in the fight against social injustice. The women in *Paradise* may have been harmed by how society weaponizes stereotypes to pathologize Black women's human experiences of hurt and misfortune and thereby ostracize them, but they heal from harm once in community with each other through a healing practice informed by Africanist spirituality and cripistemologies. Meridian's self-defining of herself also speaks to the women in Morrison's novel. Meridian says, "I am strong, actually . . . I'm just not Superwoman."[65] Morrison, like Walker, does not repudiate a harmful controlling image (the strong Black woman) nor uncritically embrace it, but by accepting her disabled bodymind, she uncovers the truth for her within it. Similarly, in *Paradise*, rather than imagine bold, bawdy, husbandless women—matriarchs—as the detriment of Black people, Morrison presents audacious women who sustain and nourish the community as matriarchs, but with matriarchy absent of the violent will to power exercised by men in a patriarchal society.

Morrison revalues the stereotypes attributed to women, especially Black women, through theorizing what she terms outlaws and pariahs. While Black nationalist discourse, as manifest in Black Aesthetic theory, urged Black creators to refute and refuse negative stereotypes, pejorative gender tropes proliferate. Black women were regularly considered Mammies, Matriarchs, Jezebels, Sapphires, and Bitches. Many Black Arts and post-Black Arts women writers actively challenged these stereotypes. However, Morrison, rather than respond defensively to the venom used to weaponize these tropes, questioned the impulse to denounce the characteristics often attributed to them. For instance, Morrison embraces the figure of the Mammy, a figure many Black people reject because of the Mammy's characterization as a fat, dark-skinned matriarch who supposedly fawns over the white children and adults who employ her to the neglect of her own family. For Morrison, though, the Mammy possesses a special, often discredited knowledge of nature. She is physically strong as well as a healer and nurturer. According to Morrison, "That stereotype is bad only when people think it's less. . . . Those women were terrific, but they were perceived of as beastly in the very things that were wonderful about them."[66] These women were wise as well as willing and able to perform care work as both employment and love praxis. While Black women whose bodies mirror that of the Mammy face harrowing lived realities due to colorism and anti-fatness, the qualities associated with the Mammy are only an insult through an elitist, sexist, sizeist, anti-Black worldview.

Likewise, Morrison values women who fail to comply with the strict prescriptions of proper womanhood as normalized and policed in a patriarchal society. These are women she identifies as "outlaws." In an interview with Anne Marie-O'Connor, Morrison explains, "Outlaw women who don't follow the rules are always interesting to me . . . because they push themselves, and us, to the edge. The women who step outside the borders, or who think other thoughts, define the limits of civilization, but also challenge it."[67] Like the Mammy, these women are capable of both providing and nurturing. They often possess what Morrison calls "the funk," traditional Black values, and "the ancient properties," traditional conceptions of Black womanhood.[68] As manifested in Morrison's fiction, the outlaw woman is often a community pariah. The pariah, for Morrison, is the unusual character, one that, when found within a community, can be "useful for the conscience of that community."[69] These women not only subvert social norms but also spirit norms. They tend to have some form of nonnormative embodiment, such as Pilate Dead's navellessness in *Song of Solomon*. It is often through navigating their gender and physical differences that nonnormative embodiment becomes a location of cripistemology.

As Walker suggests in *Meridian*, the singular focus on racial oppression obscures intra-racial violence, but, as Morrison indicates, a group pushed to the margins of the community that can absorb the fears and anxieties of the center also enables the center to ignore its ethical and moral shortcomings. Through the pariah relationship the Convent women have with Ruby, Morrison demonstrates how Black nationalist ideology relied on sexism to anchor its sense of racial unity and use the desire for racial uplift to obscure or justify sexist violence. In *Paradise*, for instance, the women who occupy the Convent are maligned because they refuse to silence and subordinate their gender-specific concerns or accept the narrow and belittled roles reserved and assigned to women. Consolata (Connie), Mavis, Grace (Gigi), Seneca, and Pallas (Divine) don't follow the rules, and/or they challenge the limits of civilization. They are women who mostly attempted to occupy and perform normative roles outlined for them but found these scripts tragically unable to hold the fullness of their life experiences, experiences like the death of children, sexual assault, state violence, and familial betrayal. They turn away from these societal expectations and, bitterly and begrudgingly (at first), toward each other at the Convent, where they settle as outlaws on the outskirts of Ruby. There, they relate to Ruby citizens as pariahs. People in Ruby, especially the men, recast these women's personal adversity and failure or refusal to embody proscriptive womanhood into generalized stereotypes levied pejoratively. For example, Gigi, who actively participated in protests, marches, and demonstrations, the memory of which haunts her, is immediately sexualized by the men of Ruby. K. D., who is engaged to Arnette, even initiates a sexual relationship with Gigi, only to callously dismiss her. Rather than contend with their inability to live up to their own rigid moral standards, the men from Ruby project their lust onto Gigi by figuring her as a Jezebel. While none of these women commit acts any more or less immoral than the other residents of Ruby—indeed, women and men from Ruby become entangled with the women from the Convent in various ways—these women become scapegoats for the political and personal problems that erupt and plague the town. As pariahs, they are useful, perhaps necessary, for the ethical consciousness of Ruby. As Anna, a woman from Ruby, thinks—". . . the Convent women had saved the day. Nothing like other folks' sins for distraction."[70]

Rather than distance themselves from their outlaw status, the women in the Convent embrace it. They find pleasure in goading the citizens of Ruby who are obvious in their contempt for them. What comes to distinguish the women from the Convent is when they begin to shift the focus onto themselves and heal, rather than hide, the self-harmful coping mechanisms they've developed to survive the physical, mental, and spiritual injuries they've sustained. As with Alice Walker's Meridian, the hardships Consolata, Mavis, Gigi, Seneca, and Pallas experience are writ on their bodymindspirits. Mavis experiences a visual and aural reality that others do not share; she sees her deceased infants and hears the twins' cries. Like Mavis, Pallas also hears infants' cries, a reality not shared with others. Pallas also restricts, binges, and purges her food until she feels ill. Seneca tries to hide that she, at times, self-harms through cutting. And Consolata loses nearly all her sight and then comes to experience her drinking as disruptive to her life. This healing process begins to take place when Consolata, the eldest ancestor figure, begins to work on her own healing, which she then uses in service of healing others.

When Consolata becomes blind, she acquires the spiritual gift to heal. Yet, the Western religion enforced on her by the nuns who kidnapped her from her home and placed her in the Convent when it was still the school for "Indian Girls" has taught her to fear her healing power. Devoutly Catholic, Consolata views her healing ability as witchcraft and shuns it. She also internalizes the sexual violence enacted against her as a child sex worker—viewing her girl-self as wanton. She remains celibate for thirty years. She ends her celibacy with Deek, a married man from Ruby, but, as K. D. will also treat Gigi, Deek abruptly ends his and Connie's affair. It is this distorted view of herself that Consolata must heal. Whereas a biomedical model, or even a traditional religious model, would focus on curing bodily impairments, Consolata's healing work has nothing to do with her blindness. She never turns her healing light towards her own eyes.[71] Instead, healing requires shedding internalized sexism and decolonizing her bodymindspirit by reintegrating her spirit and flesh. For Consolata, the two were wholly separate, and years of devotion to Christ were "transferred" to a consuming love for Deek. Whereas the nuns, Mary Magna in particular, made Consolata separate the two, even more so after Consolata's affair with Deek, healing comes when Consolata learns to "[never] break them in two. Never put one over the other."[72]

This lesson—never divide your flesh and your spirit—is one that she shares with the girls as they heal and carve a life together through interdependence and care work. They farm and cook for each other. They comfort each other. Although they do not all get along perfectly, they come to treat each other with respect and, most importantly, dignity. Unlike the men of Ruby, who believe that difference is a threat and whose mode of liberation represses and ultimately leads to murderous violence, liberation for the Convent women is healing. These women bond over the wounds they've sustained in a racist, heterosexist world and listen to how this violence manifests differently based on other, non-shared identities. Worlds of hurt injure these women's bodymindspirits; healing comes when they interrogate internalized heterosexist ideology and reconnect with their own and each other's embodied discredited knowledge.

Healing in *Paradise* involves facing and embracing the fullness of one's humanity. Unlike the Black nationalist vision of community that, much like white, Western Christianity requires one to reject (or compartmentalize) aspects of oneself, Morrison presents a community where one sees and allows others to see people in their entirety. They hold and are held. Once Consolata owns her power and the discredited knowledge that she learns from Lone, a conjure woman from Ruby, she is able to guide Mavis, Gigi, Seneca, and Pallas on their healing journey. The healing process for the women is spiritual. Healing is a practice of bearing witness to each other's pasts, reconnecting with the Divine, the land, and their own bodymindspirit in the present, and "loud dreaming" their future. Consolata's loud dreaming is that of Paradise:

> [a] place where white sidewalks meet the sea and fish the color of plums swam alongside children. She spoke of fruit that tasted the way sapphires look and boys using rubies for dice. Of scented cathedrals

made of gold where gods and goddesses sat in the pews with the congregation. Of carnations tall as trees. Dwarfs with diamonds for teeth. Snakes aroused by poetry and bells. Then she told them of a woman named Piedade, who sang but never said a word.[73]

This vision of Paradise is one of harmony, balance, and beauty. It is a deeply sensual place. It is a deeply spiritual place. It is a place of abundance, and the accouterments of wealth and the presence of the Divine are accessible to the folk and scaffolded into the everyday. It is a place where the only detailed descriptions of people are those who are nonnormative—"Dwarfs with diamonds for teeth" and "Piedade, who sang but never said a word." Morrison, as with Alice Walker, uses disability to imagine the future otherwise. Like Walker, Morrison's communities are relationships marked by care and interdependence. Unlike Walker, they need not share embodied histories but merely make space for each other's bodymindspirits, witness each other's histories, and use their embodied knowledge to cocreate the future. They destroy worlds—are destroyed by the world—and build new ones from the pieces of themselves. The women of the Convent create their own cripistemologies, a cripistemology of healing. Consolata, like Baby Sugg's from *Beloved*, creates a gospel born of the flesh that frees the women's minds and spirits.

Conclusion

Historically and in our cultural imagination, disabled people have been cast away or shut away. What we glean from Black women writers, however, is an alternative narrative, one where Black women who occupy multiple marginalized identities in this world are disabled because of their degraded status but find and forge disabled community at the margins of society. Indeed, Alice Walker claims community as her inheritance: "What the black Southern writer inherits as a natural right is a sense of community."[74] It is in this community, through Africanist spiritual onto-epistemologies, that Black women begin to heal from the spiritual wound of being societal discards. In Alice Walker's book, Meridian finds crip community in interdependent care communities among poor Black southerners, and in Toni Morrison's *Paradise*, outlaw women, pariahs, form a healing circle. In both instances, strong maternal figures and/or motherwork are central to crip community, even as each novel presents motherhood as a fraught identity for Black women. Indeed, motherhood is a central theme in Black women's writing, and the body of Black feminist literary criticism is devoted to that writing. I take up this theme in the next chapter.

Chapter 3

Cripping Motherhood

> I am black and I am female and I am a mother and I am bisexual and I am a nationalist and I am an antinationalist. And I mean to be fully and freely all that I am!
>
> —JUNE JORDAN, "A NEW POLITICS OF SEXUALITY"

As intimated at the end of the previous chapter, within rhetoric about Black community, the figure of the Black Mother is both a reified and vilified signifier. This chapter focuses on disability and motherhood as a contested point of identity in Black women's writing. On the one hand, ableism, misogynoir, poverty, and heterosexism within the Black community stripped Black women of maternal agency. On the other hand, narratives of Black maternal pathology that originated in slavery continued into the twentieth century. In the larger social discourse, Black mothers were portrayed as domineering and dominating—and disabling. The matriarchal structure they allegedly imposed in their households and within the community emasculated Black men, leading to the socioeconomic problems that plagued poor Black communities and debilitated Black social progress. Daniel Patrick Moynihan went so far as to argue that "In essence, the Negro community has been forced into a matriarchal structure which, because it is too out of line with the rest of the American society, seriously *retards* the progress of the group as a whole, and imposes a crushing burden on the Negro male and, in consequence, on a great many Negro women as well."[1] Many Black men quietly (and vocally) agreed. Moynihan went on to voice the common (fear) assessment that Black women birth too many (illegitimate) children that then become dependent on the state. Within this discourse, Black mothers are metaphorically and, as I will get to later in this chapter, physically and ontologically disabling, with ableist attitudes about dependency and care underscoring the supposed pathology of it all. He argues that it is the national government's job to establish "a stable Negro family structure."[2] Coincidently, reproductive health centers sprang up in poor, urban communities, and Black women were often targeted and coerced into long-term birth control technologies without their knowledgeable consent.[3] Consequently, many folks influenced by the Black Power Movement spurned birth control for Black women. These groups likened Black women choosing to use birth control to being complicit in the genocide of Black people. At the same time, Black nationalist discourse rhetorically appropriated Black women's reproductive capacity in service of the ongoing war for Black liberation. Black men had reduced Black women once again to breeders, this time of future generations of soldiers in the fight for Black liberation. None of these narratives took into consideration the range of thoughts, experiences, and desires of Black women.

Although Black motherhood is deeply intertwined with issues of disability, Black mothers' experiences are also largely absent in disability studies discourse. Within disability studies, much of the early scholarship on disability and motherhood focused on the experiences of white parents raising disabled children. Scholarship that privileges the experiences and concerns of disabled mothers has tended to focus on how these parents measure their mothering against white, Western able-bodied norms and expectations. For instance, most conversations about disabled motherhood focus on the early twentieth century with the rise of eugenics practices and improved gynecological and reproductive medicine and technology. Disabled white women were actively discouraged from becoming mothers, and to decrease the chance that they would spawn children with disabilities, these women were either pressured to use birth control or were often sterilized routinely without true, knowledgeable consent. As Claudia Malacrida describes in "Mothering and Disability: Implications for Theory and Practice," today, disabled women share that they are still discouraged from becoming mothers by doctors and loved ones. Additionally, disabled women share that finding romantic partners—long-term or short-term—is difficult, usually because disabled women are culturally represented as sexually undesirable and asexual. This is reinforced by the lack of information concerning sex and reproduction available to disabled people. Disabled folk who become pregnant soon learn that there is often little information about pregnancy for disabled people.

Some with physical disabilities even find gynecologists' offices inaccessible. The message is clear: disability and motherhood are incongruent.

As a result, the critical discourse on disability and motherhood reclaims maternal identity by challenging societal attitudes that assume disabled women are incapable of being good mothers. Carol Thomas argues that disabled (white) people identify three predominant themes in their experiences with motherhood: 1.) "engagement with 'risk' discourse," or the concern that their disability or disability related-issues, like whether to stay on or get off medication, will compromise their or their child's life. 2.) "The pressure . . . to demonstrate that they are, or could be, 'good enough mothers'" against societal presumptions that disabled women, often dependents themselves, are unable to care for a child, which puts them at risk of losing custody of their children. Thomas elaborates, "Living with the fear of losing the right to care for their children forces some mothers to go to great lengths to 'present' themselves and their children as managing "normally"—often at significant personal costs in terms of comfort and emotional and physical well-being. One consequence is that assistance may not be requested when it is needed because the mother feels that her request may be interpreted to mean that she is not capable." This overlaps with Thomas's last theme 3.) "the experiences of receiving unhelpful 'help' from health and social care workers." Healthcare and social workers strip away disabled women's agency when they "'[take] over' decisions about their client's pregnancy or childcare responsibilities, because they assume that they know 'what is in the patient's best interests.'"[4] However, these studies take as their starting point a maternal ideal based on white standards and constructions of family. According to Malacrida, "The ideal mother in Western culture is positioned as a woman who mothers naturally, is always and immediately present to care for her baby or child, and who does this mothering selflessly and seamlessly."[5] This reflects a paradigm that privileges a hetero-normative nuclear family where the biological mother stays at home and cares for her children or has a job with reasonable work hours and can afford childcare. Disabled white women measure their experiences with motherhood against a model from which Black women— disabled and nondisabled—have always been excluded. Moreover, this fantasy of white motherhood emerges in relation to and therefore depends on pathologized Black motherhood. Black women, however, have defined their own experiences and priorities around maternal identity.

Motherhood is often figured as an empowering identity for Black women. Black women sought and embraced the maternal agency wrested away from their enslaved foremothers yet also vied for empowered reproductive choices, even the choice not to give birth to a biological child.[6] They recognized the social and economic barriers to empowered motherhood and used them to inform their political agendas. Unlike their (white) feminist counterparts who rejected motherhood as a technology of oppression by trapping women within the domestic rather than in the political and economic sphere, Black women understood mothering as valuable labor not mutually exclusive to economic independence. As Toni Morrison affirms, "Our history as Black women is the history of women who could build a house *and* have some children, and there was no problem." For Morrison, Black women know "how to be complete human beings." According to Morrison, attaining an education or pursuing a career did not "keep us from our nurturing abilities."[7] Morrison's evaluation of Black maternal identity draws on a history where Black mothers have always had to parent and work. Moreover, mothering was a communal effort that included Black men. The family extended beyond the nuclear unit and biological bonds.[8] Motherwork became an apt and powerful figuration of the ideals of care and interdependence that contemporary Black women writers valorized. The image and rhetoric of the Black Mother came to signify the recovery of Black women's image and history and a means to articulate a tradition of Black female cultural production.[9] Thus, the figure of the Black mother became an empowering and potent metaphor for a Black feminist onto-epistemology. It was more than a role. Black motherhood was and continues to be both a practice and an identity.[10] In an anti-Black world out to maim and murder Black bodymindspirits, Black women strive to provide their children and communities with a sense of wholeness. While there are many obstacles to Black women's motherwork, nurturing and valuing the children society has tossed away as disposable remains central to Black feminist thought. Moreover, Black women draw strength from their identity as mothers and othermothers, affirming their self-worth. Mothering is healing work for self and community in Black women's writing.

A powerful example of motherhood as a healing practice is in Alice Walker's essay "Beauty: When the Other Dancer is the Self," published in both *In Search of Our Mothers' Gardens* and *The Black Women's Health Book*. In this essay, Walker theorizes the debilitating effects of racist and sexist oppression in Black women's lives through her feelings of insecurity and anger after her eye is injured, disfigured, and eventually replaced by a glass prosthetic. In the essay, histories of settler-colonialism and sexism continue to enact violence against the Black female body as Walker recalls the game of cowboy and Indians that left her, the Indian, weaponless as her brother, the cowboy, shot her with a BB gun. Walker is silenced—first by her brothers, who want to avoid accountability, and then by the rest of her family, who wish to protect her brothers. Walker is made to bear the consequences of sexist violence. She is sent away. Walker suffers—not from her eye injury and subsequent partial blindness but from diminished self-esteem and a great sense of injustice. The privilege afforded to those deemed beautiful is mutable and limited; it fails to protect women against debilitating or deathly sexist violence. Walker presents herself as broken in body, mind, and spirit by the complex constellation of racist, ableist, and patriarchal violence at work in the lives of Black women.

Healing begins for Walker through mothering. In the essay, her then three-year-old daughter notices her disfigured and blind eye for the first time. Rather than say something hurtful in childlike indifference, as Walker expects, she exclaims, "Mommy, there's a *world* in your eye . . . where did you *get* that world in your eye?"[11] The care Walker provides her child enables her toddler to witness something wonderous in Walker that Walker failed to recognize in herself: a world in her wound. Walker writes, "For the most part, the pain left. . . . There was a world in my eye. And I saw it was possible to love it: that in fact, for all it had taught me of shame and anger and inner vision, I did love it."[12] Maternal identity enables Walker to identify the embodied knowledge rendered from her experience with disability and return to self-love; it provides her with a deep sense of wholeness. By the end of the essay, Walker's drifting, rolling, floating eye is "deeply suitable to [her] personality."[13] Disability becomes an embraced part of her identity. Walker ends her essay by sharing one of her dreams, a dream of her dancing and holding and kissing herself to "As"—Black-and-blind soul icon Stevie Wonder's inspirational hit song about love. Healing is a return to acceptance and self-love experienced and expressed corporeally.

As with Walker's essay, contemporary Black women's fiction attempts to capture Black women's complex experiences of motherhood and motherwork. In this chapter, I begin to unpack this experience through an analysis of mothering a Black disabled child in Sarah E. Wright's biographical novel *This Child's Gonna Live* (1969). I then discuss disabled mothering through Octavia E. Butler's dystopic duology *Parable of the Sower* (1993) and *Parable of the Talents* (1998), and I end this chapter focusing on disabled Black mothers of disabled Black children using Sapphire's epistolary novella *Push* (1995). The breadth of work in the chapter reflects how focal mothering is within Black women's writing and how disability emerges as a multifaceted part of Black motherwork. In all of these novels, the systemic and institutional racist and sexist oppression Black women experience often works to disempower their mothering. The conditions of anti-Blackness often violently mark Black women and children as disposable. Yet Black mothers relish, nourish, and protect the beaten and broken bodymindspirits of their children and, in so doing, come to care for their own selves. In Black women's writing, mothering is an arduous yet healing practice.

Sweeping *Away* the Dirt: Mothering, Disability, and the Throwaway in *This Child's Gonna Live*

In *This Child's Gonna Live*, Mariah Upshur is a young mother in a small 1930s Maryland town called Tangierneck or "the Neck." As a mother, she doesn't have the money she needs to support her children, and her husband, Jacob, though devoted to his family, would rather hold onto the image of himself as patriarch and provider than acknowledge that his family is in dire need of help. Mariah wants to be patient and gentle with her children—she prays to be gentle with her children—but she regularly lashes out at them under the daily stress, frustration, and hopelessness of trying to raise them in abject poverty. Like many poor, southern Black women and children during the early twentieth century, Mariah and her children's material conditions leave them vulnerable to sickness and disease, and two of her children die: one choked to death from pneumonia and worms, and the other starved to death from lockjaw (tetanus). Patricia Hill Collins theorizes that ensuring their community's and their children's survival is a core aspect of Black motherwork: "African-American women's fiction contains numerous stories of mothers fighting for the physical survival both of their own biological children and of those of the larger Black community."[14] In *This Child's Gonna Live*, Mariah Upshur directs most of her motherwork to the seemingly hopeless and impossible labor of ensuring the physical survival of her children. It is in the act of mothering her physically disfigured child, Rabbit, who is born with a hair lip (cleft lip/palate), that we witness the intensity of Mariah's motherwork as well as the insurmountable obstacles and overwhelming subjugation of her maternal agency.

Despite the systemic, abject poverty that physically, psychically, and socially marks Mariah and her children as disposable, mothering provides motivation and a glimmer of light in the despairing landscape Wright depicts. As Patricia Yaeger argues in *Dirt and Desire: Reconstructing Southern Women's Writing, 1930–1990* (2000), *This Child's Gonna Live* "presents the black child as someone who is invaluable and yet becomes white culture's throwaway,"[15] the "waste product" of white racist indifference.[16] This disposability is violently inscribed on the bodies of Black children. For example, Yaeger expounds, "We stumble across torn, wounded flesh in Wright's writing," but "we also find an epistemology of astonishment, an act of wonder at the power of flesh-eating, dirt-eating kindredness in which strangeness is a permanent property of the hard-bitten every day and writing a magical theater of terror."[17] In Wright's novel, the Black child's marred, wounded flesh is the violent yet quotidian mark of anti-Blackness that Black women declare matter through their motherwork. Indeed, the survival and success of broken, Black, throwaway children's bodies is central to the project of liberation.

Stereotypes that vilify Black women's sexuality and reproductive capacity are used to pathologize the Black reproductive body and thereby justify racialized violence and subjugation. In a misguided practice of communal uplift, Black people internalize these tropes and, in turn, police Black women's sexual practices through communal injunctions to perform respectability. Respectability politics shrouds sex in silence, which breeds ignorance. Getting pregnant and giving birth becomes an exercise in beleaguered agency—at best. In *This Child's Gonna Live*, Black community institutions are complicit in disempowering Black girls' and women's sexual agency and maternal power. Mariah, as an unmarried teen mother, is herself, in many ways, a throwaway. The Tangierneck Christian community shames and shuns Mariah when they discover she is pregnant.[18] They present her before the rest of the youth as a warning and lesson: "You gotta live clean, children . . . It don't pay to be going against the will of God . . . Especially when there's white people around to see you doing it. They use any kind of an ol' excuse to take away from us what God done give us."[19] For the poor Tangierneck community, morality is a tool to secure economic resources from white benefactors; thus, the sexually immoral Black female body displaces racism as a threat to Black survival. Those who are supposed to protect and care for Mariah violently punish her instead. Mariah's mother, Mamma Effie, beats her and locks her away in a room. For Mariah, motherhood is marked by shame, isolation, and violence.

The combination of living in poverty and coping with internalized shame disempowers Mariah's motherwork. Although she deeply loves her children and cherishes them as invaluable within and against a world that treats them as disposable, she lacks the material and psychic tools to practice the model of mothering and care she envisions. Mariah's internal warring results in ambivalent, volatile oscillations in her parenting, most notably her parenting of Rabbit.

Rabbit is intelligent and loving; he is the most self-sufficient of Mariah's children and defends and cares for his mother and infant sister. Mariah finds this treatment endearing and frustrating because her desire to instill a positive sense of self in him makes her feel that she must protect him from her shameful past. For instance, when Mariah notices that her "seeing—too-much, talking—too-much, hearing—too—much" son is about to "bawl his guts out" over her yelling, she thinks, "*Little-son-of-a-bitch don't be crying over me, a no good whore!*"[20] She recognizes that Rabbit is precocious and kind but feels unworthy of his attention, affection, and care as a "bitch" and "no good whore." Mariah's internalized shame poisons her motherwork. Instead of nurturing him, she lashes out at him with hits and punches to the face, all the while battling with herself to stop and begging Jesus for help in doing so. When she is finally able to stop, she grabs Rabbit and tries to comfort and assure him: "Rabbit, . . . If I go anywhere, I'm gonna take you, Rabbit."[21] Mariah accompanies her attempt at soothing words and comfort with physical acts of care. She "[licks] the slobber and the snot and the blood from his face."[22] Mariah struggles to repair the harm she has caused and ease his fears of abandonment—she affirms that Rabbit is not disposable; Mariah, lovingly, if desperately, takes in even the abject excrements from his body. Without excusing Mariah's violence towards her children, *This Child's Gonna Live* challenges the stereotype of Black mothers as inherently aggressive. Mariah's inner voice shames her into psychic distress. Internalized misogynoir keeps Mariah and her children in a cycle of violence that undermines her efforts to empower her children and approach her parenting with gentleness.

Internalized sexism not only skews how Mariah sees herself, but it also couples with internalized ableism to distort how Mariah understands her children's embodiment. Like the Tangierneck people, Mariah can identify the societal attitudes and structural sources of her family's poverty but nevertheless blames herself for their experience of socio-political neglect and daily prejudice. Mariah focuses her motherwork on shielding her children from absorbing the stigma attached to her sexuality while also preparing them to deal with the stigma associated with their own embodiment. Sadly, Mariah believes that she *is* a whore and, as such, unworthy of kindness. This internalized sexism feeds ableist narratives about her children's socially stigmatized traits and conditions—Mary's lockjaw, Rabbit's hairlip, and, lastly, Bardetta's light skin are understood—as evidence of her lasciviousness. This disempowers her mothering, and we see this when Mariah attempts to prepare her children to confront a world that reads their bodies through both misogynoir and ableism. For instance, when Rabbit fights with neighborhood children to defend his sister and mother, Mariah herself corrects him with blows and hurtful words of her own. She scolds, "Rabbit, what you trying to do? Get yourself turned into a circus clown? Ain't your lip enough of a scar for you to be carrying around? Your whole head ain't nothing but a bunch of scars!"[23] Mariah's words are ill-phrased, misguided, and painful, and they are her attempt to protect him from violently ableist and misogynist attitudes. For Mariah, the core of Black motherwork, especially for her disabled child, is to love him and let him know that every part of him is valued. She reflects, "Rabbit just cried so pitiful after she said that thing to him. Talk about his lip hurt him worse than anything. He had a right to cry, for when Mamma won't take up for you, kiss on your sores and tell you I love you, you something—anything—who else will, Jesus?"[24] Mariah believes that, ideally, Black mothers are supposed to physically and psychically embody what bell hooks calls homeplace, a safe space where, "[despite] the brutal reality of racial apartheid, of domination, one's homeplace was the one site where one could freely confront the issue of humanization, where one could resist."[25] Although shame undermines Mariah's attempt to provide a homeplace, in Wright's novel, homeplace is theorized as the place where one goes to resist and heal from ableism. And despite her failures, Mariah never stops trying to create it.

The anti-ableist motherwork of trying to create homeplace as a lifeline for her children also becomes a lifeline for Mariah herself. It is through mothering her disabled child that Mariah is able to resist despair and hold fast to hope for a better future. She is determined to protect Rabbit from the emotional and spiritual harm of other people's ableism. Mariah caresses Rabbit's lip and thinks, "Be so glad to get him to the city where people didn't waste time making people feel bad over things like [his hairlip]."[26] To this end, Mariah resolves to leave her husband, who fails to provide financial stability and emotional support and move to the city. She is resolved to ensure that her children have a better education than she had in her hope-filled plans to see to it that Rabbit is raised with his needs met and the opportunity to attend college. Whereas disability is often excised from the future where its absence marks better, improved futures, in *This Child's Gonna Live*, motherwork changes the measure of progression to a future where her disabled child survives and thrives. Though Mariah speaks life into her children—"All my children, all you-all gonna live and be something besides ignorant country scrubs like me"[27]—In *This Child's Gonna Live*, the disabled child, Rabbit, is the child for whom Mariah holds the ultimate dreams of liberation.

For Mariah, Black motherhood is an important identity but a challenging and nearly impossible job. She lacks support. She does not have help from the larger Tangierneck community, her husband is unreliable, and her Jesus is unresponsive. Throughout the novel, we see how the systematized slow violence that usurps and upends Black motherwork blights Black women's bodymindspirits. Mariah not only experiences overwhelm by the daunting task of empowering her children through the haze of her own absence of self-worth, but she also feels dangerously debilitating psychic distress. She has anxiety, depression, and suicide ideation. Moreover, she lacks the material resources to provide basic necessities for their daily survival. She is acutely aware that her earnest and relentless motherwork has yet to keep her children alive and well: her boys are sick so often it's chronic, and her baby girl Mary starves to death in her arms. For all of Mariah's shortcomings as a mother, the novel does not reproduce violent social discourse that blames Black women alive during the setting of this novel for the illness and death of their children. Despite stereotypes of bad Black mothers, Mariah's children do not die from lack of love or care. Nor is she indifferent to their suffering. When Rabbit also dies, it's like "Mariah died in herself."[28] She psychically and spiritually comes undone. After Rabbit's death, under the weight of grief, depression, and despair, Mariah (once again) attempts suicide. She wades out into the ocean water, even though she cannot swim, echoing Kate Chopin's Edna Pontellier and Désirée.[29]

Unlike Chopin's heroines, however, Mariah refuses to give herself over to the iciness of death. Instead, half-wet, with "gritted" teeth, she returns home "to put the dough to bake in the oven" so "the children could have some nice hot bread for your dinner." Somewhere, in response to her pleads to the Lord to "Let my children live, Lord. Let 'em have a pretty day," Mariah gets a silent response, a response only noted by her reply, "Lordy, I didn't know," and her sudden determined march home to make bread for her children.[30] Mariah chooses life—her own as essential to preserving the lives of her children. Racism and sexism forge nearly insurmountable strongholds on empowered Black mothering through poverty, loneliness, and shame, yet maternal identity itself continues to serve as a lighthouse and spiritual stronghold in Wrights's novel.

In this section, I focused on mothering the throwaway child, the disabled Black child, even though it is useful to interpret the forces that disempower Mariah through disability as a frame and even read Mariah as a disabled mother. In the next section, I focus on mothering while disabled and disabled Black motherwork an experience and positionality that enables cripistemological knowledge necessary for survival.

Disabled Maternal Identity in Octavia Butler's Parable Series[31]

While Mariah Upshur internalizes misogynoir until it nearly corrupts her motherwork, the protagonist of Octavia E. Butler's *Parable of the Sower* (1993) and *Parable of the Talents* (1998), Lauren Olamina, draws on a cripistemology of motherwork to navigate misogynoir and ableism as violent mechanisms of control and power and to imagine and recreate the world otherwise. At the beginning of *Parable of the Sower*, Lauren is only fifteen but is already, and quite reluctantly, a maternal figure to her stepbrothers and other youth in her gated California community, Robledo—and "[she's] tired of it."[32] Despite her fatigue, Lauren continues to serve as a maternal figure throughout the series. When Robledo is attacked and burned down, which forces Lauren, along with two other survivors, onto the dangerous streets and highways heading northward, Lauren takes the lead of the small gang of travelers she accumulates. In *Parable of the Talents*, she serves as the community othermother in Acorn and gives birth to her daughter, Larkin. Lauren's motherwork, particularly as she directs it to carve community, demonstrates what Patricia Hill Collins observes of mothering within the matrixes of power: "A dialectical relationship exists between efforts of racial orders to mold the institution of motherhood to serve the interests of elites, in this case, racial elites, and efforts on the part of subordinated groups to retain power over motherhood so that it serves the legitimate needs of their communities."[33] Lauren not only other/mothers in the violent wake of social and economic collapse, but she also does so while living with an at times painfully debilitating condition—hyperempathy syndrome, a congenital disability that causes people with the syndrome to feel, and at times embody, what they perceive is the pain or pleasure of others. As Lauren explains, "I feel what I see others feeling or what I believe they feel." In a space where people "often have things wrong with them, they cut off each other's ears, arms, legs" and "[they] carry untreated diseases and festering wounds," Lauren is at risk of feeling more pain rather than pleasure.[34] Lauren's maternal identity and hyperempathy syndrome have activated an impressive body of criticism from a range of fields;[35] however, I am interested in how ableism shapes the discourse of motherhood within the two *Parable* novels and how Lauren mobilizes knowledge garnered from disabled maternal identity to birth a religion, Earthseed, and a community, Acorn.

In the series, misogynoir and ableism are inextricably tethered to underpin structures of oppression that disempower Black maternal and disability identity. Black women are demonized as poor and irresponsible mothers whose children and families suffer the undesirable embodied consequences of their deviant behavior. Both maternal failure and its physical evidence are contained through a culture of silence. We learn early on, for example, that within the Olamina household, Lauren's mother and hyperempathy are an interconnected source of shame for the entire family. Lauren shares:

> There's a whole range of things we never even hint about outside the family. First among these is anything about my mother, my

hyperempathy, and how the two are connected. To my father, the whole business is shameful. He's a preacher and a professor and a dean. A first wife who was a drug addict and a daughter who is drug damaged is not something he wants to boast about.[36]

Rev. Olamina is not only ashamed of his first wife, but he is also ashamed of his daughter, an emotion that Lauren internalizes. For both survival and out of shame, Lauren tries her best to pass as able-bodied, cautiously choosing when and to whom to disclose that she has hyperempathy. In these moments, Lauren's shame about her disability is tethered to her shame about her mother. For example, when Lauren decides to come out as disabled to her travel companions, she also feels compelled to come out about her mother.[37]

Lauren never separates being disabled from becoming disabled, which reinforces the negative connection between Black motherhood and disability, a connection already present in prevailing stereotypes of Black motherhood.[38] Lauren's disability not only signals her personal weakness and vulnerability in a world that values strength,[39] but it also comes to embody deviant womanhood. It's evidence of maternal failure etched into Lauren's flesh. This representation of Black mothers whose drug use is detrimental to their children's lives recalls the controlling image of the Crack Mother that proliferated headlines in the late 1980s and into the 1990s. Crack mothers were the ultimate social pariah: they threatened the moral fabric of the nation and drained it of its economic resources with their addiction and the unbridled sexuality they used to sustain it. Worse yet, they birthed and abandoned a legion of supposed defective crack babies who threatened to further tax the system. As Melissa Harris-Perry explains, "Crack babies were the living, squealing, suffering evidence of pathological black motherhood."[40] This is underscored when Zahra, one of Lauren's travel companions and another Black woman, shares:

> My mama took drugs, too. . . . Shit, where I was born, everybody's mama took drugs—and whored to pay for them. And had babies all the time, and threw them away like trash when they died. Most of the babies did die from the drugs or accidents or not having enough to eat or being left alone so much . . . or from being sick. They were always getting sick. Some of them were born sick. They had sores all over or big things on their eyes—tumors, you know—or no legs or fits or can't breathe right. . . . All kinds of things. And some of the ones

who lived were dumb as dirt. Can't think, can't learn, just sit around nine, ten years old, peeing in their pants, rocking back and forth, and dripping spit down their chins. There's a lot of them. . . . You ain't got nothing wrong with you, Lauren—nothing worth worrying about. That Paracetco shit was baby milk.[41]

The mental picture that Zahra paints of women prostituting themselves for drugs as their babies languish in filth and disease demonstrates how class inflects narratives about addiction, Black motherhood, and disability.

Sexism and ableism not only underpin stereotypes that pathologize Black motherhood, both are also mobilized to devalue care work.[42] Women are consigned to heteronormative marriage because they are considered naturally inferior and incapable of self-sufficiency. Moreover, caregiving is dismissed as undemanding and unimportant and, therefore, has historically been assigned to the weak and vulnerable.[43] The ableism and sexism embedded in this logic are brought to the fore in Butler's writing. For example, Lauren's brother Keith tells her, "You better marry Curtis and make babies . . . Out there, outside, you wouldn't last a day. That hyperempathy shit of yours would bring you down even if nobody touched you."[44] Keith's comment is supposed to be vitriolic and is intended to demean and ridicule Lauren because of her disability. Yet, as a woman, Lauren is already expected to marry and is currently assigned motherwork; indeed, most women in her gated community, including her stepmother Cory, who has a PhD, are tasked with caregiving. Keith fails to recognize the value of the care work women and disabled people provide. Moreover, Keith is not concerned about Lauren's survival, well-being, or experiences of pain and suffering; he doubts the legitimacy of her hyperempathy. Ableism simply enables him to maintain social hierarchies that privilege the able-bodied, straight male and, therefore, benefit him. Rather than perpetuate Keith's ableist and sexist logic by disavowing caregiving, motherwork, in the series, is imbued with value: without Cory and Lauren's labor, the children in Robledo would be idle and illiterate in a place where trouble beckons and every skill can be used for survival.

Yet, in a society ravished by late capitalism, environmental disasters, and war, women and disabled people of all genders are vulnerable and are more likely to be targeted for harm. Even Lauren acknowledges that her hyperempathy makes her susceptible to pain and suffering—"[a] person who knows what I am can hurt me, betray me, disable me with little effort."[45] She also knows that societal expectations and assumptions about gender inflect one's experience with disability. Lauren is aware that she will be targeted for violence as a woman before being targeted for her disability. But she also acknowledges that men with hyperempathy are vulnerable in different ways. Lauren has this sobering reflection on the first man she meets with hyperempathy and concludes, "[sharing] would be harder on a man."[46] Heterosexist masculine ideas loathe perceived weakness and vulnerability in men. Weakness in men is feminized and leaves disabled men at risk of forms of gendered violence. The California portrayed in the Parable series is dangerous for everyone, but especially those considered weak. Rape, mutilation, and murder are common quotidian occurrences, but they pose a possible lethal threat to Lauren, whether she experiences it firsthand or by proxy. Though Lauren comes harrowingly close to losing the battle for survival, especially after she is enslaved in *Parable of the Talents*, she survives, though many do not, including her father and brother, Keith. Her life as a disabled Black adolescent has taught her about the complex mechanisms of power that inform the various spaces in which she must travel. In *Parable of the Sower* and *Parable of the Talents*, Black maternal cripistemology is an invaluable resource for survival.

Claiming the creativity and knowledge from living with a disabled bodymindspirit is necessary for surviving a broken world. For instance, Lauren maintains a conscious and cautious balance between care of self and care for others to build community and manage pain. She often must decide when to be proactive, choosing to defend herself in a manner that gives her some measure of control over the pain she will experience. She is not passive. Yet, she must also be careful about inflicting harm on others. She has, as she phrases, a "biological conscience"[47]—a characteristic she realizes would benefit everyone. Her disability has also taught her that she must learn to strategically look away from other people's pain. As I discuss in chapter one, bearing witness can be debilitating. Lauren recognizes and honors that she has limitations and cannot always be the strong Black woman or mule of the world. Lauren does not overcome her disability but works with it and grows from it.

Lauren's cripistemology shapes and is shaped by her own spiritual cosmology. Lauren rejects the "big-daddy-God" that is the linchpin of her father's theology. The theological foundation of Rev. Olamina's Black church is one that bolsters patriarchal authority to the detriment of its adherents in the Robledo community. This understanding of God fails to provoke an honest yet caring engagement with the world and the people around them as they are. It disempowers its believers from proactive survival preparation by encouraging them to trust and rely on a benevolent Divine patriarch and his earthly auxiliary. Despite performances of paternalist benevolence, Rev. Olamina's dogma reproduces the valorization of social stratification and patriarchal will to power, as well as promotes an unrealistic and unsustainable brand of individualism. Yet rather than renounce spiritual practice and guidance, Lauren instead establishes her own belief system and her own definition of what God is and does—Earthseed. With Earthseed, Lauren intuits that God is Change. It is revealed to and through her that God is a powerful, indifferent force that "can't be resisted or stopped, but can be shaped and focused." Lauren's theology is not a product of intellect, as most have come to know. She's not "making any of this up."[48] Earthseed is borne of critical observation and deep feeling that Lauren then pens as powerfully and simply as she can. It is a crip, Erotic, as theorized by Audre Lorde, spiritual system.[49] Moreover, Earthseed reflects and revises Africanist cosmologies. Like many Africanist deities and supernatural agents, Lauren describes her God as a "Trickster," a "teacher," and "chaos."[50] Although Lauren's God does not display conscious intelligence, her God, like many Africanist deities, is shapable. People have some measure of spiritual control in and over their lives. Furthermore, "shaping," like the magic of many Africanist spiritual practices, is an exercise of personal and communal will, power, and agency.[51]

Not only that, Earthseed is Lauren's cripistemology of the spirit. God as mutable and indifferent yet consciously and unconsciously malleable parallels how Lauren comes to understand living with hyperempathy. She is powerless over whether or not she has the syndrome, nor does she invest her illness with moral significance. Like her God, Lauren's disabled bodymind-spirit just is. However, also like God, hyperempathy is shapeable. Lauren can leave herself vulnerable to the vicissitudes of painful stimuli around through an unconscious, passive engagement with the world, or she can co-shape her embodied experience by seeking pleasure and mitigating the likelihood of harm. With the embodied knowledge of Earthseed, Lauren upsets the investment in individualism and the myth of progress to which her father, right-wing despotic leader Andrew Steele Jarret, and others cling. The world, like her body, is dynamic and vulnerable and powerful. Existence is empowered through shaping—motherwork is a political and spiritual practice.

Motherwork as a political and spiritual practice is the foundation of Lauren's understanding and project of community building. For example, sharing, the ethical core of Acorn, is reflected in mutual respect, caregiving, and interdependence manifested through communal motherwork. As an Earthseed community, everyone can be a shaper; everyone has ideas and knowledge that can and should be shared for the benefit of the group.

Moreover, in Acorn, the entire community, men and women alike, collectively rear children and provide for each other. Senior denizens assist and teach new residents. If someone needs help, they are encouraged to ask. Lauren explains, "Acorn is a community of people who have saved one another in all kinds of ways ... Acorn is home."[52] Acorn is not only a community of people engaged in motherwork, but it is also a space transformed by that work. It is a homeplace. Whereas maternal identity and labor are held in mutual contempt by the surrounding patriarchal society, Lauren uses care work to create a refuge.

Motherwork and interdependence are oppositional to patriarchal systems and structures. They are transgressive. As such, they are targeted for domination and destruction by those invested in patriarchal power. Acorn, as a transgressive space, inevitably succumbs to the patriarchal violence of the state. This begins when Marc, Lauren's other brother, decides to leave Acorn. Although Acorn serves as a safe space to recover and heal after he is liberated from enslavement, he resents that he holds no patriarchal privilege or power. Acorn also becomes the target of the far-right political administration of Andrew Steel Jarret, Christian America. Through Christian America, Jarret uses his political and military might to subjugate the Acorn community. Through the benevolent paternalistic rhetoric of Christian morality and family values, Jarret wrests away maternal power from Lauren and others: he steals their children. Through *Parable of the Talents*, Butler exposes how this paternalist discourse of care works to conceal and enable violence against women and children. Lauren's daughter Larkin, later Asha Vere, is kidnapped and placed with "good Christian American parents," who emotionally and sexually abuse her.[53] Although her uncle Marc finds her, he is fooled by the veneer of morality bestowed upon them through their adherence to patriarchal doctrine. He decides it is best for Larkin to stay with her Christian American parents rather than return her to Lauren, with whom he is in contact and knows is searching for her. Institutionalized patriarchy forever robs Lauren of the opportunity to mother and connect with her biological daughter.

Ultimately, Christian America's influence dissolves, though never fully disappears, as Earthseed's influence increases. Lauren's intuition that humans need a destiny and a project larger than themselves—in this case, the stars—to recover proves correct. Earthseed eventually spreads like wildfire. However, her relationship with her daughter is forever fractured. Lauren becomes the mother of a movement but at the cost of losing her biological daughter.

In both *This Child's Gonna Live* and the *Parable* duology, disability enriches Black motherhood, but the forces of oppression that disempower Black mothers prove nearly insurmountable. Much of these novels' focus is on basic survival. In the next and final section, focusing on *Push*, the barriers disabled Black mothers face while trying to mother disabled Black children also appear impregnable, and the central characters are also very much engaged in the core motherwork of survival. In addition to survival, however, we also get to see the healing power of disabled mothering.

Motherwork as Healing and Empowering in Sapphire's *Push*

In *Push* (1995), motherhood is yoked to violence. Whereas Lauren Olimina's motherwork is done within the oppressive and disempowering contexts of state violence, the protagonist of *Push*, Claireece Precious Jones (Precious), becomes a mother through familial violence and has her motherwork disempowered by state violence. Precious has her first baby at just twelve years old and her second baby at sixteen; her father, Carl Kenwood Jones, is the father of both children. Mary, Precious's mother, does nothing to stop the continual rapes. Instead, she accuses Precious of stealing her husband and then goes on to sexually, physically, and emotionally abuse Precious. She gives Mongo, Precious's first child, to her mother, Toosie, to raise, yet claims to be Mongo's primary caretaker to increase her welfare benefits. At school, Precious gets no relief. She is illiterate but has made it to the ninth grade, and though she is eager to learn, her peers tease her about her fatness and dark skin, and her teachers ignore or dismiss her as disruptive. Moreover, the school punishes her for her father's abuse by expelling her due to her second pregnancy, and her mother follows suit by kicking her out on the streets with her newborn son, also parented by her father, as a jealously-infused punishment for the same said abuse. Precious's experiences of Black girlhood become debilitating through her own traumatized, nonnormative bodymindspirit as well as through normalizing forces. Therefore, like Lauren Olamina, Precious is also disabled, albeit by societal neglect, as it abuts societal expectations. This is particularly apparent through Precious's literacy—or lack thereof. Much like Gayl Jones's *Eva's Man*, *Push* is a disabled novel as it is told only through Precious's first person, at times very difficult to read, journal entries. These experiences as a Black, femme laboring body nearly destroy Precious. Precious is a throwaway child trying to care for throwaway children. We see, in *Push*, Patricia Hill Collins's argument that "Racial ethnic women's motherwork reflects the tensions inherent in trying to foster a meaningful racial identity in children within a society that denigrates people of color."[54] We also see the power of the labor of nurturing "meaningful racial identity" in *Push*. Precious finds empowerment in her maternal identity only after it is nurtured by the mothering she receives from her teacher and othermother, Blue Rain, at the alternative school, Each One, Teach One. Moreover, it is Ms. Rain's maternal, queer Black feminist disability consciousness that enables her to create homeplace for Precious as she navigates the process of becoming a disabled Black mother.

In *Push*, there is no way to disentangle issues of disabled motherhood from issues of Black motherhood. Although sexual violence robs Precious of the bodily autonomy to choose if and when to conceive, as well as makes the experience of being pregnant distressing (Pregnancy triggers flashbacks of being raped), Precious wants to mother her children in a society that has deemed them disposable. However, ongoing domestic violence and exploitation, in addition to systemic and institutionalized misogynoir disempower Precious's motherwork. For instance, Mongo is immediately rendered defective and dispensable; after giving birth, before Precious can even hold Mongo, a nurse tells Precious that "[something] is wrong with your baby . . .Mongoloid."[55] After that, Precious rarely gets to bond with and care for Mongo, which is a source of sadness and regret for Precious, as expressed through her frustrated desire to breastfeed her daughter. This time, it is Mary, Precious's mother, who decides that Mongo is not worthy of maternal love and care, of life-affirming sustenance. Instead, Mary seizes maternal power from Precious to further her own aims, like claiming primary guardianship of Mongo to increase the financial assistance she receives from the state, but then casually yielding over care work to her mother, Toosie, who then places Mongo in a facility. At each juncture, it is others with more power, even if marginally so, who have deemed Mongo a throwaway and who have the power to control the material conditions of Mongo's life. Precious's esteem and desires for her daughter make no difference and are summarily dismissed. Indeed, Mary and Toosie only have the power that they do because they similarly devalue Mongo and exploit her and divest from her wellbeing in ways that reflect and align with the structural and institutionalized anti-Black ableism manifest in the dominant society. Jina B. Kim brilliantly articulates the relationship between ableism and misogynoir at work here: "the unexpected affinity between Precious as welfare mother and her disabled baby daughter is not incidental. Rather, it reflects how ableist reasoning anchors antiwelfare rhetoric, casting entire categories of people as undeserving of public support."[56]

Institutionalized ableism divests Precious of agency to self-determine and mother her children. Precious must contend with ableism as the mother of a disabled child but also as a person with disabilities herself. Her own mental health and intellectual disability diagnoses are used to disqualify Precious from shaping her life and the lives of her children. For instance, though Precious treasures Mongo as invaluable and worthy of love, freedom, and care, the medical state emphatically insists on Mongo's disposability and Precious's inability to parent. When Precious tries to take Mongo out of the institution she's incarcerated in, administrators disparage Precious, arguing that Mongo "is in really bad shape" and "even if she could be help, take a lot more than [her], and ain't [she] got full load with Abdul."[57] Like Marc decides Lauren is incapable of mothering Larkin in *Parable of the Talents*, other people tell Precious whether or not she is capable of mothering her child and have the power to enforce their evaluation.

Moreover, as Michelle Jarman aptly points out, these same institutions also divest Precious of access to economic mobility through systemic ableism.[58] As Precious and Jermaine, her transgender peer from Each One, Teach One, read the notes in the file Precious steals from her caseworker, Ms. Weiss, they recognize that Ms. Weiss uses standardized tests to diagnose Precious as intellectually disabled and therefore justify assigning her work that would exploit her labor. Ms. Weiss does not feel that Precious is worth the "considerable" resources needed to help her get even a GED but does believe that "[despite] [Precious's] obvious intellectual limitations, she is quite capable of working as a home attendant."[59] Precious perceptively recognizes home health care work as domestic labor that would leave little free time to mother her child. As Precious's social worker, Ms. Weiss decides what quality and level of education Precious deserves, what jobs to make available to her, and how much access to and influence over her children she can attain. She uses historically racist diagnostic tools to label Precious disabled and thereby justify her choices to divest Precious of resources that would empower her and her motherwork.

Precious's struggles highlight how ableism underpins the institutionalized misogynoir that has circumscribed Black women to domestic labor and other work that pirates away time and energy from their families and fuels stereotypes that pathologize Black motherhood. From slavery and into the present, different iterations of care work are often the only jobs open to poor, Black women. These women have been maligned in the popular imagination as Mammies—asexual, fat Black women who are more dedicated to caring for white families than their own. In the Black community, the Mammy is a sellout. In the white imagination, the Mammy is the safer alternative to the angry Sapphire and hypersexual Jezebel stereotypes. She is the affective opposite of the Matriarch.[60] For all the wit and wisdom she offers to her White employers, the Mammy is presented as in need of the patriarchal guidance of her white charges because she lacks the intellectual capacity to care for herself. The Mammy figure is encapsulated by her large-bodied, slow-witted gentleness. She is the Black female version of John Steinbeck's "gentle giant," Lennie. Annie Johnson, in the 1959 rendition of *Imitation of Life*, is an excellent example. To be clear: fat embodiment, intellectual disability, and even asexuality are not degrading or shameful traits. Fatphobia, ableism, heterosexism, and misogynoir meld to construct the Mammy as a demeaning cultural trope that has had material consequences in Black women's lives. In *Push*, Ms. Weiss understands Precious's fat Black female body and supposed intellectual disability as particularly suited to exploitative care work.

Despite all these obstacles, Precious is motivated by her identity as a mother and eventually comes to find motherhood empowering after she, herself, receives the healing touch of motherwork. After Mary evicts Precious, Precious's teacher at Each One, Teach One steps up as an othermother. Ms. Rain invests in Precious's and Precious's son Abdul's survival: she encourages Precious to seek prenatal care and helps Precious secure housing. Moreover, she invests in Precious's psychic and spiritual wellbeing and wholeness by guiding Precious towards accepting and loving her Black disabled bodymindspirit. Ms. Rain affirms Precious and tells Precious that she is a "beautiful" and "wonderful girl" who "was born for a purpose,"[61] and importantly, Ms. Rain explicitly addresses the anti-Black ableist discourse that has been hurled at Precious in the institutional narratives about her. Ms. Rain assures Precious that these evaluations of her do not define her. She also provides Precious with language to rearticulate disability from an inherent flaw or pathology. Ms. Rain is what Carole Boyce Davies calls a mother-healer, who "take[s] on the responsibility of nurturing when biological mothers are unable to sustain the emotional support of their daughters." Davies theorizes maternal healing directed toward psychic and spiritual wholeness that is mutually sustaining. Davies explains "Significantly, much of this mothering is directed at releasing the inner self being suffocated by race and sex oppression. As Each participates in the other's healing they, by extension, heal themselves in a kind of symbiotic unity." What Davies describes is a community of mutual caregiving, a community built upon an ethos of motherwork and healing work.[62] This community of mutual mothering and caregiving is fostered and nurtured in Ms. Rain's class. Moreover, in *Push*, literacy provides Precious with a community of literary othermothers as Black women's writing becomes an additional source of wisdom and strength and healing. For instance, Ms. Rain encourages Precious to read Alice Walker's *The Color Purple*, which reflects Precious's experiences while also providing hope for healing. Ms. Rain also introduces

Precious to other Black feminist foremothers, such as Harriet Tubman and Audre Lorde, women who had to learn to deal with their own disabilities and come to terms with motherhood. At Each One, Teach One, Ms. Rain creates a space that is what Alexis Pauline Gumbs theorizes as motherful, the queer, Black feminist work of collective mothering.[63]

Moreover, all of the young women in Ms. Rain's class eventually learn to support each other as chosen family in the challenging work of healing. For instance, Precious is met with love and support when she entrusts her sisters with her HIV-positive status. Precious writes:

> Rita Romero hug me like I'm her chile and I cry and Ms Rain rub my back and say let it out, Precious, let it out. I cry for every day of my life. I cry for Mama what kinda story Mama got to do me like she do? And I cry for my son, the song in my life. The little brown penis, booty, fat thighs, roun' eyes, the voice of love say, Mama, Mama he call me.[64]

Being a mother uplifts Precious, even after she is dealt what many believe is a death blow—her father gives her HIV. At the same time, being mothered also sustains her. In this dark moment, Precious is surrounded by a community of care. Moreover, Ms. Rain pushes her to write, recognizing that writing is a healing act.

Mothering is a healing act that empowers motherwork. Receiving the love, care, and nurturance long denied her provides Precious with the security and self-confidence she needs to lay claim to her own maternal identity and vie for maternal agency. Not long after attending Each One, Teach One, Precious stops trying to dissociate from her pregnant body. She has the opportunity to decide whether or not to keep her second child and does: "This is my baby. My muver took Little Mongo but she ain' taking this one. I am comp'tant."[65] She feels confident in her ability to mother, and this confidence is strengthened the more she provides care for Abdul.

Although Precious feels more empowered as a mother, ableism and misogynoir are still overwhelming phenomena that threaten her motherwork. For instance, although she decides she is "not going to give Abdul up," and, though much more hesitantly, that she "is gonna get Little Mongo back one day, maybe," Precious realizes that, she "hardly even know what [Mongo] look[s] like, aside from retarded, that is."[66] Here, Precious does not question whether or not to reclaim Mongo because Mongo is disabled; she is hesitant because she realizes that the only thing she knows about Mongo, the only thing she has been allowed to know about her daughter, is that she has Down's Syndrome. Moreover, she hints that she is afraid for her girl child. She is afraid that Mongo will end up like her. But as Abdul grows and Precious realizes that she is more than capable of taking care of his needs, she feels empowered enough in her motherwork to decide that, "One day I going back for Little Mongo. Maybe I make the day sooner than I had thought."[67] Precious, as many mothers diagnosed with learning disabilities share, feels empowered through caregiving, by realizing she is able to do that work.[68]

Push presents healing as acceptance and moving forward in one's crip maternal power. Like Mariah, she not only sees her disabled Black child in the future but also her disabled Black self. By the end of the novella, Precious is thinking about and planning for her future. She believes she has a future. She feels ready and worthy of love and sex within the dynamics of a healthy relationship. She is getting an education. She is mothering her son. She is healing from her trauma but recognizes that the trauma will never completely go away. She testifies to her truth and bears witness to sisters. Together, they form a crip community of other/mothers that support, sustain, and empower each other. Yes, being HIV positive during the late eighties is a grim reality for Precious, but as her peer-sister Rita tells her: "forgit the WHY ME shit and git on to what's next."[69] This is not to invalidate Precious's right to be sad, angry, distressed, and however else she feels about her diagnosis, but it is a loving reminder from someone else with the illness not to forget she still has some living to do. And we are reminded of this in the last scene of the novel proper:

> It's Sunday, no school, meetings. I'm in dayroom . . . sitting on a big leather stool holdin' Abdul. The sun is coming through the window splashing down on him . . . When the sun shine on him like this, he is an angel child. Brown sunshine. And my heart fill. Hurt. One year? Five? Ten years? Maybe more if I take care of myself. Maybe a cure. Who knows, who is working on shit like that? Look his nose is so shiny, his eyes shiny. He my shiny brown boy. In his beauty I see my own. He pulling on my earring, want me to stop daydreaming and read him a story before nap time. I do.[70]

The thought of dying and leaving Abdul hurts Precious, but the act of mothering and loving in the here and now fills her heart. While I do not aim to turn Precious's story into inspiration porn, there is no denying the sadness yet hope—bliss, even—in this last passage. There is a balance of realism, which Ms. Rain argues is missing from works like *The Color Purple*, and serenity and joy brought about by her own healing through the motherwork of others and sustained by her love of mothering her son.

Conclusion

Black women's representation of disabled motherhood brings to the fore how complex and fraught mothering while Black and disabled can be. Mariah internalizes the controlling images that are used to pathologize and mark the actions of Black girls and women as deviant. The shame she feels threatens to completely disempower her motherwork, work that she finds important, if nearly impossible, to do. Nevertheless, her work creates homeplace for her disabled children and demonstrates her belief in their value in a world that has discarded them as throwaways. If motherwork is valuable to one's sense of being in *This Child's Gonna Live*, motherwork proves valuable to survival and imagining the world otherwise in Octavia E. Butler's *Parable* duology, and in *Push*, motherwork does effectively create a healing homeplace for the child-mother protagonist. These works demonstrate that motherhood and motherwork are valuable and, indeed, necessary for Black/crip futures. As Alexis Pauline Gumbs affirms, "The queer thing is that we were born; our young and/or deviant and/or brown and/or broke and/or single mamas did the wrong thing. Therefore, we exist: a population out of control, a story interrupted. We are the guerrilla poems written on walls, purveyors of a billion dangerous meanings of life."[71] These portrayals of brokenbeautiful motherwork as validating and community-sustaining are far from the image of the Black nationalist revolutionary trope. In all their flaws, the Black mothers of Black women's writing are also a far cry from the grotesque, demeaning, and pathologizing controlling images that stand in for the lived realities of actual Black mothers. Indeed, these selections demonstrate that misogynoir marks them for debilitation and disempowers their motherwork, but mothering is a spiritual identity that calls to them and buoys them even in the midst of great despair. Indeed, motherwork is so spiritually powerful that it is healing for the self and the community.

Chapter 4

Sexual Healing

> If I was to ever get to a place where I was able to own my own sexuality, sensuality, and desirability, my whole world would change.
> —OLAJUMOKE "JAY" ABDULLAHI OF TRIPLE CRIPPLES

The problem of Black women's sexuality has touched on each topic discussed in this book so far. As I demonstrate in my analysis of Gayl Jones's *Corrigedora* and *Eva's Man*, the tension between witnessing and testifying erupts as Jones's Black female characters attempt to exercise sexual self-determination in a world where psychically debilitating sexual violence is normalized. In chapter two, I address how Black nationalist ideology left little to no room for Black women who attempt to exercise sexual autonomy. Indeed, women who do are demeaned as outlaws and pariahs in relation to the Black community—at least as conceptualized by heterosexist Black nationalist rhetoric. Moreover, motherhood is a fraught identity for Black women because limited reproductive agency renders heterosexual sex often negatively consequential. The rhetorical and material manipulation of Black women's sexual practices is the center that defines and delimits nearly every other facet of Black women's lives. A central and creative preoccupation in Black women's writing has been how to emerge from under the debilitating weight of external social, cultural, and political investments in their sexuality and into inhabiting their own experiences of themselves as erotic beings. Thus, Black women's sexuality has been a central focus of Black feminist theory—from analyzing the negative stereotypes used to justify the sexual abuse of the Black female body[1] to theorizing how Black women have protected themselves against this violence through the cultures of dissemblance and silence,[2] to the move to reclaim Black women's sexual agency.[3]

Whereas Black women's sexuality is rhetorically over-determined in our cultural imagination, the sexuality of (white) disabled people remains largely unimaginable. Whereas Black women's sexuality is overly represented in modern society, representation of disabled people's sexuality is virtually absent. These seeming binaries render the sexual subjectivity of disabled Black women theoretically incomprehensible. And yet, more and more disabled Black women have been speaking up and speaking out about the sexual landscapes of their lives. For instance, Olajumoke Abdullahi, one-half of the podcast duo Triple Cripples, shares, "There's a presumption because of me being a Black woman, people think, she's always ready to go all the time for anything and everything . . . But then when coupled with a disability, it's like okay, but will her body—her physicality—allow this presumption that I have in my head of her always being ready for anything?"[4] Abdullahi's experiences reveal how prevailing stereotypes continue regardless of her disability. What shifts is the ableist, male-centered discourse of ability and limits: can you perform the acts I want you to perform? Like Alice Walker's representation of heterosexual sex while disabled in *Meridian* (see chapter 2), there is no consideration given to Black women's pleasure, in this case, about Abdullahi's desires. Despite growing conversations on social media, blogs, and podcasts, we have yet to theoretically and critically account for disabled Black women's experiences of sex and sexuality, not even in the sexual archive. The critical discourse around Saartjie Baartman, the so-called "Hottentot Venus," is a case in point. In Black feminist theory, Baartman's subjection to exhibition for the sexualized white gaze both in life and death is not the first location of Black women's sexual exploitation in the white cultural imagination but comes to stand as exemplary of the violent cultural politics of representing Black women as sexual objects. As Janell Hobson's work suggests, Baartman has also proved a useful hermeneutic for considering dis/ability as other than a static medical fact of the body but an experience of shifting relations of access and power.[5] Attention to the intersections of Black womanhood and disability would draw our attention to how the nonnormative Black woman's body is "a site for intense fetishization." As Kym Oliver, the second half of Triple Cripples, explains, "The moment you sit down on something with wheels, it bugles the mind. It's like 'You're a fetish to me but now you're sitting on this thing which dehumanises you so you're not really a person anymore but unfortunately my loins are reacting to my imagination.' People don't know what to do with this."[6] Oliver's insight speaks volumes to the complex, clashing feelings of disgust, desire, and dehumanization that erects from the sexualized Black disabled female body on display.

And yet, as suggested in Oliver's and Abdullahi's analysis of race, sexuality, and disability, there is the need to not only attune to subjection but also pleasure. Through advocating for sexual access, Black disabled women necessarily shift the critical inquiry from how Black women have been robbed of sexual agency, no doubt important, to how can and do Black women experience pleasure, also important. Therefore, in this chapter, I want to use sex and disability to explore alternative ways of engaging Black women's sexuality. Specifically, I am stricken by how Jennifer C. Nash's work on race and pornography attempts to move away from thinking through Black women's sexuality and representation in terms of injury to focusing on ecstasy.[7] Nash clarifies, "By ecstasy, I refer both to the possibilities of female pleasures within a phallic economy and to the possibilities of black female pleasures within a white-dominated representational economy."[8] In other words, in what ways have Black women accessed sexual pleasure in spite of it? This seems counter-productive in a book about debilitating injury, and yet I imagine my conversation about healing as akin to Nash's analysis of ecstasy and pleasure. This chapter considers what happens when we acknowledge injury yet also make space for Black women's pleasure. What ways of being and knowing have Black women theorized through pleasure, through deeply feeling the ecstasy of one's body, mind, and spirit? In contemporary Black women's essays, life writing, and fiction, Black women theorize sexual agency as a spiritual practice that is informed through the embodied knowledge of queercrip bodymindspirits. I first discuss Audre Lorde's theorizing of the Erotic, then analyze the Erotic in Alice Walker's *By the Light of My Father's Smile*. Both writers reveal how heterosexist ideology has damaged Black women's relationship between their bodies and spirits. The erotic and the divine have been violently severed in ways detrimental to Black women's well-being. Healing in their works involves a return to Africanist spiritual beliefs that respect and honor the erotic as an affective and spiritual onto-epistemology.

But Why Spirituality?

I center spirituality in this discussion of sexual pleasure and the erotic because of the central role of spiritual practice in the everyday lives of Black women and the theories of sexual agency in Black women's writing.

Many Black women's spiritual practices involve and are informed through the theologies espoused in the Black Church. "The Black Church emerges from the religious, cultural, and social experience of Black people. With its roots on the continent of Africa and the Middle Passage, the Black Church provided structure and meaning for African people and their descendants in the Americas who struggled to survive the ravages and brutality of slavery and racial oppression."[9] The Black Church has historically been the fulcrum of the Black community as a provider of services and resources in the absence of social and economic equity. It has been the site and organizing body of Black politics, including its centrality in the civil rights movement. It has been the womb of Black popular cultural production as the spirituals and gospel tradition branched into the blues and R&B. In ways that are more and more forgotten, the Black Church has also preserved non-Christian Africanist spiritual beliefs and practices.[10] As such, the Black Church has been a space of liberation. It has also been a space of subjugation, primarily for its queer and female body, the latter of whom, by and large, constitute the regular and consistent demographic of the institution.

As Black women and womanist theologians have bemoaned, heterosexism has resulted in skewed power dynamics. Black men are granted institutional power as church leaders, while women constitute a disproportionate percentage of the membership yet are typically assigned (and, within some denominations, confined) to the daily operations of administering and managing the church. Moreover, these male preachers uphold double standards around Black sexuality: cisheterosexual Black men are often given a pass for their sexual indiscretions while demonizing Black queer folks' and straight Black women's sexuality is a homiletic mainstay. The results have been devastating. On the one hand, as scholars like Cathy Cohen have noted, issues that stem from supposed deviant sexual practices, like the HIV/AIDs crises in the Black community, were far too often ignored, neglected, or tabled within larger political organizations.[11] Moreover, there has been a crisis around queer/women's sexual subjectivity and sexuality. It has been shrouded in secrecy, silence, and shame. As Black feminist theorist Brittney Cooper so candidly shares of her experience as "single, saved, and sexin," "I was caught in a continual cycle of self-denial, self-indulgence, guilt, confession, rinse, and repeat, topped off by five years of celibacy. I was treating sex as if it were a bad habit that I desperately needed to break."[12] As Cooper goes on to proclaim in her academic contribution to Black feminist theology, *"I rebuke this."*[13]

Audre Lorde's Queercrip Erotic of the Spirit

I turn to Audre Lorde to consider Black women's ecstasy because a Lordian perspective refuses to view Black women's pleasure as suspect or unimportant and insists on the integration of knowledge and affect, body and spirit. Moreover, Lorde writes extensively from the position of the queer, disabled (queercrip) body in pain. She navigates, mourns, adapts, and shares this pained body through the erotic as an affect deeply rooted in African-derived spirituality. Lorde's essay, "Uses of the Erotic: The Erotic as Power," frames the erotic as affective, as a powerful epistemological tool that roots knowledge in feeling and the self, which in the case of queercrip women and femmes of color, is always discredited knowledge. The erotic is a crip way of knowing because it was theorized over, in, and through Lorde's disabled body. Cancer profoundly changed Lorde's body, her relationship to her body, and her relationship to her body in relating with other bodies. Surviving cancer, especially within a deeply racist and sexist medical system, required that Lorde connect deeply with her body, that she listen to and trust her experience in her body and what it has to teach her. The practice of feeling, listening, and trusting the female body is a truly subversive act. It challenges and, therefore, exposes the deep-seated distrust of the body, particularly the body in pleasure, that women have been conditioned to practice. The practice of distrust and disavowal of embodied knowledge, particularly embodied knowledge rooted in the erotic, has been especially cultivated among Black women fearful of the ongoing social, cultural, and political consequences that the (hyper)sexualization of the Black female body has wrought on Black women's lives. The erotic is dangerous. Of course, it's powerful.

According to Lorde, it is the goal of oppression to evacuate the oppressed of their power. The erotic has been distorted and so rendered invisible to women. For women, this has meant vilifying the erotic. The erotic has been conflated with superficial sexuality interminably appropriated for male satisfaction. What has come to pass as the erotic is largely sexual thingafication mobilized in service of patriarchy's will to power. This slippage and substitution has been weaponized and used to violently diminish, dominate, and injure women. Consequently, women have sought strength by suppressing the erotic. Reclaiming erotic power involves reacquainting one's self with the self. Lorde explains, "The erotic is a resource within each of us that lies in a deeply female and spiritual plane, firmly rooted in the power of our unexpressed or unrecognized feeling."[14] Moreover, the erotic merges two forms of discredited knowledge: bodily sensation and deep feeling. Those who oppress have mobilized ableism and sanism—preference for the able body and mind—to diminish the knowledge that comes from physical and psychic feeling in order to discredit the oppressed as mindless bodies and unruly, mindless affect. The erotic, therefore, is a mad cripistemology. It rejects the violence of Reason in favor of "our deepest and nonrational knowledge"[15] and demands that we make a home—"our sense of self"—in "the chaos of our strongest feelings."[16] The deepness and fullness of feeling from the erotic is a compass, a compass that directs us towards "that joy which we know ourselves to be capable of."[17] Erotic power makes us dissatisfied with "suffering and self-negation."[18] It drives us towards pleasure. Moreover, the erotic also rejects the individualism of rationality in favor of relationality. The erotic is experienced most intensely when shared. The erotic holds us accountable to ourselves and to each other: "When we look the other way from our experience, erotic or otherwise, we use rather than share the feelings of those others who participate in the experience with us. And use without consent of the used is abuse."[19] The erotic demands that we both testify and witness as we exercise our will to self-define.

The erotic is also a spiritual power. The erotic, including the sexual, is an aspect of one's spiritual life, which is unlike what is so often the case in Western religious and spiritual practices. The erotic as physical, mental, and spiritual orients all three aspects of the self as informative and political:

> The dichotomy between the spiritual and the political is also false, resulting from an incomplete attention to our erotic knowledge. For the bridge which connects them is formed by the erotic—the sensual—those physical, emotional, and psychic expressions of what is deepest and strongest and richest within each of us, being shared: The passions of one in its deepest meanings.[20]

The spirituality of the erotic is an Africanist spiritual knowing, a queercrip Black orientation of the relationship to the Spirit. In her poetry and essay, for example, Lorde frequently references and relates to African-derived Orisha and goddesses. Though Lorde began expressing her Africanist spirituality prior to her diagnosis, it is, as Meredith F. Coleman Tobias argues, after her diagnosis with breast cancer that we see Lorde increase her writing about her spirituality.[21] Moreover, Lorde's queercrip erotic spirituality is, as Coleman-Tobias also argues, an African Atlantic spiritual orientation.[22] Lorde's spirituality links her to a diasporic and potentially transnational community. Thus, to reiterate, Erotic power is a political tool rooted in a Black feminist affect. This power, I argue, is a technology in service of queer femme afro futures.

To be clear, my discussion of disability, affect, and spirituality in Lorde's theorization of the erotic is not meant to supplant or circumscribe the place of sexual pleasure in Lorde's theory. They are all mutually constitutive of the erotic. This is important to note because, as Black feminist pleasure theorist Joan Morgan explains, Black feminist theory has severed Lorde's theory of the erotic from Black women's sex and sexuality. Like Morgan, I want to bring sex and Black women's sexual pleasure back into focus in theorizing the erotic. Like Morgan, "I want an erotic that demands space be made for honest bodies that like to also fuck."[23] I want to take seriously that the queercrip body in sexual ecstasy is deeply spiritual. A location of healing. Therefore, I enter my discussion of the erotic in a text that opens with a Black woman getting fucked, and fucked well—Alice Walker's 1998 novel *By the Light of My Father's Smile*. Although the intense and multiple scenes of fucking and its so-called "New-Age hocus pocus goddess religion baloney" led to its lukewarm, at times negative, critical reception,[24] it is the intertwining of the Goddess baloney and the fucking that makes Walker's *By the Light of My Father's Smile* compelling. Walker's spirituality, like Lorde's, is a merging of the Erotic, African, and Indigenous spiritualities and queercrip sensibilities that come together to articulate a Black feminist love praxis attuned to accountability and justice.

The Erotic in Alice Walker's Early Writing

Before transitioning into my discussion of the erotic as a queercrip healing power in *By the Light of My Father's Smile*, Walker's later fiction, I want to draw out how, as a contemporary of Audre Lorde, who was also disabled, Walker began fleshing out the erotic as an Afro-Indigenous spiritual power in her early work, primarily in *The Color Purple*, *In the Temple of My Familiar*, and *Possessing the Secret of Joy* trilogy. What Walker suggests in *The Color Purple* through Celie and Shug's mutual caregiving that guides them towards their erotic power, Walker makes explicit in *In the Temple of My Familiar* and *Possessing the Secret of Joy* as Shug appropriates prophetic power and articulates her own theology. In *The Color Purple*, Shug and Celie, together and separately, embark on a healing journey. This journey begins with a queercrip ethics of care as Celie provides care for Shug's sick bodymindspirit. Although Shug is initially "evil" towards Celie (and everybody else), Celie is enamored with Shug and, through daily, intimate acts of care work, comes to sense her own sexuality. In these moments, which Celie writes in her letters to God, she articulates an innate, embodied queercrip spirituality: "I wash her body, it feel like I'm praying."[25] Eventually, Shug comes to reciprocate Celie's affection and attraction. As Shug comes to know Celie (specifically that Celie has never consented to any sexual activity or found sex pleasurable), Shug encourages

Celie to shift her understanding of sex: "Why Miss Celie" Shug exclaims, "you still a virgin."[26] Shug, quite significantly, divorces sexual violence from sex; rape and sexual slavery are not sexual intimacy. Although misogynistic men have devalued Celie as spoiled goods for being a teenage mom out of wedlock, Shug cleanses Celie of that shame and thereby suggests to whom that shame truly belongs—predatory men. From there, Shug teaches Celie to connect with her sexuality using a lesson about pussy and pleasure. Both, for Shug, are manifestations of the Divine. According to Shug, God takes joy in her delight. God loves what brings her joy. God is one's birthright: "God is inside you and inside everybody else,"[27] Shug tells Celie: "You come into the world with God. but only them that search for it inside find it. And sometimes it just manifest itself even if you not looking, or don't know what you looking for. Trouble do it for most folks, I think. Sorrow, lord. Feeling like shit."[28]

For Shug, "God is in everything." She explains to Celie that a relationship with God is being connected to one's deep feelings and feeling a connection with all the life around: "that feeling of being part of everything, not separate at all. I knew that if I cut a tree, my arm would bleed."[29] Moreover, being with God is like sex, which God loves for her and everyone else to enjoy. Shug's gospel is a queercrip erotic relationship that helps her feel secure that it is her divine purpose to do what brings her joy.

These ideas are elaborated upon in *In The Temple of My Familiar*. While there are many spiritual beliefs and practices expressed throughout this novel, Shug has also fleshed out her own theology in a pamphlet she called "The Gospel According to Shug." These beatitudes articulate a spiritual philosophy rooted in a queercrip erotic:

> Helped are those who love the lesbian, the gay, and the straight, as they love the sun, the moon, and the stars. None of their children, nor any of their ancestors, nor any parts of themselves, shall be hidden from them.
>
> Helped are those who love the broken and the whole; none of their children, nor any of their ancestors, nor any parts of themselves shall be despised.[30]

A queercrip erotic spiritual practice is a process of empowered self-discovery and discovery of their connection to all the world—material and spiritual—around them.

Like Lorde's theory of the erotic, Walker, through Shug, theorizes an erotic that is deeply spiritual. It is a spiritual power of deep connection and acceptance of all of creation. It is also an erotic rooted in transformative justice:[31] there is no space in the beatitudes for the oppression and harm of others.

Black Pleasure as Transformative Justice in *By the Light of My Father's Smile*

By the Light of My Father's Smile is a story about injury, healing, and reconciliation. It is also a story about intense and fully felt pleasure. Told through the perspective of multiple spirits, it traces the childhood injuries of two sisters—Magdelena, also known as Mad Doc, Mad Dog, and June,[32] and Susannah—after their father severely beats Magdelena for her sexual life with Manuelito (Mannie), one of the boys in the fictional Afro-Indigenous Mundo tribe Magdelena and Susannah's parents have come to study. Though Susannah only witnesses the violent act, both she and June are harmed into adulthood. While both sisters are successful in their respective careers, June as a professor and Susanna as a writer, only Susanna is able to have a robust (queer) sexual life. June, who holds on to her rage, dies alone, even after reconnecting with Mannie. While the scant critical attention afforded *By the Light of My Father's Smile* is focused on Walker's exploration of father-daughter relationships, the damage wrought on the psyche by internalizing Christianity, and the violence of anthropological work, to name a few, the most notable theme of the novel is the merging of the sexual (erotic) and the Afro-spiritual as healing.[33]

Walker's novel denaturalizes Black sexual politics as inherently and naturally conservative while also refusing to represent Black sexual subjects as racist caricatures such as Brutes and Jezebels. Sexual expression and pleasure are naturalized, while Black men as violently heterosexist, is denaturalized. The process of inverting these truths is positioned as a traumatic and debilitating injury. Soul murder. Through the character of Mr. Robinson, Walker demonstrates that adopting violent heterosexism is a process. In the novel, Mr. Robinson and Mrs. Robinson pose as Christian missionaries to fund their anthropological studies of the Mundo people, an Afro-Indigenous Mexican tribe. As his wife and daughters embrace the Mundo's customs and ways of knowing, Mr. Robinson begins to internalize the white hetero-patriarchy of the Catholic faith. Although self-consciously always more sexually conservative than his wife, he transitions from pretending and performing his role as a Christian missionary to believing in his position. This transformation culminates when he beats Magdalena with a belt of leather and metal, a gift from her young lover, to "tame" not only Magdalena's refusal to abide by gender norms but also her bold, burgeoning sexuality. Langley, Mr. Robinson's wife, explicitly links his compulsion to violently tame and control Magdalena to the racial violence used to control and exert power over enslaved bodies. Moreover, this violence is experienced as a betrayal by the entire household. The agency and need to determine one's own gender expression and experience of sexuality is self-evidently natural to all but Mr. Robinson. Magdalena's wild audaciousness and experience of sexual ecstasy are not inherently self-harmful; heterosexist will to power is.

In Walker's writing, patriarchal violence results in mental and spiritual injury. This injury reaches beyond the individual into the community and is worsened and prolonged when the schism between body and spirit is sustained. June never recovers from the beating. She transitions from a vivacious, inquisitive, sexually and spiritually empowered adolescent to a bitter and stultified woman. The broken place within June is presented as a consuming anger and a gaping hole that she attempts to fill with food and transpose with piercings. Erotic power has been replaced with what Sianne Ngai calls ugly feelings. Ugly feelings are the ambivalent "*amoral* and *non*cathartic" affects that are often indicative of a "general state of obstructed agency."[34] June experiences the ugly feelings of envy, greed, and irritation. These low-heat, simmering affects speak to how heterosexism and patriarchy insidiously infiltrate even the seeming safest spaces to destroy girls' and women's erotic power. The cleaving of body and spirit, the erotic from the self, is not only disempowering but it is also a violent act of displacement. As June later reflects: "Moving to Mexico was, as far as my relationship with my father was concerned, a falling away from the home in myself that my father himself represented."[35]

The mental and spiritual displacement that Walker presents is also felt physically. Without access to the erotic as a source of physical and affective pleasure and spiritual knowing and power, the bodymindspirit itself fails to serve as an ontological homeplace. The disconnect is experienced as discordance. In *By the Light of My Father's Smile*, June's ontological houselessness is experienced as an embodied houselessness—one in which she actively participates. June's sense of displacement and dis-ease is signaled by her fat body. Drawing on and perpetuating anti-fat and fatphobic attitudes about (Black femme) bodies, Walker presents the fat, Black, queer, sexless body as grotesque. June is presented as "very fat," as "Aunt Jemima disguised as Punk Dyke" with her multitudinous piercings and flamboyantly colored hair.[36] Moreover, June expresses no remorse for her fatness. Fat people are expected to perform public displays of self-hatred and shame for lack of discipline—moral failing—as manifested in their intractable bodies.[37] June doesn't. In fact, she finds her pained, "suffering" body fascinating.[38] And she quite conscientiously and carefully invites the pain to the chagrin of those closest to her. Her body not only registers her psychic pain caused by her ontological houselessness through her grotesque body and ugly feeling of greed, but June herself signals and forces others to share her dis-ease through her body and greed. For instance, she intentionally performs abject gluttony when around her father to stoke his guilt. During these performances, she tests his readiness to hold himself accountable for his actions; she questions if he is indeed aware of when and how he has caused injury. He's hopelessly ignorant every time. June manipulates how her greed as a fat Black woman triggers anti-fat and fatphobia to agitate ugly feelings in everyone around her—including the reader. More specifically, June's fatness is supposed to elicit disgust.

Disgust is a politically efficacious ugly feeling because, as Ngai explains, disgust is clear and direct. It "is never ambivalent about its object." Moreover, disgust is an affect that begs concurrence: "it seeks to include or draw others into its exclusion of its object."[39] Walker intentionally, explicitly, and repeatedly positions violent heterosexist patriarchy as the root of June's fatness, so much so that to feel disgust at her greedy and voluminous body is to feel disgust at the system of patriarchy that so routinely and nearly absent-mindedly (Mr. Robinson doesn't pinpoint until after death how and what, precisely, his actions broke) injures and kills the spirits of Black girls and women. Disgust is a politically powerful literary tool because disgust is experienced as "urgent," "dangerous," "intolerable,"[40] as our understanding of and attitude towards patriarchy should be. Disgust doesn't solicit sympathy but action. In Walker's text, it must be done away with immediately. June dies from a massive heart attack as the organ "buckle[s] under the strain of pumping blood through so much weight."[41] Patriarchy is spiritually and psychically lethal. It is also physically deadly. Patriarchy destroys the self as homeplace; it makes the bodymindspirit inhospitable.

Sankofa: A Return to the Erotic, Afro-femme Futures

By the Light of My Father's Smile is ultimately a book about healing. Healing is a process and an experience possible only through the queer cripistemology of the erotic. Healing and the erotic are epistemologically queercrip not only as a theory born of Audre Lorde's queercrip body but because it also demands a reckoning with debilitating injury to move past it. This is not the same as overcoming debility and disability but rather an acceptance and adamant refusal to sit in suffering. The erotic is a spiritual transformation catalyzed through its mining wisdom from pain but insistence on pleasure where pleasure doesn't necessitate the complete absence of pain. For instance, we see Lorde draw on erotic power in her battle against cancer in *The Cancer Journals* (1980). For Lorde, erotic pleasure through masturbation becomes a way of reconnecting to her postmastectomy body, a way to feel fully and deeply the physical, mental, and spiritual pain that marks that moment in her life but not remain stuck in that pain. June attempts to exercise power, particularly over Susannah and her father, but fails to access the deeply personal power of the erotic. For instance, Walker's novel suggests that June rejects her sister and thinness because they both, in June's mind, are equated with suffering. Susannah's disgust at June's fatness, a disgust disguised as concern and care, leads her to say, "merrily, thoughtlessly, stupidly: You see, suffering makes you thin!"[42] June secures a portrait of Susannah and her thin body to her refrigerator to stew her irritation and disdain for Susannah. Yet, for all June rejects of suffering and finds her body in pain fascinating, she fails to find joy and pleasure. She does not move past the moment of injury to fashion a life of her own design. She meets external markers for success but does not feel "acutely" or "fully" "in the doing."[43] Despite singing and humming for most of her life, she does not, presumably, die in song.

June approaches healing when she reconnects with Mannie by chance. Like June, Mannie has also been debilitated by violent heterosexist patriarchy. He has internalized Western paradigms of masculinity, evident by assuming the more Anglo-sounding name Mannie. He fights in the Vietnam War and returns home in pieces stitched back together with wire. His life has become unmanageable without and within because of his drinking. He is never sober. Healing, for both Mannie and June, requires a different orientation to the past, an orientation that asks one to look back in order to move forward. After she meets Mannie while on a flight (they are nearly strangers to each other; both experience a tinge of recognition but cannot quite place the other), Magdalena writes to Manuelito, "from the past," to reveal herself to him as his seatmate and shares her plans for moving forward with her life (she now wants to attempt to diet). For Magdalena, this changed orientation to the past and future marks a step on the journey toward healing, which is less about losing weight and more about returning to the self. Magdalena writes, "you and I have both come back to me." This coming to self and each other is experienced most deeply when they meet and have sex with each other once again. Their sexual intimacy is a reaching for erotic power, a power accessed through their disabled bodies. Magdalena comes to recognize the presence of Manuelito, not just the horror of his violence as a soldier in the Vietnam war and the spectacle of his inebriated, shoddily stitched together-again body. She comes to recognize herself as Manuelito remembers the crook in her little finger, no matter how much larger and relishes her now thick legs and large breasts. Healing does not cure their crip bodies, but they find beauty and potential in their bodies as they navigate the moment. It is through deeply felt and sincerely shared pleasure that both Manuelito and Magdalena come to know each other and themselves again.

It is by reconnecting with their erotic power that they begin to imagine a future for themselves with each other.

Also central to Walker's vision of erotic healing is making amends for the harm one has caused others and forgiving those who make amends for harming you, including yourself. This vision of forgiveness, however, does not substitute amends from those who harm with forgiveness from victims of racist, heterosexist harm, as is often performed and expected.[44] Instead, Walker's model is about acknowledging the fact that we, as humans, will inevitably hurt those closest to us. We all have actions for which we must atone. This is an exercise of erotic power that demonstrates deep and honest self-knowing and maturity. For instance, Susannah, as she sorts through June's belongings and recalls her anti-fat remarks, acknowledges the callousness of her words and actions. She also recognizes how she, too, punished her father even as he tried to make amends. Most of all, she comes to understand how she betrayed herself by rebuffing a relationship with him. She allows herself to fully feel her guilt, sadness, and regret. Susannah's moment of deep feeling and atonement is rewarded with Peace. Moreover, she accesses her erotic power to refuse to allow June to emotionally manipulate and abuse her and to stand in her own truth. After, "Susannah felt herself complete the process of becoming an adult."[45] Both Mr. Robinson and June fail to atone and forgive while alive and, therefore, fail to access the fullness of their erotic power. However, Walker's erotic healing, as a spiritual source of power not rooted in Western religious frames, envisions erotic healing work as continuing even after we cease to be enfleshed and become spirit.

This understanding of erotic healing work draws on Africanist and Indigenous paradigms of ancestor reverence and work: part of our work as newly minted ancestors is to continue to atone for the harm that we have caused while enfleshed. While Black religious and spiritual systems do not escape critique in Walker's writing, particularly those ideas and practices steeped in misogynoir, Walker, like other post-1970s Black women writers, turn to Africanist cosmologies to imagine the world otherwise. Interestingly, while scholars tend to pick up on the Indigenous roots of Walker's spirituality, less attention has been paid to the Africanist influences of Walker's spiritual vision, despite its equally central place in her work. For instance, in *By the Light of My Father's Smile*, the Mundo people, the vehicle Walker uses to articulate her spiritual vision in this novel, is an *Afro*-Indigenous tribe in Mexico. Their spiritual wisdom and insight are an amalgamation and revision of both African-derived and Indigenous-American spiritual cosmologies, particularly evidenced through the significance of the ancestral presence in the work. This concept of the ancestor varies from the popular genealogical understanding of ancestry and differs from Toni Morrison's concept of the ancestor as wise and timeless but mostly enfleshed. Ancestors, as presented in *By the Light of My Father's* smile, reflect the more traditional Africanist-Indigenous understanding of ancestors as enspirited. In many spiritual paradigms throughout Africa and the African diaspora, death is not the end of living. Though not enfleshed, life, as renowned scholar of African Religions John Mbiti explains, "continues more or less the same in the hereafter as it did in this world."[46] The recently dead remain physically and affectively close to their physically alive families. These ancestors may visit living family members, and many cultures honor these ancestors with food, drinks, and other items they enjoyed in life. These newly transitioned relatives can protect, advise, and bless as well as warn, punish, and block blessings.[47] In many African cosmologies, this is part of the work one does as an ancestor before one can move on to the next phase of spiritual life, which is often a version of paradise. Just as a family and community must adjust after the death of a loved one, so too must the recent ancestor adjust to the afterlife.[48] It is in this phase of adjustment that Mr. Robinson, Magdalena, and Manuelito return. Their healing work as ancestors shapes both the novel form and story plot; it operates at the level of *fabula* and *szujet*. Mr. Robinson and Magdalena, and at times Manuelito, alternate as narrators, and the words and experiences of the living characters are focalized through them. Other chapters are told in the first person "I" of the living. The relationship between the living and the dead of Africanist-Indigenous cosmologies is reflected in the formal elements of the novel.

Our power comes from our ability to harness the erotic power of the spirit, like the Orisha Oshun, and transform it into material change. This power—for Walker, accessible both in the physical and spiritual realms—is not only available to women and femmes but also to men. Mr. Robinson and Magdalena, as ancestors, are able to travel between both worlds and can exert limited agency in the living. While they at times use this agency to assist their living relatives, they mostly observe and reflect, sometimes with the assistance, guidance, and wisdom of a more established spirit. Like the living, Mr. Robinson and then Magdalena must also learn to access their erotic power to atone and forgive in order to find peace and pleasure in the spirit world. By making Mr. Robinson the primary narrator and the one most in need of atonement and by inviting him to access his own erotic power, Walker makes the powerful argument that those who exercise violent heterosexism and patriarchal power can and must make amends for their role in stripping women of their erotic power and connection to the Spirit. In Walker's novel, the work of bearing witness is lovingly thrust onto Black men. Mr. Robinson, to witness to the entirety and fullness of his daughters' being, must also witness moments of his daughters engaged in sexual intimacy. In so doing, he realizes that their erotic power is not something to fear and contain but to support and celebrate. Men are made to take up the erotic as a love praxis, as a practice of ongoing accountability. In Walker's spiritual vision, there is no end to transformative justice work. It is work that continues.

Conclusion: Afro-Femme Futures

Audre Lorde's and Alice Walker's queercrip erotic spiritual power is deeply invested in transformative justice. They propose a healing modality in service of everyone's wellness, even those who perpetuate harm. Moreover, it is a vision of Black queercrip futurity that altogether revises and redefines healing and survival. Healing is both deeply personal and communal. None of the characters in *By the Light of My Father's Smile* heal in isolation. Moreover, healing is less about treating the body and more about coming into power. It's about reconciliation with self and the world around us. As Walker comments in *Warrior Marks*, "Those of us who are maimed can tell you it is possible to go on. To flourish. To *grow*. To love and be loved, which is the most important thing. To feel pleasure and to know joy."[49] One does not need to be physically intact to be whole. Although wholeness, for Walker, is our birthright in the physical world, in the here and now, *By the Light of My Father's Smile* projects wholeness into the spiritual realm. In a world hostile to Black femme aliveness, imagining life as continuing and transformative justice work as ongoing is a radical vision of Afro-femme futurity.

Conclusion

Towards a Crip Technoscience of the Spirit

> "IT MEANS, FOR ME, RECOGNIZING THE ENEMY OUTSIDE, AND THE ENEMY WITHIN, AND KNOWING THAT MY WORK IS PART OF A CONTINUUM OF WOMEN'S WORK, OF RECLAIMING THIS EARTH AND OUR POWER, AND KNOWING THAT THIS WORK DID NOT BEGIN WITH MY BIRTH NOR WILL IT END WITH MY DEATH."
> —AUDRE LORDE, *THE CANCER JOURNALS*

In chapter three of this book, I analyze disabled community in Toni Morrison's *Paradise*, noting how a community of wounded women come together and, under the leadership of the blind, spiritually gifted matriarch, Consolata, undergo a healing ceremony. The book's understanding of healing and wholeness rests not on curative logic but on a spiritual reconciliation with one's flesh, one's body. Healing, for Consolata, is used in service of imagining the future otherwise:[1] "a place where white sidewalks met the sea," where "fruit . . . tasted the way sapphires look," with "Dwarfs with diamonds for teeth," where "a woman named Piedade" resides and sings "but never said a word."[2] As the opening of the novel foretells and the rest of the story reveals, the women of the Convent will not only have to heal in order to reach this paradisiac future, but they will also have to redefine survival as their dream for a world otherwise abuts deathly patriarchal violence. The men of Ruby, armed with guns, storm the women's safe haven and hunt down the women, one-by-one. Whether or not Consolata, Mavis, Gigi, Seneca, and Pallas survive is initially ambiguous. The narrative suggests that perhaps one got away. At the end of the novel, all the women re-emerge, radicalized and ready for combat. Yet it is unclear if they are enfleshed or spirit. The text strongly suggests the latter. The section that marks this conclusion starts with each person, other than Consolata, visiting a living loved one. Consolata, we read, is resting her head on the lap of "a woman black as firewood," whose song possesses an unmatched solace.³ Piedade. Those versed in Africanist spiritual beliefs recognize that Mavis, Gigi, and Seneca are recent ancestors there to visit a loved one shortly after they've transitioned. Consolata, with no kin left in the material plane and furthest along in her healing journey, rests on the shores of paradise. This concluding scene, however, is no eulogy or textual epitaph. Each scenic snapshot is alive, anticipatory of living and work left to be done. Even in paradise, there is "endless work they were created to do."⁴ Through Africanist cosmologies, *Paradise* can imagine life and liberation work continuing from the material into the spiritual world. The assault on murderously violent heterosexist patriarchy must continue. Indeed, Africanist spirituality is a technology that extends community and activism from this version of life into the next. In this conclusion, I want to think about futurity. I want to consider the multiple technologies Black women writers mobilized to imagine Black aliveness as ongoing.

Ritual: Crip Technoscience of the Spirit

A crip technoscience of the Spirit merges then extends the theoretical world-making by crip trouble makers in feminist technoscience.⁵ Kelly Fritsch and Aimi Hamraie crip the field of feminist technoscience by challenging the presumption that disabled people are only beneficiaries of technoscientific innovation. While acknowledging and accounting for the, at times, contentious relationship disabled people have had with technoscience—technoscience has and continues to be used to police, surveil, and develop eugenics-based tools to eradicate disabled people⁶—Fritsch and Hamraie contend that disabled people also participate in technoscientific production.⁷ As Fritsch and Hamrai affirm, "Disabled people design our own tools and environments, whether by using experiential knowledge to adapt tools for daily use or by engaging in professional design practices. Crip technoscience conjures long histories of daily adaption and tinkering with built environments."⁸ Whether "smashing curb cuts," "direct actions with mobility devices," or "occupying media space," disabled people "remake the material world."⁹ Crip technoscience requires a reconfiguration of our common understandings of technological innovation, one divested of the classism that underpins so much of ableism. Crip technoscience also demands that we shift the relationship between technological knowledge, the body, and the surrounding world. Most consider technology in service of making bodies bend to the demands of the surrounding environment. Crip technoscience uses embodied knowledge, discredited knowledge, to carve spaces in the environment accessible to various bodyminds. In other words, "Disabled peoples' activist practices . . . constitute a kind of critical world-building."[10]

The discredited yet innovative technological manipulation of inaccessible environments in crip technoscience reminds me of the survival strategies Black folks throughout the diaspora have practiced, the Africanist spiritual practices used to "[tinker] with built environments." This has taken shape in the rumors of supernatural interventions in uprisings against slavery in the eighteenth and nineteenth centuries,[11] to the ongoing daily healing practices through plant medicine, and beyond. Although largely dismissed as irrational and superstitious, Africanist cosmological beliefs that spiritual power can be used to affect people and the world around us have worked as an epistemological technology that has aided everyday Black survival in a climate of anti-Blackness. Isiah Lavender III's definition of liberation technology is useful in clarifying this relationship. According to Lavender III, "[any] kind of practical knowledge that helps black people solve problems with their environment and in their society, abetting their escape from physical and psychological bondage and thereby allowing them control of their own actions, qualifies as a freedom technology."[12] For many writers we study in the African American literary tradition, such as Fredrick Douglass, literacy has been a freedom technology, as Lavender III explains.[13] Yet even within Douglass's now canonical narrative, we see a seed of faith in Africanist spirituality as technology: Douglass procures a root from a rootworker right before his transformational and transitional fight with the slave-breaker Covey. As Kameelah L. Martin so illuminatingly points out in her reading of the scene as a conjuring moment, "Douglass never fully attributes the changing dynamic of his and Covey's relationship to the root; rather, he leaves the reader to make his or her own conclusions."[14]

Contemporary Black women writers, invested in personal, communal, and global healing, have incorporated Africanist spirituality as a literary technology with the aims of Black world-building and survival. They have largely turned to Africanist spirituality as a helping and healing technology, though the powerful women characters who yield this power often serve as a reminder and warning that, at times, healing comes through dismantling. Tellingly, the characters and writers who wield the technological power of Africanist spirituality for world tinkering and making are often disabled or display a crip sensibility. Returning to my reading of Toni Cade Bambara's genre-transforming novel, *The Salt Eaters*, Minnie Ransom, the revered and celebrated healer, comes to access her spiritual power through her mad identity. Similarly, by the end of the novel, Velma, too, comes to access the reserve of Black spiritual technology through her experience of surviving deathly psychic distress. To be clear: this is more than a literary trope. For Bambara, spiritual technology is necessary in the fight for liberation: "I was trying to figure out as a community worker why political folk were so distant from the spiritual community... I wondered what would happen if we could bring them together as Bookman brought them together under Toussaint, as Nan brought them together in Jamaica. Why is there that gap? Why don't we have a bridge language so that clairvoyants can talk to revolutionaries?"[15] Bambara not only considers the future possibilities of powerful spiritual technology for political change, but she also considers it in navigating her crip identity as a woman with cancer. Bambara brandishes the spiritual crip technology that is *The Salt Eaters* in her battle to survive cancer. In a 1994 interview with Louis Massiah, she shares, "I was writing that book in 1981 so I could kick cancer's ass in 1993. That book taught me how to get well. If I hadn't written it, I'm not quite sure I'd be sitting here. I was writing beyond myself in that sense."[16] As I will discuss later in this conclusion, Bambara was writing beyond herself in more ways than one.

Weaving together these discordant threads, I articulate a crip technoscience of the Spirit as a range of sacred technological tools discredited by modern science yet nevertheless mobilized by Black and Indigenous people against systems of violence and domination. Crip technoscience of the Spirit is an African and Indigenous "politicized practice of non-compliant knowing-making: world-building and world-dismantling practices." It is cripistemology manifest in Black women's writing to shape Black presents and ensure Black futures.

Black Death, Black Aliveness, and Black Futures

In Black women's writing, crip technoscience of the Spirit is most often used in service of reimagining survival when faced with the reality of Black death, far too often their own. Drawing on Africanist technoscientific paradigms that understand life as ongoing even as one transitions from the material world into the spiritual, Black women writers imagine healing and liberation work as ongoing and one's work and legacy, as well as one's ancestral self, as a technology available in the fight for liberation.[17] A crip technoscience of the Spirit does not undercut the necessity of abolishing the institutions and transforming the conditions that forestall Black life, but rather it is a mechanism of circumscribing the present reality of Black death in service of Black futurity. At stake in this argument is further consideration of what it means to constantly confront deathly violence against Black bodymindspirits in the streets, in the archives, in literature, and in scholarly criticism. The focus on deathly violence against Black bodymindspirits significantly brings our attention to the afterlives of slavery: from the bullet's rapid snuffing out of Black life to the slow dying that accompanies environmental racism and the slow, yet at times rapid speed at which Black bodies can die due to racist medical neglect. There is no denying that so much of Black life is marked by unremarked and unremarkable Black death. But what does the focus on Black death elide? What gets erased and looked over? My query is not a repudiation of lines of theoretical query on Black death as one of the most devastating consequences of slavery's ongoing reach, such as Afropessimism; indeed, my line of thought corrals Afropessimist critique of Enlightenment humanism and narratives of progress as ongoing histories of white violence to arrest Black life. Yet I also want to spotlight the attention and intention with which Black women have breathed into Black life. In chorus with Kevin Quashie, I want to engage with how Black texts "*assume* Black being."[18]

There are many ways our collective fascination with Black death invisibilizes disability in ways that reify the ableist overlaying of premature death and disability. For instance, the bullet-ridden body of young Black men is the dominating image in the Movement for Black Lives.[19] While the Movement for Black Lives proposes a dynamic social and political platform that encompasses a range of issues and institutional practices—from prison abolition to health care—detrimental to Black life, in the public imaginary, the movement has largely been reduced to demonstration against deathly state violence. The social uprisings protesting the unjust murders of men and boys such as Michael Brown, George Floyd, and Freddy Gray largely focus on their brutal deaths by law enforcement while unarmed.[20] Yet, as Black disability studies scholars and activists have pointed out, many of the victims targeted for violence were also disabled: Kajime Powell had a mental disability, Deborah Danner also had a mental disability, and Elijah McClain was neurodivergent. Thanks to the fastidious work of disabled Black intellectuals and activists, more and more people are becoming aware of the deathly danger the state poses to Black people with disabilities.[21] I worry, however, that this new attention to the disabled victims of police murder will perpetuate the equation of disability and death in the popular imagination. Moreover, state violence not only kills but also disables. Bullets fired by police paralyzed Randy Cox, Jacob Blake Jr., and Jajuan R. Henderson. This doesn't account for the ongoing experiences of psychic distress caused by the encounters. Without dismissing the gravity yet the necessity of bearing witness to and fighting against the climate of anti-Blackness that re-produces Black death, I also want to make space for celebrating Black crip aliveness, Black crip survival. We can hold on to both truths. We see Black women do so in their writing.

"That the pain not be wasted": The Erotic as a Crip Technoscience of the Spirit

In this section, I return to my discussion of Audre Lorde's theorization of the erotic. In the previous chapter, I identified the Erotic as queercrip technology of the spirit. While I used Lorde's theory to unpack the conversations around Black women's sexuality and shame, here I want to expand on the argument I made that the Erotic is a spiritual tool to ensure Black femme futures. In fact, I argue that Lorde is a preeminent theorist of marshaling a crip technoscience of the Spirit towards Black futurity. In her poetry, essay, and life writing, Lorde uses Black spirituality as a scientific technology against oppressive forces that never intended for her to survive. Through a crip technoscience of the Spirit, Lorde extends the reach of her activism from one realm of existence into another. In the "Uses of the Erotic: The Erotic as Power," Lorde frames the erotic as a powerful epistemological tool that roots knowledge to feeling and the embodied self. The erotic is not merely a sexual experience or theoretical concept, but, as Lorde explains, it's "a resource within each of us," one "that lies in a deeply female and spiritual plane, firmly rooted in the power of our unexpressed or unrecognized feeling."[22] In other words, the erotic is a spiritual tool that we can tap into as we come into greater self-consciousness and give voice to our affective knowledge. Moreover, the erotic is a political resource, a tool available to manifest material changes in the world around us. For Lorde, the world of the spirit and the inner landscape of our feelings are not mutually exclusive to our political lives but rather deeply imbricated and informative to them; the erotic, "the sensual—those physical, emotional, and psychic expressions of what is deepest and strongest and richest within each of us, being shared" is "the bridge which connects" the spiritual and the affective.[23] Erotic power is a queercrip technoscience of the Spirit.[24]

Indeed, Lorde mobilizes the erotic as crip technoscience of the Spirit in her own transformative justice praxis of simultaneous world-destroying and world-building. After treating her cancer through a mastectomy, Lorde grieves a significant loss—the material loss of a limb (her breast) and the ontological loss of self as able-bodied and immortal. However, Lorde draws on the erotic as a crip technoscience of the Spirit to re-evaluate her relationship to her transformed body and contemplate her new awareness of her mortality. She comes to realize that her experience with cancer affirmed and deepened the confidence she has in herself to listen to and understand what her bodymindspirit communicates to her. It confirmed her ability to listen to her body and heed its message. For instance, before her medical diagnosis, Lorde already suspects that she has cancer. Moreover, Lorde attunes to the guidance from her bodymindspirit as she plots a course for treatment and draws on her erotic power to advocate for herself, to affirm that she is capable of making informed decisions—drawing on multiple knowledges—about the care of her wellbeing. This is not to disparage people who did not and do not sense changes in their health or to discourage people from seeking a medical diagnosis. This is an affirmation of cripistemology in a world that suspects and discredits the ways of knowing about being, even of one's own being, that disabled people have. Thus, in her essay "Breast Cancer: A Black Lesbian Feminist Experience," Lorde thanks her pain for knowledge "*direct and different from all other certainties.*"[25] Although Lorde admittedly would rather not have the knowledge born from the pain and precarity of cancer (particularly as a consequence of racist, heterosexist slow violence), it is, even as an "unwanted" weapon, nevertheless "useful." Lorde's cripistemology fuels her desire to live—to live consciously, to live fully. It compels her to engage in work that destroys and then rebuilds the world into a space less deathly and more inhabitable for herself and others.

Through the erotic as crip technoscience of the Spirit, Lorde becomes more aware of the healing power of crip community, both enfleshed and spirit. In *The Cancer Journals*, for instance, Lorde rejects prostheses as a product of racist, heterosexist patriarchy and as an obstruction to accessing the erotic and forming community. The prosthetic, for Lorde, prohibits the honest and deep feeling of one's body. It assumes, as she argues, "that women are too weak to deal directly and courageously with the realities of our lives,"[26] and "it encourages her not to deal with herself as physically and emotionally real."[27] The erotic as a crip technoscience of the Spirit combats the minimization of women's concerns as cosmetic by demanding that "we begin to feel deeply all the aspects of our lives."[28] Additionally, the prosthesis keeps women invisible to each other. Without this visibility, it is impossible to draw strength from each other as a collective and turn our combined power into action.[29] Through the strength of the erotic, Lorde makes herself visible, makes herself a beacon to others, which connects her to a transnational Afro-diasporic community of women. Lorde understands that together, women have power, power to effect change, and power to heal each other's deepest wounds. Indeed, it is Lorde's former lover's, Eudora Garrett's, mastectomy scars, scars Lorde encounters long before acquiring her own, that make her aware of the restorative vulnerability and strength in women loving women. Lorde makes it clear that it took the "loving support of other women before I could once again look at and love my altered body with the warmth I had done before."[30]

Garrett is not only a source of crip connection in life but also in death: Lorde shares that Garrett's spirit visits and comforts her after her surgery. Lorde's crip technoscience of the Spirit connects her with a healing community of women both in the material world and the spiritual. Lorde's crip community extends and is indeed deepened, through her connection to the Divine. Although Lorde began creatively expressing Africanist spiritual beliefs prior to her official cancer diagnosis,[31] it is, as Meredith F. Coleman-Tobias argues, after her diagnosis with breast cancer that we see Lorde increase her writing about her spirituality.[32] It is through Lorde's connection with Spirit that she prepares for the transformation cancer will initiate in her own bodymindspirit. As playwright, poet, novelist, and biographer Alexis De Veaux quotes of Lorde, "I never thought Seboulisa would overtake me in this fashion—that I would become her so completely that even the symbol of her breast eaten away by worms of sorrow should become mine."[33] In addition to deeper self-knowledge, Lorde's spiritual community of powerful women inspires Lorde's activist work. For instance, in "The Winds of the Orisha," Lorde evokes and likens herself to the Yoruba Orishas Yemonja, Oshun, and Oya, female deities associated with motherhood and creation, sensuality and/as political efficacy, and transformative power. As they "ride" Lorde in her poem, Lorde's connection to them becomes embodied as "Impatient legends speak through [her] flesh."[34] Transformed and empowered by her spiritual community, the reach of her body extends until "leaping out of the almanacs/instead of an answer to their search for rain/ they will read me/ the dark cloud/meaning something entire/and different."[35] Through a crip technoscience of the Spirit, Lorde channels her "rage" to survive into power to unmake the world.[36]

However, if we were to focus only on Lorde's (Black) death, we would elide Lorde's queercrip survival. Even faced with the possibility then imminence of (Black) death, Lorde, herself, still makes space for Black crip aliveness and survival in her writing. For one, as a sistah-conjurer,[37] Lorde draws on Africanist understandings of the spiritual power of the word to speak life and strength back into herself to continue her liberation work and writing. Lorde testifies that "The existence of that paper ["The Uses of the Erotic"] enabled me to pick up and go . . . it enabled me to start working again. I don't know when I'd have been able to write again, if I hadn't had those words."[38] Lorde's words are imbued with self-edifying *nommo*, ashé—ashé that she accesses in times of need and crises, ashé that she bestows to other women as well. Moreover, *A Burst of Light* is brimming with living in the physical world in the time she has left as she shares evenings dreaming of futurity with other Black lesbians, watches films, gives talks, visits doctors, travels, swims, reflects on dying, reflects on living. *A Burst of Light* is overflowing with Black crip survival. Moreover, Lorde rejects the ways of knowing and being that enable her oppression and destruction. In *The Cancer Journals*, Lorde concludes, "*I do not have to win in order to know my dreams are valid, I only have to believe in a process of which I am a part.*"[39] Later, in *A Burst of Light*, Lorde makes a similar reflection, "Our battle is to define survival in ways that are acceptable and nourishing to us, meaning with substance and style. . . . Racism. Cancer. In both cases, to win, the aggressor must conquer, but the resisters need only survive. How do I define that survival, and on whose terms?" Lorde comes to redefine survival by drawing on an Africanist onto-epistemology that understands the continuity of life as not only *between* the living world and that of the spirit but also as one *transitions* from one sphere into the next. Survival, within this frame, is Lorde's ability, even after her health fades and her body dies, to continue to work toward meaningful change through her written legacy: "I want to move toward death if I must with the certain knowledge that I leave something rich and part of the Great Going Forward behind me."[40]

Crip survival, in part, means living each day fully and intentionally. It is putting one's existence to use, to work. And, when living in this world no longer appears likely, redefining survival. The erotic becomes a crip technoscience of unmaking a world where misogynoir, capitalism, and environmental racism succeed in their efforts to eradicate Black life with their own technologies of destruction. It is an exercise in Black queercrip refusal of death in favor of an Afro-femme understanding of survival.

"Wholeness is no trifling matter": Crip Technoscience Of The Spirit As Healing Affect

I opened this book with Toni Cade Bambara's work, and I would like to close it with Bambara's vision as well. Like Lorde, Toni Cade Bambara's understanding of spirituality as technoscience reaches every facet of her work and her life. Like Lorde, Bambara, too, faced cancer. Also, like Lorde, Bambara draws healing strength from connection, connections in this realm, and extended out into the next. As Bambara proclaims in an interview with Louis Massiah: ". . . I am connected with the most powerful something or others—spirit guides—let's call them angels, if you like. I also have a tremendous feeling of attachment to friends all over who are the people who got me out of that bed and got me well . . . Your [the surgeon's] scalpel is only a physical manifestation of the love and affection of my friends. They got me off the table."[41] For Bambara, love is a crip technoscience of the Spirit.

Toni Cade Bambara understands her writing, her work, as in service for the liberation for Black people. This work does not cease because she transitions into the spiritual world. Only now, she performs this work as an ancestor. As Thabiti Lewis explains in his essential book on Toni Cade Bambara's activist legacy, *Black People Are My Business*, "At the core of these practices of liberation is an embrace of the interrelated roles of ancestral intelligence and political activism to sustain unity of community, self, and social change."[42] We see Bambara illustrate this in her short story "Going Critical." In the story, the protagonist, Clara, has developed cancer from radiation exposure during government weapons testing. After trying multiple healing modalities—spiritual and medical—she has accepted that she will transition into the next phase of her existence sooner than she expects. The main storyline takes place on a sunny day at the beach where Clara wants to talk to her daughter, Honey, about their future. The tension in the story is not that Clara has cancer and will soon die, but what to do with the money Clara will receive as redress from the state. Clara wants Honey to embrace her spiritual gifts and continue Clara's grassroots activist legacy by investing the money into the community center that Clara has founded. Honey, however, feels pressure from her husband's middle-class family to invest in liquor stores in Black communities. At the core of this story is the continuation of liberation work as crip survival.

As in Lorde's writing, "Going Critical" teems with moments of crip survival that spill over in flashbacks and interrupt the main plotline. In "Going Critical," Honey and Clara, bald from her cancer treatments, fold sheets while singing and dancing. They share intimate, tender moments as Clara receives her radiation and chemotherapy treatments. Clara and Honey frolic and get into other silly shenanigans while strolling the beach boardwalk. All of these are moments of Black joy and crip survival in the interstitial narrative space of the story, reflecting on the psychic and communal effects of violent Black death. However, these are moments not to be subsumed and erased by the reality of Clara's impending transition but to be celebrated, remembered, and used as a resource of strength to continue the work of Black, crip worldbuilding. These moments are so easy to look over in the grand narrative of dying yet so essential to understanding the relationships and the modes of relating that have informed and will continue to inform, Clara's work. Like Lorde, Clara sees her work continuing into her next phase of existence; thus, the importance of Honey confirming her commitment to keeping the center running rather than engaging in the further destruction of poor Black communities. For Clara, the energy she puts into the center while in the physical realm sets the foundation for the liberation work she will continue as an ancestor. She exclaims to Honey, "I've still my work to do, whatever shape I'm in. I mean whatever form I'm in, you know? So OK, Honey? And don't mess up, damnit."[43]

While conversations about Black death are important, we have to ask ourselves what gets erased. All too often, it's crip survival, for however long that may be. We see this in Audre Lorde's fire for living consciously and purposefully, even if that may not be long in this realm. We see this in Toni Cade Bambara's zest for life and activism, even as death seems imminent. We see this in the way these Black women imagine their work continuing on by turning to Black spirituality as a crip technology to redefine survival, to upend the finality of unjust death.

These women's relationships to spirituality as a crip technoscience are fascinating as more and more women of color return to the discredited knowledge of their African and/or Indigenous foremothers for inspiration, for a roadmap. While we must be attentive to Afro-femme futures that no longer create deathly illness and injury in Black women's bodies, we must also craft a future that makes space for all the varieties of bodies that exist—a crip future. Work towards that future must accommodate all bodymindspirits. For instance, current understandings of activism assume one inhabits an able bodymindspirit, but, as Black disability activist Vilissa Thompson reminds us,[44] not everyone can march, engage in nonviolent direct action, and the like.[45] Technology removes these barriers. Black women have used technology to tear down these barriers.[46] Expanding our definitions of technology expands the multitudinous ways that different bodymindspirits have worked to manipulate physical, digital, and spiritual environments toward transformative justice.

To that end, I have strived, in this book, to demonstrate and celebrate the magnitude of Black women's strength, resilience, and fortitude as encapsulated in their writing. Standing on the shoulders of Black feminist and critical disability studies scholars, and through my engagements with Black women's essays, life-writing, and fiction, I've attempted to call out the debilitating violence that proliferates the daily lives of Black women. And yet, I tried to capture the healing practices and re/visions of wholeness encapsulated in their writing as well. In their will to self-define, Black women's writing and creating in the contemporary period have managed to look reverently yet critically to the past without being trapped in it, to speak truth to life to our present and breathe life into better futures.

Postscript

> Audre was a freedom fighter
> And she taught us how to fight
> —JAMILAH WOODS, "BLACK GIRL SOLDIER"

Over the years-long process of writing this book manuscript, the world has undergone drastic and frightening changes. In 2016, while writing my dissertation, and the seeds for this book were being planted in the inchoate ideas and early drafts of chapters, Donald Trump shocked the world by being elected as the forty-fifth president of the United States. As I continued to write and revise this manuscript, I bore witness as he and his administration unleashed a whirlwind of chaos, hatred, and harm. I secured a contract with the University Press of Mississippi in 2019 on the precipice of a world-undoing and remaking pandemic unfolding amidst the ongoing state-sanctioned assaults on Black life and social progress. I was in my Texas apartment submitting my initial draft to the press only days after the Supreme Court of the United States voted to overturn Roe v. Wade. And I submit this most recent draft of this manuscript after anti-DEI and CRT bills have nearly banned this type of work in Texas universities, as well as other measures to rapidly deteriorate free speech rights in the US in the wake of the US-supported genocide of Palestinian people. We are indeed in our dark hour of night.

And yet, even though largely ignored, I bore witness to Black, femme crip calls for care, interdependence, and love praxis. I joined others who put their bodymindspirits on the line for a joint vision of racial reckoning and liberation for all. I relished in the (brief) moment when access, empathy, and grace were institutionally supported and encouraged. I started this book in 2016 to strengthen my resolve and resilience today. In these moments of collective exhaustion, mourning, terror, and anger, I turn toward the queercrip knowledge of the women in these pages for strength, guidance, support, and hope. From Toni Cade Bambara, I remember that this darkness, too, is part of the fight, but we are armed with the strength to help our comrades in this world in the next. Thanks to Audre Lorde, I implore myself to sit with others in the fullness of our feelings. It is only when we face the sources of our oppression with honesty and courage that we take action against them. I treasure the opportunity to continue to learn from Alice Walker's ever-growing wisdom. From her, I remember anything we loved can be saved. Octavia E. Butler reminds me that this, too, shall pass; yet it is up to us to determine to what extent and into what shape we'll transform this moment. Toni Morrison challenges me to continue my personal healing work so that I may continue to be in service in the fight to liberate all. And with Gayl Jones, I bear witness to the darkness of this moment but refuse to forfeit my will to self-define a brighter future.

Notes

Introduction

1. Moya Bailey coined the term misogynoir to "[describe] the anti-Black racist misogyny that Black women experience." Moya Bailey and Trudy, "On Misogynoir: Citation, Erasure, and Plagiarism," *Feminist Media Studies* 18, no. 4 (March 13, 2018): 1–7, https://doi.org/10.1080/14680777.2018.1447395.

2. Rosemarie Garland-Thomson, *Extraordinary Bodies: Figuring Physical Disability in American Culture and Literature* (New York: Columbia University Press, 1997), 8.

3. Rebecca Ann Wanzo, *The Suffering Will Not Be Televised: African American Women and Sentimental Political Storytelling* (Albany, NY: State University of New York Press, 2009), 160.

4. Hortense J. Spillers, "Mama's Baby, Papa's Maybe: An American Grammar Book," *Diacritics* 17, no. 2 (July 1, 1987): 67, https://doi.org/10.2307/464747.

5. Spillers, 67.

6. Nirmala Erevelles, *Disability and Difference in Global Contexts: Enabling a Transformative Body Politic* (New York: Palgrave Macmillan, 2011), 25.

7. Therí A. Pickens, *Black Madness:: Mad Blackness* (Durham: Duke University Press, 2019), 25.

8. Here, my use of the phrasing "climate of anti-Blackness" draws on Christina Sharpe's analysis of slavery's ongoing vilence. Sharpe writes, "In my text, the weather is the totality of our environments; the weather is the total climate; and that climate is antiblack" (104). Christina Sharpe, *In the Wake: On Blackness and Being* (Duke University Press Books, 2016).

9. R. L. "Wanderings of the Slave: Black Life and Social Death," June 5, 2013. https://www.metamute.org/editorial/articles/wanderings-slave-black-life-and-social-death.

10. Pickens, *Black Madness*, 11.

11. Douglas Baynton, "Disability and the Justification of Inequality in American History," in *The Disability Studies Reader*, ed. Lennard J. Davis (London, United Kingdom: Taylor & Francis Group, 2016), 17–34.

12. Jennifer C. Nash, *Black Feminism Reimagined: After Intersectionality*, Next Wave New Directions in Women's Studies (Durham: Duke University Press, 2019).

13. Pickens, *Black Madness*, 25.

14. Nash, *Black Feminism Reimagined*, 5.

15. Audre Lorde, *Sister Outsider: Essays and Speeches* (Potter/TenSpeed/Harmony, 2012), 110.

16. Toni Cade Bambara, *The Black Woman: An Anthology* (Simon and Schuster, 2010), 1.

17. Bambara, 2.

18. James Berger, "Trauma Without Disability, Disability Without Trauma: A Disciplinary Divide," *JAC* 24, no. 3 (2004): 572.

19. Rachel Adams, Benjamin Reiss, and David Serlin, eds., *Keywords for Disability Studies* (New York: NYU Press, 2015), 17.

20. Erevelles, *Disability and Difference in Global Contexts*, 17.

21. Jasbir K. Puar, *The Right to Maim: Debility, Capacity, Disability* (Durham, NC: Duke University Press, 2017), xi.

22. Christopher M. Bell's collection of essays and Therí A. Pickens's two special issues are excellent places to begin learning more about Black disability studies. Christopher M. Bell, *Blackness and Disability: Critical Examinations and Cultural Interventions* (LIT Verlag Münster, 2011); Therí A. Pickens, "Blue Blackness, Black Blueness: Making Sense of Blackness and Disability," *African American Review* 50, no. 2 (2017): 93–103, https://doi.org/10.1353/afa.2017.0015; Therí A. Pickens, "Blackness and Disability: The Remix," *CLA Journal* 64, no. 1 (2021): 3–10, https://doi.org/10.1353/caj.2021.0004.

23. Here, and elsewhere, I adopt Sami Schalk's use of the parenthesis to refer to "the overarching social system of bodily and mental norms that includes ability and disability" (6). Samantha Dawn Schalk, *Bodyminds Reimagined: (Dis)Ability, Race, and Gender in Black Women's Speculative Fiction* (Durham: Duke University Press, 2018), 4–5.

24. Jane Dunhamn et al., "Developing and Reflecting on a Black Disability Studies Pedagogy: Work from the National Black Disability Coalition," *Disability Studies Quarterly* 35, no. 2 (May 19, 2015), http://dsq-sds.org/article/view/4637; Moya Bailey and Izetta Autumn Mobley, "Work in the Intersections: A Black Feminist Disability Framework," *Gender & Society* 33, no. 1 (February 2019): 19–40, https://doi.org/10.1177/0891243218801523.

25. Moya Bailey, Izetta Mobley, Anna Hinton, Jina B. Kim, and Sami Schalk have all identified Black feminist writing as theorizing disability. Moya Bailey and Izetta Autumn Mobley, "Work in the Intersections: A Black Feminist Disability Framework," *Gender & Society* 33, no. 1 (February 2019): 19–40, https://doi.org/10.1177/0891243218801523; Anna Hinton, "On Fits, Starts, and Entry Points: The Rise of Black Disability Studies," *CLA Journal* 64, no. 1 (2021): 11–29, https://doi.org/10.1353/caj.2021.0005; Jina Kim, "Toward a Crip-of-Color Critique: Thinking with Minich's 'Enabling Whom?,'" *Lateral* (blog), May 15, 2017, https://csalateral.org/issue/6-1/forum-alt-humanities-critical-disability-studies-crip-of-color-critique-kim/; Samantha Dawn Schalk, *Bodyminds Reimagined: (Dis)Ability, Race, and Gender in Black Women's Speculative Fiction* (Durham: Duke University Press, 2018).

26. Joan Morgan, *When Chickenheads Come Home to Roost: A Hip-Hop Feminist Breaks It Down*, 1999, 65.

27. For a more detailed alternative geneaology of Black disability studies, see Anna Hinton, "On Fits, Starts, and Entry Points: The Rise of Black Disability Studies," *CLA Journal* 64, no. 1 (2021): 11–29, https://doi.org/10.1353/caj.2021.0005.

28. Bailey and Mobley, "Work in the Intersections," 2.

29. Bailey and Mobley, 3.

30. See Bailey and Mobley, "Work in the Intersections"; Sami Schalk, *Black Disability Politics* (Durham, NC: Duke University Press, 2022).

31. See Sami Schalk, *Black Disability Politics* (Durham, NC: Duke University Press, 2022).

32. For a Black disability studies analysis of HIV/AIDs in Cleage's work, see Timothy S. Lyle, "Tryin' to Scrub That 'Death Pussy' Clean Again: The Pleasures of Domesticating HIV/AIDS in Pearl Cleage's Fiction," *African American Review* 50, no. 2 (2017): 153–68, https://doi.org/10.1353/afa.2017.0019.

33. Brittney Cooper, "How Sarah Got Her Groove Back, or Notes Toward a Black Feminist Theology of Pleasure," *Black Theology* 16, no. 3 (September 2, 2018): 196, https://doi.org/10.1080/14769948.2018.1492299.

34. For an example of Africanism in (white) American literature, see Toni Morrison, *Playing in the Dark* (Knopf Doubleday Publishing Group, 2007).

35. When considering the relationship amongst these beliefs and practices, I find Joseph Murphy's metaphor of kinship apt and illuminative. These systems are "a family of traditions, cousins sharing common ancestors and set apart by the 'intermarriages' made in the line." These are each distinct and should be honored as such. Joseph M. Murphy, *Working the Spirit: Ceremonies of the African Diaspora*, Reprint Edition (Beacon Press, 1995), 4.

36. See *A Joyous Revolt* and *Black People are My Business* for an in-dept discussion on spirituality in *The Salt Eaters* as well as Toni Cade Bambara's personal spiritual beliefs. Linda Janet Holmes, *A Joyous Revolt: Toni Cade Bambara, Writer and Activist*, Women Writers of Color (Santa Barbara, California: Praeger, 2014).

37. Kameelah L. Martin, *Envisioning Black Feminist Voodoo Aesthetics: African Spirituality in American Cinema* (Lexington Books, 2016), xx.

38. Theophus Smith's *Conjuring Culture* is a thorough dissection of African belief in Black Christian theology. Theophus Harold Smith, *Conjuring Culture: Biblical Formations of Black America*, Religion in America Series (New York: Oxford University Press, 1994).

39. Judylyn S Ryan, *Spirituality as Ideology in Black Women's Film and Literature* (Charlottesville: University of Virginia Press, 2005), 1.

40. Alice Walker, *In Search of Our Mothers' Gardens: Womanist Prose* (San Diego, CA: Harcourt, 1983), xii.

41. Schalk, *Bodyminds Reimagined*; Margaret Price, "The Bodymind Problem and the Possibilities of Pain," *Hypatia* 30, no. 1 (February 1, 2015): 268–84, https://doi.org/10.1111/hypa.12127.

42. M. Jacqui Alexander, *Pedagogies of Crossing: Meditations on Feminism, Sexual Politics, Memory, and the Sacred*, Perverse Modernities (Durham [NC]: Duke University Press, 2005), 298.

43. Alexander, *Pedagogies of Crossing*; Christina Garcia Lopez, *Calling the Soul Back: Embodied Spirituality in Chicanx Narrative* (Tucson: The University of Arizona Press, 2019).

44. Johan Wedel, *Santería Healing: A Journey into the Afro-Cuban World of Divinities, Spirits, and Sorcery*, Contemporary Cuba (Gainesville, FL: University Press of Florida, 2004), 2.

45. Toni Cade Bambara, *The Salt Eaters*, 1st Vintage contemporaries ed, Vintage Contemporaries (New York, NY: Vintage Books, 1992), 148.

46. Clare Barker and Stuart Murray, eds., *The Cambridge Companion to Literature and Disability* (Cambridge, United Kingdom; New York, NY: Cambridge University Press, 2017), 156.

47. Stephanie Y. Mitchem, *African American Folk Healing* (New York: New York University Press, 2007), 35.

48. Omise'eke Natasha Tinsley, *Ezili's Mirrors: Imagining Black Queer Genders* (Durham: Duke University Press, 2018), 19. Original emphasis.

49. Mitchem, *African American Folk Healing*, 29.

50. Schalk, *Bodyminds Reimagined*, 3.

51. Ryan, *Spirituality as Ideology in Black Women's Film and Literature*, 4.

52. For more about how religious attitudes lead to prejudice against disabled people on the African continent, see: Baker, Charlotte, and Elvis Imafidon. "Traditional Beliefs Inform Attitudes to Disability in Africa. Why It Matters." The Conversation. Accessed November 8, 2021. http://theconversation.com/traditional-beliefs-inform-attitudes-to-disability-in-africa-why-it-matters-138558, and Nyangweso, Mary. "Disability in Africa: A Cultural/Religious Perspective." In *Disability in Africa: A Cultural/Religious Perspective*, 2018.

53. Mary Nyangweso, "Disability in Africa: A Cultural/Religious Perspective," in *Disability in Africa: A Cultural/Religious Perspective*, 2018, 7.

54. Patrick Ojok and Junior B. Musenze, "A Defence of Identity for Persons with Disability: Reflections from Religion and Philosophy versus Ancient African Culture," *African Journal of Disability* 8, no. 0 (April 23, 2019): 4, https://doi.org/10.4102/ajod.v8i0.490; Jennifer F Byrnes and Jennifer Lynn Muller, *Bioarchaeology of Impairment and Disability: Theoretical, Ethnohistorical, and Methodological Perspectives*, 2018. Jennifer Barclay also makes this observation in her essay, "Differently Abled: Africanism, Disability, and Power in the Age of Transatlantic Slavery."

55. Nancy L. Eiesland, *The Disabled God: Toward a Liberatory Theology of Disability* (Nashville: Abingdon Press, 1994); Amos Yong, *The Bible, Disability, and the Church: A New Vision of the People of God* (Grand Rapids, Mich: W.B. Eerdmans Pub. Co, 2011); Deborah Creamer, "Theological Accessibility: The Contribution of Disability," *Disability Studies Quarterly* 26, no. 4 (September 15, 2006), https://doi.org/10.18061/dsq.v26i4.812.

56. Henri-Jacques Stiker, *A History of Disability*, Corporealities (Ann Arbor: University of Michigan Press, 1999), 27.

57. Stiker, 25.

58. Some theologians, influenced by disability studies interventions, are rereading biblical canon against the grain to craft an empowered disabled Christian identity and push churches to be more inclusive and accessible—in other words, to create a liberation theology of disability. For examples, see Eiesland, Nancy L. *The Disabled God: Toward a Liberatory Theology of Disability*. Nashville: Abingdon Press, 1994 and Yong, Amos. *The Bible, Disability, and the Church: A New Vision of the People of God*. Grand Rapids, Mich: W.B. Eerdmans Pub. Co, 2011.

59. There has been a move to find a liberatory theology of disability. For more, see: Eiesland, Nancy L. *The Disabled God: Toward a Liberatory Theology of Disability*. Nashville: Abingdon Press, 1994, Creamer, Yong, Amos. *The Bible, Disability, and the Church: A New Vision of the People of God*. Grand Rapids, Mich: W.B. Eerdmans Pub. Co,

2011, and Deborah. "Theological Accessibility: The Contribution of Disability." *Disability Studies Quarterly* 26, no. 4 (September 15, 2006). https://doi.org/10.18061/dsq.v26i4.812.

60. Gay Alden Wilentz, *Healing Narratives: Women Writers Curing Cultural Dis-Ease* (New Brunswick, NJ: Rutgers University Press, 2000); Donna Weir-Soley, *Eroticism, Spirituality, and Resistance in Black Women's Writings* (Gainesville: University Press of Florida, 2009).

61. Schalk, *Bodyminds Reimagined*, 34.

62. Schalk, *Bodyminds Reimagined*; Pickens, *Black Madness*.

63. Toni Morrison, *Conversations with Toni Morrison* (Jackson, MS: University Press of Mississippi, 1994), 226.

64. AnaLouise Keating, "'I'm a Citizen of the Universe': Gloria Anzaldúa's Spiritual Activism as Catalyst for Social Change," *Feminist Studies* 34, no. 1/2 (2008): 55.

65. For an analysis of the the relationship between Enlightenment investments in reason and rationality and anti-Blackness and madness, see Therí A. Pickens, *Black Madness:: Mad Blackness* (Durham: Duke University Press, 2019); La Marr Jurelle Bruce, *How to Go Mad Without Losing Your Mind Madness and Black Radical Creativity*, 2021.

66. Gloria T. Hull, *Soul Talk: The New Spirituality of African American Women* (Rochester, Vt: Inner Traditions, 2001), 19.

67. Jonathan Metzl, *The Protest Psychosis: How Schizophrenia Became a Black Disease* (Boston, Mass: Beacon, 2011); Pickens, *Black Madness*; Bruce, *How to Go Mad Without Losing Your Mind Madness and Black Radical Creativity*.

68. La Mar Jurelle Bruce does a marvelous job of distinguishing the multiple, instersecting registers of madness levied against Black people in *How to Go Mad*.

69. Hull, *Soul Talk*, 1–2.

70. Alexander, *Pedagogies of Crossing*, 299.

71. Valerie Lee, *Granny Midwives and Black Women Writers: Double-Dutched Readings* (New York: Routledge, 1996), 16.

72. Lee, 16.

73. Lennard J. Davis, ed., *The Disability Studies Reader*, 4th ed (New York, NY: Routledge, 2013), 11.

74. Karla F. C. Holloway, "Revision and (Re)Membrance: A Theory of Literary Structures in Literature by African-American Women Writers," *Black American Literature Forum* 24, no. 4 (1990): 626, https://doi.org/10.2307/3041792.

75. Holloway, 627.

76. Winston Napier, ed., *African American Literary Theory: A Reader* (New York: New York University Press, 2000), 349.

77. Elizabeth Alexander, "'Coming out Blackened and Whole': Fragmentation and Reintegration in Audre Lorde's Zami and The Cancer Journals," *American Literary History* 6, no. 4 (1994): 697.

78. Alexander, 697.

79. Alexander, 696.

80. Several foundational scholars of literary and cultural disability studies have highlighted the connection between embodiment and aesthetic. Rosemarie Garland-Thomson, "Shape Structures Story: Fresh and Feisty Stories about Disability," *Narrative* 15, no. 1 (2007):

113–23; Tobin Anthony Siebers, *Disability Aesthetics* (Ann Arbor: University of Michigan Press, 2010); Michael Bérubé, *The Secret Life of Stories: From Don Quixote to Harry Potter, How Understanding Intellectual Disability Transforms the Way We Read* (NYU Press, 2016).

81. Gayl Jones, "From The Quest for Wholeness: Re-Imagining the African-American Novel: An Essay on Third World Aesthetics," *Callaloo* 17, no. 2 (1994): 508, https://doi.org/10.2307/2931773.

82. Therí A. Pickens, "Octavia Butler and the Aesthetics of the Novel," *Hypatia* 30, no. 1 (February 1, 2015): 168, https://doi.org/10.1111/hypa.12129.

Chapter 1

1. Margaret Price, *Mad at School: Rhetorics of Mental Disability and Academic Life, Corporealities* (Ann Arbor: University of Michigan Press, 2011), 1. I am grateful for the inspiration of Margaret Price's provocation at the open their book.

2. Cheryl A. Wall, "Extending the Line: From 'Sula' to 'Mama Day,'" *Callaloo* 23, no. 4 (2000): 1450.

3. Patricia Hill Collins, *Black Feminist Thought: Knowledge, Consciousness, and the Politics of Empowerment*, Rev. 10th anniversary ed. 2nd ed (New York: Routledge, 2000), 69.

4. Collins, 98.

5. Throughout, I will use "testifying" to refer to telling one's own story and "witnessing" or "bearing witness" to refer to listening to another's, except when quoting or summarizing another scholar. While it is common to refer to both actions as bearing witness, I differentiate the two to reduce confusion as I put the two actions in productive conflict.

6. Ann duCille, "Phallus(Ies) of Interpretation: Toward Engendering the Black Critical 'I,'" *Callaloo* 16, no. 3 (1993): 564, https://doi.org/10.2307/2932256.

7. Eldridge Cleaver, *Soul on Ice* (Laurel/Dell, 1992), 14.

8. Ashley Taylor's analysis of the discourse around teenage pregnancy to exemplify her argument about the use of able-mindedness and cognitive and mental disability as part of racialization speaks directly to the sanism inherent in the figuration of the Jezebel. See, Taylor, Ashley. "The Discourse of Pathology: Reproducing the Able Mind through Bodies of Color." *Hypatia* 30, no. 1 (February 1, 2015): 181–98. https://doi.org/10.1111/hypa.12123.

9. June Jordan, "All About Eva (Published 1976)," *The New York Times*, May 16, 1976, sec. Archives, https://www.nytimes.com/1976/05/16/archives/all-about-eva-evas-man.html.

10. For critical readings on memory, history, trauma, and the blues, see: Donia Elizabeth Allen, "The Role of the Blues in Gayl Jones's 'Corregidora,'" *Callaloo* 25, no. 1 (2002): 257–73; Caroline Brown, "Of Blues and the Erotic: Corregidora as a New World Song," *Obsidian III: Literature in the African Diaspora* 5, no. 1 (Spring-Summer 2004): 118–38; Clara Escoda Agustí, "Strategies of Subversion: The Deconstruction of Madness in Eva's Man, Corregidora, and Beloved," *Atlantis: Revista de La Asociación Española de Estudios Anglo-Norteamericanos* 27, no. 1 (June 2005): 29–38; Joanne Lipson Freed, "Gendered Narratives of Trauma and Revision in Gayl Jones's Corregidora," *African American Review* 44, no. 3 (Fall 2011): 409–20; Madhu Dubey, *Black Women Novelists and the Nationalist Aesthetic* (Bloomington: Indiana University Press, 1994).

11. To name a few who remark on the physical, in addition to the psychic, inscription of historical trauma in Corrigedora, see: Jennifer L. Griffiths, *Traumatic Possessions: The Body and Memory in African American Women's Writing and Performance* (Charlottesville: University of Virginia Press, 2009); Casey Howard Clabough, "'Toward an All-Inclusive Structure': The Early Fiction of Gayl Jones," *Callaloo* 29, no. 2 (August 9, 2006): 634–57, https://doi.org/10.1353/cal.2006.0093; Deborah M. Horvitz, *Literary Trauma: Sadism, Memory, and Sexual Violence in American Women's Fiction*, SUNY Series in Psychoanalysis and Culture (Albany: State University of New York Press, 2000).

12. For an example of a psychoanalytic reading of Corregidora, see: Deborah M. Horvitz, *Literary Trauma: Sadism, Memory, and Sexual Violence in American Women's Fiction*, SUNY Series in Psychoanalysis and Culture (Albany: State University of New York Press, 2000).

13. Clabough, Casey Howard. "'Toward an All-Inclusive Structure': The Early Fiction of Gayl Jones." *Callaloo* 29, no. 2 (August 9, 2006): 636. https://doi.org/10.1353/cal.2006.0093.

14. I am indebted to the work of scholars like Moya Bailey and Izetta Mobley and Sami Schalk for outlining Black Feminist Disability Studies as a theoretical, critical, and methodological framework. Here, I specifically draw on Sami Schalk's argument in her fabulous debut monograph, *Bodyminds Reimagined (Dis)ability, Race, and Gender in Black Women's Speculative Fiction* (2018). In *Bodyminds Reimagined*, Schalk makes a "loving, critical intervention into black feminist theory and disability studies" by demonstrating that disability in Black women's fiction is both metaphor and material. I also draw on Nirmala Erevelles's groundbreaking work, *Disability and Difference in Global Contexts: Enabling a Transformative Body Politic*. By contextualizing disability within a transnational context, Erevelles reminds white disability studies scholars that disability does not emerge in a vacuum but within specific material contexts.

15. I use the terminology of slavery's afterlives in conversation with Saidiya Hartman's theorization of the ongoing resonances of the slave trade. For an example, see Saidiya V. Hartman, *Lose Your Mother: A Journey Along the Atlantic Slave Route*, 1st ed (New York: Farrar, Straus and Giroux, 2007).

16. Gayl Jones, *Corregidora* (Beacon Press, 1987), 6.

17. Dubey, *Black Women Novelists and the Nationalist Aesthetic*, 29.

18. Jones, *Corregidora*, 3.

19. Alison Kafer, *Feminist, Queer, Crip* (Bloomington, IN: Indiana University Press, 2013), 1.

20. Michael Bérubé, *The Secret Life of Stories: From Don Quixote to Harry Potter, How Understanding Intellectual Disability Transforms the Way We Read* (NYU Press, 2016), 43.

21. Hortense J. Spillers, "Mama's Baby, Papa's Maybe: An American Grammar Book," *Diacritics* 17, no. 2 (July 1, 1987): 65, https://doi.org/10.2307/464747.

22. Spillers, 65.

23. Jones, *Corregidora*, 9.

24. Indeed, Simon Corregidora's whiteness is questioned throughout Great Gram's and Gram's memory. They often remark on how he looked "Indian" and would "get mad and beat you" or "stick a poker up your ass" or "have [your] ass off" if you mentioned this (Jones 11, 23, and 124). While Great Gram suggests that he may have had a swarthy complexion (a "light black man looked more like a white man than he did" (Jones 124), it is his "big" size and "greasy," "straight," and "black" hair that raises suspicions (Jones 11).

25. Jones, *Corregidora*, 42.

26. Jones, 117.

27. Jones, 81.

28. Roy Sieber et al., eds., *Hair in African Art and Culture* (New York : Munich: Museum for African Art; Prestel, 2000), 15.

29. The free mulatta concubine has historically been presented as attentive to her "hair and toilet." For more on the figure of the mulatta concubine, see Lisa Ze Winters, *The Mulatta Concubine: Terror, Intimacy, Freedom, and Desire in the Black Transatlantic*, 2016.

30. Jones, *Corregidora*, 57.

31. Jones, 57.

32. Jones, 22.

33. Jones, 7.

34. As Kameelah M. Martin importantly notes, the griot is usually a position held by men. Jones presents a specifically feminized version of this figure by linking oral historical work with reproduction.

35. For more about griots as formative of community identity see Waltraud Kokot Alfonso, Carolin and Khachig Tölölyan, "Diaspora, Identity and Religion: New Directions in Theory and Research" (Abingdon: Taylor & Francis).

36. Kalí Tal, *Worlds of Hurt: Reading the Literatures of Trauma* (Cambridge England: Cambridge University Press, 1995).

37. Tal.

38. Angela M. Carter, "When Silence Said Everything: Reconceptualizing Trauma through Critical Disability Studies," *Lateral* 10, no. 1 (2021), https://doi.org/10.25158/L10.1.8. original emphasis.

39. Carter.

40. Carter.

41. Nirmala Erevelles, *Disability and Difference in Global Contexts: Enabling a Transformative Body Politic* (New York: Palgrave Macmillan, 2011), 25.

42. Jones, *Corregidora*, 59.

43. For more about how Black motherhood has been demonized for reproducing disability, see Anna Hinton, "Making Do with What You Don't Have: Disabled Black Motherhood in Octavia E. Butler's Parable of the Sower and Parable of the Talents," *Journal of Literary & Cultural Disability Studies* 12, no. 4 (2018): 441–57,507, http://dx.doi.org.libproxy.library.unt.edu/10.3828/jlcds.2018.35.

44. Saidiya V. Hartman, *Scenes of Subjection: Terror, Slavery, and Self-Making in Nineteenth-Century America*, Race and American Culture (New York: Oxford University Press, 1997), 25.

45. Jones, *Corregidora*, 59.

46. Christina Elizabeth Sharpe, *Monstrous Intimacies: Making Post-Slavery Subjects*, Perverse Modernities (Durham, NC: Duke University Press, 2010), 45 and 47.

47. Jones, *Corregidora*, 61.

48. Anna Mollow, "Criphystemologies: What Disability Theory Needs to Know about Hysteria," *Journal of Literary & Cultural Disability Studies* 8, no. 2 (July 5, 2014): 186.

49. La Marr Jurelle Bruce, *How to Go Mad Without Losing Your Mind Madness and Black Radical Creativity*, 2021. Here, I align my use of the capital "R" reason with La Marr Jurelle Bruce. According to Bruce, "... reason, signifies a generic process of cognition within a given system of logic and the 'mental concerned with forming conclusions, judgments, or inference.' Meanwhile, Reason is a proper noun denoting a positivist, secularist, Enlightenment-rooted episteme purported to uphold objective 'truth' while mapping and mastering the world" (4). In his study of madness and Blackness, Bruce, as others before him like Theri Pickens, explains how Enlightenment definitions and preference for Reason was used to justify racialized slavery and therefore underscores the violence committed in the name of Reason.

50. Marta Caminero-Santangelo, *The Madwoman Can't Speak, or, Why Insanity Is Not Subversive*, Reading Women Writing (Ithaca: Cornell University Press, 1998); Jess Waggoner, "'Oh Say Can You ___': Race and Mental Disability in Performances of Citizenship," *Journal of Literary & Cultural Disability Studies* 10, no. 1 (March 4, 2016): 87–102; Sami Schalk, *Bodyminds Reimagined: (Dis)Ability, Race, and Gender in Black Women's Speculative Fiction* (Durham: Duke University Press, 2018), 59–83; Cynthia Lewiecki-Wilson, "Rethinking Rhetoric through Mental Disabilities," *Rhetoric Review* 22, no. 2 (2003): 156–67.

51. Jones, *Corregidora*, 11.

52. Éva Tettenborn, "Melancholia as Resistance in Contemporary African American Literature," *MELUS* 31, no. 3 (September 1, 2006): 102, https://doi.org/10.1093/melus/31.3.101.

53. Tettenborn, 102.

54. Bruce, *How to Go Mad Without Losing Your Mind Madness and Black Radical Creativity*, 137.

55. In *Worlds of Hurt: Reading the Literatures of Trauma*, Kali Tal identifies "mythologization," "medicalization," and "disappearance" as three methods of what she calls "cultural coping" with trauma, or how "reflected and revised in the larger, collective political and cultural world." Tal examines traumatic events that society culturally codifies by essentially combining these coping mechanisms. Importantly, slavery and its afterlives are outside the scope of Tal's work. In the US, slavery is immediately and compulsorily dismissed as a past idiosyncrasy. The primary (white) cultural coping response to the trauma slavery wrought—and continues to inflict today—has largely disappeared. While African American communities have mythologized enslaved Black women's experiences of sexual subjugation, white American society has largely attempted to erase it. The Corregidora women's story is one that, arguably, even resists incorporation into Black collective memory because of the taboo around incest. Nancy Tauna argues that communities are persistently willfully ignorant about incest, as well as racism. Christina Sharpe, who discusses incest in *Corregidora*, reveals how US chattel slavery likened and, in some ways, displaced incest with amalgamation (28) and how, in the case of master-slave dynamics, property relations "subordinated" kinship relations, complicating (erasing?) enslaved Black women's experiences as incest (34–35).

56. Gayl Jones, *Eva's Man*, Reprint edition (Boston: Beacon Press, 1987), 5.

57. Tal, *Worlds of Hurt*.

58. Jones, *Corregidora*, 127.

59. Jones, 51.

60. Jones, 20.
61. Jones, 38.
62. Jones, 75.
63. Jones, 76.
64. Elizabeth Swanson Goldberg, "Living the Legacy: Pain, Desire, and Narrative Time in Gayl Jones' Corregidora," *Callaloo* 26, no. 2 (2003): 446–72, https://doi.org/10.1353/cal.2003.0046.
65. Claudia C. Tate, "Corregidora: Ursa's Blues Medley," *Black American Literature Forum* 13, no. 4 (1979): 139, https://doi.org/10.2307/3041480. Other critical readers of Jones's novel, such as Donia Elizabeth Allen, Caroline Brown, and Ana María Fraile-Marcos, to name a few, consider Corregidora a blues novel, but Claudia Tate explicitly links the experimental formal elements to blues conventions such as the blues break.
66. For more about the influence of mad people on blues music, see La Marr Jurelle Bruce, *How to Go Mad Without Losing Your Mind: Madness and Black Radical Creativity*, 2021; Read about blind blues men in Terry Rowden, *The Songs of Blind Folk: African American Musicians and the Cultures of Blindness*, Corporealities. Discourses of Disability (Ann Arbor: University of Michigan Press, 2009).
67. Bruce, *How to Go Mad Without Losing Your Mind Madness and Black Radical Creativity*, 77.
68. Jones, *Corregidora*, 41.
69. Allen, "The Role of the Blues in Gayl Jones's 'Corregidora.'"
70. Jones, *Corregidora*, 75.
71. Sharon L. Snyder and David T. Mitchell, *Cultural Locations of Disability* (Chicago: University of Chicago Press, 2006).
72. Petra Kuppers, "Disability Culture Poetry: The Sound of the Bones. A Literary Essay," *Disability Studies Quarterly* 26, no. 4 (2006): 10–10. Here, Petra Kuppers offers an excellent discussion of disability culture.
73. Angela Yvonne Davis, *Blues Legacies and Black Feminism: Gertrude "Ma" Rainey, Bessie Smith, and Billie Holiday* (New York: Vintage, 1999); Terry Rowden, *The Songs of Blind Folk: African American Musicians and the Cultures of Blindness*, Corporealities. Discourses of Disability (Ann Arbor: University of Michigan Press, 2009). Angela Davis's definitive study of Black women blues singers, as well as Terry Rowden's groundbreaking book on blind blues men, discuss both the financial freedom yet creative confines blues singers met in the midcentury music industry.
74. While pregnancy can cause some changes to the singing voice, Ursa may more likely have damaged her vocal cords at the hospital. Tad reports to Ursa that she had the nurses "scared to death" because she was "cussing them out" (8). This detail is relayed several times across Ursa's story either by Ursa herself or Tadpole. While these passages do not mention whether or not Ursa was yelling, Tad does note that the nurses are regularly confused as to *what* Ursa is. This questioning not only reflects unsurety of Ursa's racial and ethnic identity—nurses mistake her for a "gypsy," for instance—but also of Ursa's ontology.
75. Jones, *Corregidora*, 44.
76. Angelyn Mitchell and Danille K Taylor, *The Cambridge Companion to African American Women's Literature*, 2009. Several scholars of Black literature and culture

liken the blues singer to the African griot. For examples, see Keith D. Leonard's chapter "African American Women Poets and the Power of the Word."

77. Jones, *Corregidora*, 92.

78. Neil William Lerner and Joseph Nathan Straus, eds., *Sounding off: Theorizing Disability in Music* (New York: Routledge, 2006), 176.

79. Neil William Lerner and Joseph Nathan Straus, eds., *Sounding off: Theorizing Disability in Music* (New York: Routledge, 2006), 179. Stras also highlights how the conditions of blues venues and the demand for the rougher singing voice created or further impaired blues singers' focal chords. Singers like Ethel Waters eventually had to have surgeries to remove nodules.

80. LaMonda Horton-Stallings, *Mutha' Is Half a Word: Intersections of Folklore, Vernacular, Myth, and Queerness in Black Female Culture*, Black Performance and Cultural Criticism (Columbus: Ohio State University Press, 2007).

81. Yvonne Patricia Chireau, *Black Magic: Religion and the African American Conjuring Tradition*, 1. paperback printing, The George Gund Foundation Imprint in African American Studies (Berkeley, Calif.: University of California Press, 2006), 144.

82. Kameelah L. Martin, *Conjuring Moments in African American Literature: Women, Spirit Work, and Other Such Hoodoo*, 1st ed (New York: Palgrave Macmillan, 2013), 2.

83. Jones, *Corregidora*, 54.

84. Carter, "When Silence Said Everything."

85. Therí A. Pickens, "Octavia Butler and the Aesthetics of the Novel," *Hypatia* 30, no. 1 (February 1, 2015): 167–80, https://doi.org/10.1111/hypa.12129. Therí Pickens outlines Octavia E. Butler's aesthetic practices and links them to the complex representations of race, gender, and dis/ability. Pickens identifies open-ended conclusions, intricate depictions of power, and "contained literary chaos that troubles ontological fixity" (176) as characteristics of Butler's aesthetic. I argue, as Pickens suggests, that the aesthetic practices can be found across the body of Black women's writing concerned with race, gender, and dis/ability.

86. I say within the fabric of her life as opposed to in her life because some of the people in her stories aren't in her life—they aren't friends, family, or people she personally knows—but the presence and the mythos around them are part of her psychic and social landscape. Most notable of these folk are The Queen Bee and Freddy Sloot's mom. She doesn't know them, but they are—and become—intimately familiar to her.

87. Jordan, "All About Eva (Published 1976)," 217.

88. Roseann P. Bell, Bettye J. Parker, and Beverly Guy-Sheftall, *Sturdy Black Bridges: Visions of Black Women in Literature* (Garden City, NY: Anchor Press/Doubleday, 1979), 215, http://archive.org/details/sturdyblackbridgoobell.

89. RICK BRAGG, "Author's Downward Spin Rivals Tragedies in Her Novels of Black America," *New York Times*, 1998, sec. National Report.

90. Bernard W. Bell, *The Contemporary African American Novel: Its Folk Roots and Modern Literary Branches* (Amherst: University of Massachusetts Press, 2004), 162.

91. Martha Stoddard Holmes et al., *Embodied Rhetorics: Disability in Language and Culture*, ed. James C. Wilson and Cynthia Lewiecki-Wilson, 1st edition (Carbondale:

Southern Illinois University Press, 2001), 53. In her contribution, Prendergast contends, "that the these polarized positions effectively place the mentally ill and schizophrenics in particular in a rhetorical black hole." The language of black holes also recalls Evelyn C. Hammonds's discussion of Black women's sexuality and the culture of silence.

92. David T. Mitchell and Sharon L. Snyder, *Narrative Prosthesis: Disability and the Dependencies of Discourse*, Corporealities (Ann Arbor: University of Michigan Press, 2001), 6.

93. Jordan, "All About Eva (Published 1976)."

94. Catherine Prendergast, "The Unexceptional Schizophrenic: A Post-Postmodern Introduction," in *The Disability Studies Reader*, ed. Lennard J Davis (Taylor and Francis, 2016), 232–41, https://doi.org/10.4324/9781315680668-25.

95. Jones, *Eva's Man*, 4–5.

96. Jones, 3.

97. Jones, 81.

98. Kevin Everod Quashie, *The Sovereignty of Quiet: Beyond Resistance in Black Culture* (New Brunswick, NJ; London: Rutgers University Press, 2012), 4.

99. Quashie, 6.

100. Jones, *Eva's Man*, 173.

101. Jones, 3.

102. Jones, 4.

103. Rosemarie Garland-Thomson, *Staring: How We Look* (Oxford; New York: Oxford University Press, 2009), 194.

104. Lorde, Audre. *Sister Outsider: Essays and Speeches*. Potter/TenSpeed/Harmony, 2012.38.

105. Morrison, Toni. *Sula*. Reprint edition. New York: Vintage, 2004. 14.

Chapter 2

1. In this chapter, I do not distinguish between cultural nationalism and revolutionary nationalism, the former referring to emphasis on embracing African culture and the latter referring to radical political transformation through, if necessary, armed resistance. The writing I discuss in this chapter addresses both forms of Black nationalist discourse. Amy Ongiri provides an excellent distinction between the two. See, Amy Abugo Ongiri, *Spectacular Blackness: The Cultural Politics of the Black Power Movement and the Search for a Black Aesthetic* (Charlottesville: University of Virginia Press, 2010), 49.

2. I borrow the term "brokenbeautiful" from Alexis Pauline Gumbs's blog, brokenbeautiful press. I borrow this term for how it encapsulates the philosophy espoused in the works under consideration in this chapter.

3. Mel Watkins, "Sexism, Racism and Black Women Writers," *The New York Times*, June 15, 1986, sec. Books, https://www.nytimes.com/1986/06/15/books/sexism-racism-and-black-women-writers.html.

4. Stephanie Y. Mitchem, African American Folk Healing (New York: New York University Press, 2007), 36.

5. *Sick from Freedom* provides another in-depth discussion about the health impacts of racism and how white supremacists mobilized Black health outcomes to argue in-favor of slavery and present the enslaved past as nostalgic. Jim Downs, *Sick from Freedom: African-American Illness and Suffering during the Civil War and Reconstruction* (Oxford; New York: Oxford University Press, 2012).

6. Douglas Baynton, "Disability and the Justification of Inequality in American History," in *The Disability Studies Reader*, ed. Lennard J. Davis (London, United Kingdom: Taylor & Francis Group, 2016), 17–18.

7. Stephen Knadler, "Dis-Abled Citizenship: Narrating the Extraordinary Body in Racial Uplift," *Arizona Quarterly: A Journal of American Literature, Culture, and Theory* 69, no. 3 (September 29, 2013): 113, https://doi.org/10.1353/arq.2013.0023.

8. Rosemarie Garland-Thomson, "Shape Structures Story: Fresh and Feisty Stories about Disability," *Narrative* 15, no. 1 (2007): 115. My emphasis.

9. For a general history of disabled folk in the US, Kim E. Nielsen's *A Disability History of the United States* is an excellent start. For a historical overview of disabled people's political organizing, see Joe Shapiro's *No Pity*. If you're interested in the emergence of critical disability studies as an academic field, check out Lennard J. Davis's essay "Crips Strike Back." For a loving yet incisive critique of the constitutional whiteness of disability studies, Christopher M. Bell's "White Disability Studies: A Modest Proposal" in the Disability Studies Reader is *the* starting place, and see Anna Hinton's article "On Fits, Starts, and Entry Points." Therí A. Pickens's special edition of African American Review (50.2) and CLAJ (64.1) are essentials for entering into the field of Black disability studies. Kim E. Nielsen, *A Disability History of the United States*, Paperback edition, Revisioning American History (Boston: Beacon Press, 2012); Joseph P. Shapiro, *No Pity: People with Disabilities Forging a New Civil Rights Movement*, 1 edition (New York: Broadway Books, 1994); Lennard J. Davis, "Crips Strike Back: The Rise of Disability Studies," *American Literary History* 11, no. 3 (1999): 500–512; Lennard J. Davis, ed., *The Disability Studies Reader*, 4th ed (New York, NY: Routledge, 2013); Anna Hinton, "On Fits, Starts, and Entry Points: The Rise of Black Disability Studies," *CLA Journal* 64, no. 1 (2021): 11–29, https://doi.org/10.1353/caj.2021.0005; Therí A. Pickens, "Blue Blackness, Black Blueness: Making Sense of Blackness and Disability," *African American Review* 50, no. 2 (2017): 93–103, https://doi.org/10.1353/afa.2017.0015; Therí A. Pickens, "Blackness and Disability: The Remix," *CLA Journal* 64, no. 1 (2021): 3–10, https://doi.org/10.1353/caj.2021.0004.

10. Margaret Rose Torrell, "Plural Singularities: The Disability Community in Life-Writing Texts," *Journal of Literary & Cultural Disability Studies* 5, no. 3 (January 1, 2011): 322, https://doi.org/10.3828/jlcds.2011.25.

11. Throughout her body of essays, Walker underscores how Black women forced to have many children find financial precarity nearly insurmountable.

12. Merri Johnson and Robert McRuer, "Cripistemologies," *Journal of Literary & Cultural Disability Studies* 8, no. 2 (January 1, 2014): 130, https://doi.org/10.3828/jlcds.2014.12.

13. Merri Johnson and Robert McRuer, "Cripistemologies," *Journal of Literary & Cultural Disability Studies* 8, no. 2 (January 1, 2014): 127–48, https://doi.org/10.3828/jlcds.2014.12. In their introduction to this special issue of JLCDS on cripistemologies, Johnson and McRuer open with "Southerisms" quoted from Randall Kenan's 1989 novel *A Visitation of Spirits*—a

novel itself filled with southern Black cripistemologies. Moreover, it was at a conference in Spartanburg, SC, that Duggan and McRuer sparked the conversation that would continue in academia elsewhere and develop into a nascent theory of cripistemologies.

14. Johnson and McRuer, 130.

15. Johnson and McRuer, "Cripistemologies," 128.

16. Johnson and McRuer, 128.

17. Alice Walker, *In Search of Our Mothers' Gardens: Womanist Prose* (San Diego, CA: Harcourt, 1983), 231.

18. Walker, 231.

19. Johnson and McRuer, "Cripistemologies," 128.

20. Walker, *In Search of Our Mothers' Gardens*, 17.

21. Walker, 380.

22. For examples of discussions of *Meridian* as a civil rights or protest novel, see Shermain Jones's "Presenting Our Bodies, Laying our Case" and Karen Stein's "Meridian: Alice Walker's Critique of Revolution." For feminist readings/readings of Gender in *Meridian*, read "Alice Walker's Meridian, Feminism, and the 'Movement,' Guy Foster's "Looking Good," and Lindsey Tucker's "Walking the Red Road." Shermaine M. Jones, "Presenting Our Bodies, Laying Our Case: The Political Efficacy of Grief and Rage during the Civil Rights Movement in Alice Walker's Meridian," *The Southern Quarterly* 52, no. 1 (Fall 2014): 179–95; Karen F. Stein, "Meridian: Alice Walker's Critique of Revolution," *Black American Literature Forum* 20, no. 1/2 (1986): 129–41, https://doi.org/10.2307/2904556; Susan Danielson, "Alice Walker's Meridian, Feminism, and the 'Movement,'" *Women's Studies* 16, no. 3/4 (March 1989): 317; Guy Mark Foster, "Looking Good: Neutralizing the Desiring (Black Male) Gaze in Alice Walker's Meridian," *Symbiosis: A Journal of Anglo-American Literary Relations* 13, no. 2 (October 2009): 127–57; Lindsey Tucker, "Walking the Red Road: Mobility, Maternity and Native American Myth in Alice Walker's Meridian," *Women's Studies* 19, no. 1 (July 1991): 1.

23. Essays on Meridian's broken body include Pamela Barnett's "Miscegenation, Rape, and Race in Alice Walker's Meridian" and Alan Nadel's "Reading the Body." Pamela E. Barnett, "'Miscegenation,' Rape, and 'Race' in Alice Walker's Meridian," *Southern Quarterly: A Journal of the Arts in the South* 39, no. 3 (Spring 2001): 65–81; Alan Nadel, "Reading the Body: Alice Walker's Meridian and the Archeology of Self," *MFS Modern Fiction Studies* 34, no. 1 (January 1, 2009): 55–68, https://doi.org/10.1353/mfs.0.0162.

24. Walker, *In Search of Our Mothers' Gardens*, 17.

25. Here, I draw on Hortense Spillers's foundation essay "Mama's Baby, Papa's Maybe: An American Grammar Book." Zahi Zalloua's *Being Posthuman* offers an insightful expansion of Spillers's argument. Hortense J. Spillers, "Mama's Baby, Papa's Maybe: An American Grammar Book," *Diacritics* 17, no. 2 (July 1, 1987): 65–81, https://doi.org/10.2307/464747; Zahi Anbra Zalloua, *Being Posthuman: Ontologies of the Future* (London, UK; New York, NY, USA: Bloomsbury Academic, 2021).

26. Alice Walker, *Meridian* (Harcourt, 1976), 49. In *Meridian*, Alice Walker also explores Black people's relationship and responsibility to other marginalized and oppressed communities. For instance, collaboration and conflict emerge between Black and Jewish, Indigenous, white women, and Roma communities. Histories of enslavement, settler

colonialism, and anti-Blackness have enmeshed and implicated all in shifting and varying degrees of harm and repair. As Walker's fictional father explains, "Her father sighed. "I never said either side was innocent or guilty, just ignorant. They've been a part of it, we've been a part of it, everybody's been a part of it for a long time" (49).

27. Alice Walker, *Meridian* (Harcourt, 1976), 120. Original Emphasis.

28. The sexually abusive and coercive nature of Mr. Raymonds's interactions with Meridian is especially problematic when considered with her own disability. For one, Meridian, while at Saxton, experiences instability in her ability to stay fed. She tolerates Mr. Raymonds's abuse because she needs food. Moreover, Meridian, by this point in her life, already lives with chronic illness, making her more vulnerable to sexual abuse. As a social worker and disability activist, Vilissa Thompson exposes, in "Domestic Violence & Disabled Women—The Silent Epidemic within Our Community" (2014), Black women with disabilities are three times more likely to be sexually assaulted than nondisabled women. The intersections of race, poverty, and disability make women less likely to report these crimes, as we see with Meridian.

29. Walker, *Meridian*, 113.

30. Walker, 217.

31. Erica R Edwards, *Charisma and the Fictions of Black Leadership* (Minneapolis: University of Minnesota Press, 2012), xv, http://site.ebrary.com/id/10555680.

32. Seongho Yoon, "Gendering the Movement: Black Womanhood, SNCC, and Post-Civil Rights Anxieties in Alice Walker's Meridian," *Feminist Studies in English Literature* 14, no. 2 (December 2006): 179~207.

33. See the introduction to this book for a readings of movement work and psychically debilitating burnout in *The Salt Eaters*.

34. Evelyn Brooks Higginbotham, "African-American Women's History and the Metalanguage of Race," *Signs* 17, no. 2 (1992): 251–74; Darlene Clark Hine, "Rape and the Inner Lives of Black Women in the Middle West," *Signs* 14, no. 4 (1989): 912–20. In their often-cited essays, Darlene Clark Hine and Evelyn Brooks Higginbotham contend that during the nineteenth century, Black, middle-class women protected themselves against sexual violence—justified by stereotypes of Black women as hypersexual—by not discussing sexual violence, sexuality, or sex. Hine understands this coping mechanism as a culture of silence. Higginbotham builds on Hine's work by claiming Black women appear open while actually hiding their inner lives, what Higginbotham calls a culture of dissemblance.

35. In this chapter, Walker also challenges Black nationalist anti-abortion attitudes and platitudes about motherhood by emphasizing how Meridian is made a victim of motherhood through her sheer ignorance about the physiological and power mechanisms of sex: Meridian who, for instance, experienced no pleasure and understanding of sex became pregnant as a teenager. The primary takeaway from this chapter is that it is impossible to experience motherhood as empowering when it is compulsory from either or both expected gender roles or utter ignorance.

36. Walker, *Meridian*, 62.

37. Walker, 64.

38. Walker, 64. Here, I quite intentionally use "exchange." As a child, Meridian is treated as prostitute. For instance, Daxter starts off giving her candy in exchange for sexually

molesting her, and as Meridian ages, he offers her cash money for more intrusive violations. While The Assistant boasts of his sexual prowess and ability to sexually please girls (he and the narrator say "women" but, besides his wife, he seems to mostly target early-to-mid adolescent girls), his so-called "gift" "to make a woman come by using nothing but his penis and his beautiful voice," he fails to offer Meridian physical pleasure, and the other teenage girl Meridian watches him fuck. Moreover, these girls clearly want affection that he callously denies. In turn, Meridian exchanges unspecified sexual acts for affection: she'll continue to see him if he agrees to shut up and hold her."

39. Walker, 61.

40. La Marr Jurelle Bruce, *How to Go Mad Without Losing Your Mind Madness and Black Radical Creativity*, 2021, 74.

41. Walker, *Meridian*, 50.

42. Walker, 51.

43. Walker, 51

44. Walker, 53.

45. La Marr Jurelle Bruce, *How to Go Mad Without Losing Your Mind: Madness and Black Radical Creativity*, 2021, 6. La Marr Jurelle Bruce defines phenomenal madness as "an intense unruliness of mind—producing fundamental crises of perception, emotion, meaning, and selfhood—as experienced in the consciousness of the mad subject" (6).

46. Mann, Barbara Alice. *Spirits of Blood, Spirits of Breath: The Twinned Cosmos of Indigenous America.* Oxford University Press, 2016, 209.

47. See chapter four of this book, "Sexual Healing: A Queercrip Spirituality of the Erotic" for a detailed discussion of the erotic as an Africanist spiritual practice.

48. Tarrell A. A. Portman and Michael T. Garrett, "Native American Healing Traditions," *International Journal of Disability, Development and Education* 53, no. 4 (December 1, 2006): 456, https://doi.org/10.1080/10349120601008647.

49. For just a couple of scholars of nonwestern spiritual practices, see Stephanie Y. Mitchem's *African American Folk Healing* and Tarrall Portman and Michael Garret's essay "Native American Healing Traditions." Tarrell A. A. Portman and Michael T. Garrett, "Native American Healing Traditions," *International Journal of Disability, Development and Education* 53, no. 4 (December 1, 2006): 453–69, https://doi.org/10.1080/10349120601008647; Stephanie Y. Mitchem, *African American Folk Healing* (New York: New York University Press, 2007).

50. Walker, *Meridian*, 53.

51. Leah Lakshmi Piepzna-Samarasinha, *Care Work: Dreaming Disability Justice* (Vancouver: Arsenal Pulp Press, 2018), 33.

52. bell hooks, *All About Love: New Visions*, 1st ed (New York: William Morrow, 2000), 5–6.

53. Walker, *Meridian*, 29.

54. Walker, 131.

55. Walker, 122

56. Walker, 154.

57. Walker, 153–54.

58. Rosemarie Garland-Thomson, *Extraordinary Bodies: Figuring Physical Disability in American Culture and Literature* (New York: Columbia University Press, 1997), 115.

59. Walker, *Meridian*, 10.

60. Susan Wendell, *The Rejected Body: Feminist Philosophical Reflections on Disability* (New York: Routledge, 1996). For more about Susan Wendell's intervention into disability studies through her discussion of chronic illness, read *The Rejected Body*. Moreover, it is important to note that Alice Walker's understanding of enslaved people working through sickness complicates the argument that many disabilities are a product of modernity's shift from agriculture to industry. According to disability studies scholars such as Sharon Snyder and David T. Mitchell, modernity shifted to a more rigid workday and demand for labor that is more intellectual, thereby producing disabilities by erecting a more exclusionary labor standard. Walker's reminder that enslaved people did not often have the option to be ill or disabled suggests that Snyder and Mitchell's idyllic view of the past may be incomplete.

61. For an expanded discussion of cripistemology, check out the special issue of the *Journal of Literary & Cultural Disability Studies*, guest edited by Merri Johnson and Robert McRuer. Theodora Danylevich and Alyson Patsavas expand on Johnson and McRuer as they contemplate our current moment of global crisis in their essay, "Cripistemologies of Crisis." Merri Johnson and Robert McRuer, "Cripistemologies," *Journal of Literary & Cultural Disability Studies* 8, no. 2 (January 1, 2014): 127–48, https://doi.org/10.3828/jlcds.2014.12; Theodora Danylevich and Alyson Patsavas, "Cripistemologies of Crisis: Emergent Knowledges for the Present," *Lateral* 10, no. 1 (2021), https://doi.org/10.25158/L10.1.7.

62. It is also important to note the gentle exploration of what, exactly, Black folks desire to access from new legislation.

63. Lauren S. Cardon, "From Black Nationalism to the Ethnic Revival: 'Meridian's' Lynne Rabinowitz," *MELUS* 36, no. 3 (2011): 159–85.

64. Walker, *Meridian*, 3.

65. Walker, Alice. *Meridian*. Harcourt, 1976, 20.

66. Toni Morrison, *Conversations with Toni Morrison* (Jackson, MS: University Press of Mississippi, 1994), 82.

67. Anne-Marie O'Connor, "'Love' and the Outlaw Women," *Los Angeles Times*, October 15, 2003, http://articles.latimes.com/2003/oct/15/entertainment/et-oconnor15.

68. Andrea O'Reilly, *Toni Morrison and Motherhood: A Politics of the Heart*, annotated edition edition (State University of New York Press, 2010), 20.

69. Morrison, *Conversations with Toni Morrison*, 168.

70. Toni Morrison, *Paradise*, First Vintage International edition (New York: Vintage International, 2014), 159.

71. Morrison, 247.

72. Morrison, 263.

73. Morrison, 263–64.

74. Walker, Alice. *In Search of Our Mothers' Gardens: Womanist Prose*. San Diego, CA: Harcourt, 1983. 17

Chapter 3

1. Emphasis added, "The Negro Family: The Case for National Action | U.S. Department of Labor," accessed July 4, 2022, https://www.dol.gov/general/aboutdol/history/webid-moynihan.

2. "The Negro Family: The Case for National Action | U.S. Department of Labor."

3. For an introduction to the history of Black women's experience of reproductive injustice, see Dorothy Roberts's *Killing the Black Body* is foundational, and the essays in *Undivided Rights* insightful. Dorothy Roberts, *Killing the Black Body: Race, Reproduction, and the Meaning of Liberty*, 6486 4th edition (Vintage, 1998); Jael Miriam Silliman, ed., *Undivided Rights: Women of Color Organize for Reproductive Justice* (Cambridge, Mass: South End Press, 2004).

4. Carol Thomas, "'The Baby and the Bath Water' Disabled Women and Motherhood in Social Context," in *Maternal Theory: Essential Readings*, ed. Andrea O'Reilly, 2007, 573 and 584, http://search.ebscohost.com/login.aspx?direct=true&scope=site&db=nlebk&db=nlabk&AN=940481.

5. Claudia Malacrida, "Mothering and Disability: Implications for Theory and Practice," in *Routledge Handbook of Disability Studies*, ed. Nick Watson, Alan Roulstone, and Carol Thomas (New York: Routledge, 2012), 392.

6. Here, I am gesturing toward reproductive justice. For more on Black women and reproductive justice, see Ross, Loretta. "Understanding Reproductive Justice: Transforming the Pro-Choice Movement." Off Our Backs 36, no. 4 (2006): 14–19.

7. Toni Morrison, *Conversations with Toni Morrison* (Jackson, MS: University Press of Mississippi, 1994), 135.

8. bell hooks's essay "Revolutionary Parenting" provides an overview of this history of communal parenting. bell hooks, *Feminist Theory: From Margin to Center*, 2015, http://search.ebscohost.com/login.aspx?direct=true&scope=site&db=nlebk&db=nlabk&AN=862044.

9. Jennifer C. Nash has made an important and compelling argument about the image of the Black mother, particularly the Black mother in crisis, that "the crisis frame has transformed Black mothers into a distinct form of Left political currency" (4). Nash, Jennifer C. *Birthing Black Mothers*. Durham: Duke University Press, 2021.

10. For a more in-depth discussion of motherhood as an identity, see Anna Hinton's essay "You've already got what you need, sugar": Southern and maternal identity in Toni Morrison's Song of Solomon in the collection *Toni Morrison on Mothers and Motherhood*. Lee Baxter and Martha Satz, eds., *Toni Morrison on Mothers and Motherhood* (Bradford, ON: Demeter Press, 2017).

11. Alice Walker, *In Search of Our Mothers' Gardens: Womanist Prose* (Harcourt Brace Jovanovich, 1983), 393. Original emphasis.

12. Walker, 393.

13. Walker, 393.

14. Patricia Hill Collins. "Shifting the Center: Race, Class, and Feminist Theorizing about Motherhood." In *Maternal Theory: Essential Readings*, edited by Andrea O'Reilly, 2007.

15. Patricia Yaeger, *Dirt and Desire: Reconstructing Southern Women's Writing, 1930–1990* (Chicago: University of Chicago Press, 2000), xi.

16. Yaeger, 64.

17. Yaeger, x.

18. For close readings of sexual shaming in *This Child's Gonna Live*, see Jennifer Campbell, "'It's a Time in the Land': Gendering Black Power and Sarah E. Wright's Place in the Tradition of Black Women's Writing," *African American Review* 31, no. 2 (Summer 1997): 211–22; Trudier Harris, "Three Black Women Writers and Humanism: A Folk Perspective," in *Black American Literature and Humanism*, ed. R. Baxter (ed.) Miller, viii, 114 pp. vols. (Lexington: UP of Kentucky, 1981), 50–74.

19. Sarah E. Wright and Thulani Davis, *This Child's Gonna Live*, 2nd ed. edition (New York: The Feminist Press at CUNY, 2002), 87.

20. Wright and Davis, 43.

21. Wright and Davis, 43.

22. Wright and Davis, 43.

23. Wright and Davis, 231.

24. Wright and Davis, 231.

25. bell hooks, "Homeplace: A Site or Resistance," in *Maternal Theory: Essential Readings*, ed. Andrea O'Reilly, 1 Edition edition (Toronto: Demeter Press, 2007), 308.

26. Wright and Davis, *This Child's Gonna Live*, 40.

27. Wright and Davis, 39.

28. Wright and Davis, 251.

29. In both her novella *The Awakening* and short story "Désirée's Baby," Kate Chopin's heroines, for different reasons related to marriage and mother, commit suicide by surrendering themselves to water.

30. Wright and Davis, 265.

31. A version of this section has been published in the Journal of Literary and Cultural Disability Studies. Anna Hinton, "Making Do with What You Don't Have: Disabled Black Motherhood in Octavia E. Butler's *Parable of the Sower* and *Parable of the Talents*," *Journal of Literary & Cultural Disability Studies* 12, no. 4 (2018): 441–57,507, http://dx.doi.org.libproxy.library.unt.edu/10.3828/jlcds.2018.35.

32. Octavia E. Butler, *Parable of the Sower* (Open Road Media, 2012), 34.

33. Patricia Hill Collins. "Shifting the Center: Race, Class, and Feminist Theorizing about Motherhood." In *Maternal Theory: Essential Readings*, edited by Andrea O'Reilly, 2007.

34. Butler, 10.

35. For close readings of hyperempathy syndrome in the novels, see Therí Pickens's essay "Octavia Butler and the Novel Aesthetics," Gregory Hamptoms *Changing Bodies in the Fiction of Octavia Butler*, and Sami Schalk's *Bodyminds Reimagined*. Check out Clara Agustí's essay "The Relationship Between Community and Subjectivity in Octavia E. Bulter's *Parable of the Sower*" for a close reading of Lauren's motherwork in the novel. Clara Escoda Agustí, "The Relationship Between Community and Subjectivity in Octavia E. Butler's *Parable of the Sower*," *Extrapolation* 46, no. 3 (January 1, 2005): 351–59, https://doi.org/10.3828/extr.2005.46.3.7; Gregory J. Hampton, "Migration and Capital of the Body: Octavia Butler's

Parable of the Sower," *CLA Journal* 49, no. 1 (September 2005): 56–73; Therí A. Pickens, "Octavia Butler and the Aesthetics of the Novel," *Hypatia* 30, no. 1 (February 1, 2015): 167–80, https://doi.org/10.1111/hypa.12129; Samantha Dawn Schalk, *Bodyminds Reimagined: (Dis) Ability, Race, and Gender in Black Women's Speculative Fiction* (Durham: Duke University Press, 2018); Gregory Jerome Hampton, *Changing Bodies in the Fiction of Octavia Butler: Slaves, Aliens, and Vampires* (Lanham, Md: Lexington Books, 2010).

36. Butler, *Parable of the Sower*, 12.

37. For more about the process of "coming out" with an invisible disability, read Ellen Jean Samuels, "My Body, My Closet: Invisible Disability and the Limits of Coming-Out Discourse," *GLQ: A Journal of Lesbian and Gay Studies* 9, no. 1 (April 10, 2003): 233–55.

38. For a lengthier discussion of ableism in tropes about bad, Black motherhood, see Anna Hinton's "Making Do with What You Don't Have." Anna Hinton, "Making Do with What You Don't Have: Disabled Black Motherhood in Octavia E. Butler's *Parable of the Sower* and *Parable of the Talents*," *Journal of Literary & Cultural Disability Studies* 12, no. 4 (2018): 441–57,507, http://dx.doi.org.libproxy.library.unt.edu/10.3828/jlcds.2018.35.

39. Trudier Harris provides an excellent critique of the Strong Black Woman trope in her foundation book of literary theory, *Saints, Sinners, and Saviors*. Trudier Harris, *Saints, Sinners, Saviors: Strong Black Women in African American Literature* (New York: Palgrave, 2001).

40. Melissa V. Harris-Perry, *Sister Citizen: Shame, Stereotypes, and Black Women in America* (Yale University Press, 2011), 282.

41. Butler, *Parable of the Sower*, 193.

42. For a fuller discussion of care work, see the previous chapter of this book, "Black Community, Communities of Care." Also see Leah Lakshmi Piepzna-Samarasinha's *Care Work*. For an analysis of care work in Octavia E. Butler's *Parable* series, check out Derek Thiess's "Care Work, Age, and Culture in Butler's Parable Series." Leah Lakshmi Piepzna-Samarasinha, *Care Work: Dreaming Disability Justice* (Vancouver: Arsenal Pulp Press, 2018); Derek Thiess, "Care Work, Age, and Culture in Butler's Parable Series," *FEMSPEC: An Interdisciplinary Feminist Journal Dedicated to Critical and Creative Work in the Realms of Science Fiction, Fantasy, Magical Realism, Surrealism, Myth, Folklore, and Other Supernatural Genres* 15 (2015): 63–99.

43. For instance, historian of race and disability Jenifer Barclay discusses how enslaved Black folks with disabilities were often assigned care work on plantations. Jenifer L. Barclay, "Mothering the 'Useless': Black Motherhood, Disability, and Slavery," *Women, Gender, and Families of Color* 2, no. 2 (2014): 115+.

44. Butler, *Parable of the Sower*, 110.

45. Butler, 178.

46. Butler, 324.

47. Butler, 115.

48. Butler, 78.

49. I will discuss Audre Lorde's theory of the Erotic as a queercrip spiritual technology in chapter 4 and the conclusion.

50. Butler, 25.

51. For a discussion of magic as spiritual agency and the trickster figure in Africanist spirituality, see Yvonne Chireau's *Black Magic*. For further discussion on magic and the trickster figure in African cosmology, see Theophus Smith's *Conjuring Culture*. Smith's text offers a compelling analysis of the traces of (non-Christian) spiritual practices in the theology of the Black church. Yvonne Patricia Chireau, *Black Magic: Religion and the African American Conjuring Tradition*, 1. paperback printing, The George Gund Foundation Imprint in African American Studies (Berkeley, Calif.: University of California Press, 2006); Theophus Harold Smith, *Conjuring Culture: Biblical Formations of Black America*, Religion in America Series (New York: Oxford University Press, 1994).

52. Octavia E. Butler, *Parable of the Talents* (Open Road Media Sci-Fi & Fantasy, 2012), 175.

53. Butler, 377.

54. Patricia Hill Collins. "Shifting the Center: Race, Class, and Feminist Theorizing about Motherhood." In *Maternal Theory: Essential Readings*, edited by Andrea O'Reilly, 2007.

55. Sapphire, *Push: A Novel* (New York: Vintage Contemporaries, 2009), 17.

56. Jina B. Kim. "Cripping the Welfare Queen." *Social Text* 39, no. 3 (September 1, 2021): 79–101. https://doi.org/10.1215/01642472-9034390.

57. Sapphire, 84.

58. Michelle Jarman, "Cultural Consumption and Rejection of Precious Jones: Pushing Disability into the Discussion of Sapphire's Push and Lee Daniels's Precious," *Feminist Formations* 24, no. 2 (August 24, 2012): 170, https://doi.org/10.1353/ff.2012.0019.

59. Sapphire, *Push*, 119.

60. For a discussion of controlling images, or stereotypes, about Black women, including the Mammy, see Patricia Hill Collins, *Black Feminist Thought: Knowledge, Consciousness, and the Politics of Empowerment*, Rev. 10th anniversary ed. 2nd ed (New York: Routledge, 2000); Melissa V. Harris-Perry, *Sister Citizen: Shame, Stereotypes, and Black Women in America* (Yale University Press, 2011).

61. Sapphire, *Push*, 70, 71, 75.

62. Davies, 43.

63. Indeed, Ms. Rain transforms Each One, Teach One into a space that mirrors Sisterhood of Black Single Mothers, the organization that inspired Gumbs's theorizing of queer, Black feminist community work, as well as the term "motherful." See, Gumbs, Alexis Pauline, China Martens, and Mai'a Williams, eds. Revolutionary Mothering: Love on the Front Lines. Oakland, CA: PM Press, 2016. 23.

64. Sapphire, *Push*, 96.

65. Sapphire, 64.

66. Sapphire, 75.

67. Sapphire, 88.

68. For stories of mothers with intellectual disabilities, see Rachel Mayes, Gwynnyth Llewellyn, and David McConnell, "'That's Who I Choose to Be': The Mother Identity for Women with Intellectual Disabilities," *Women's Studies International Forum* 34, no. 2 (March 2011): 112–20, https://doi.org/10.1016/j.wsif.2010.11.001.

69. Sapphire, *Push*, 139.

70. Sapphire, 140.

71. Gumbs, Alexis Pauline, China Martens, and Mai'a Williams, eds. *Revolutionary Mothering: Love on the Front Lines*. Oakland, CA: PM Press, 2016.13.

Chapter 4

1. Foundational texts on stereotypes and sexual subjugation are: Deborah Gray White, *Ar'n't I a Woman?: Female Slaves in the Plantation South* (W. W. Norton & Company, 1999); Bell Hooks, *Ain't I a Woman: Black Women and Feminism* (South End Press, 1981); Patricia Hill Collins, *Black Feminist Thought: Knowledge, Consciousness, and the Politics of Empowerment*, Rev. 10th anniversary ed. 2nd ed (New York: Routledge, 2000).

2. See, Darlene Clark Hine, "Rape and the Inner Lives of Black Women in the Middle West," *Signs* 14, no. 4 (1989): 912–20.

3. To shave the tip of the iceberg on writings about reclaiming Black women's sexuality, check out: Shayne Lee, *Erotic Revolutionaries: Black Women, Sexuality, and Popular Culture* (Government Institutes, 2010); Patricia Hill Collins, *Black Sexual Politics: African Americans, Gender, and the New Racism* (New York: Routledge, 2004); LaMonda Horton-Stallings, *Funk the Erotic: Transaesthetics and Black Sexual Cultures*, The New Black Studies Series (Urbana, Chicago: University of Illinois Press, 2015).

4. "What Sexual Health Looks Like For These Black Disabled Women," Daye, accessed July 4, 2022, https://yourdaye.com/vitals/cultural-musings/the-triple-cripples-sexual-health/.

5. Hobson, Janell. *Venus in the Dark: Blackness and Beauty in Popular Culture*. Oxford, United Kingdom: Taylor & Francis Group, 2018. http://ebookcentral.proquest.com/lib/unt/detail.action?docID=5259834.

6. "What Sexual Health Looks Like For These Black Disabled Women."

7. See Jennifer C. Nash, *The Black Body in Ecstasy: Reading Race, Reading Pornography*, Next Wave (Durham; London: Duke University Press, 2014).

8. Nash, 2.

9. Stacey M. Floyd-Thomas, ed., *Black Church Studies: An Introduction* (Nashville, TN: Abingdon Press, 2007), xxiii.

10. See Theophus Harold Smith, *Conjuring Culture: Biblical Formations of Black America*, Religion in America Series (New York: Oxford University Press, 1994).

11. Cathy J. Cohen, *The Boundaries of Blackness: Aids and the Breakdown of Black Politics* (Chicago: University of Chicago Press, 1999).

12. Brittney C. Cooper, Susana M. Morris, and Robin M. Boylorn, eds., *The Crunk Feminist Collection*, First Feminist Press edition (New York: The Feminist Press at CUNY, 2017), 181.

13. Brittney Cooper, "How Sarah Got Her Groove Back, or Notes Toward a Black Feminist Theology of Pleasure," *Black Theology* 16, no. 3 (September 2, 2018): 199, https://doi.org/10.1080/14769948.2018.1492299. My emphasis.

14. Audre Lorde, *Sister Outsider: Essays and Speeches* (Potter/TenSpeed/Harmony, 2012), 53.

15. Lorde, 53.

16. Lorde, 54.

17. Lorde, 57.

18. Lorde, 58.

19. Lorde, 58.

20. Lorde, 56.

21. Meredith F. Coleman-Tobias, "Audre and Africa: Reconsidering Lorde's Rites/Rights," *Journal of Interreligious Studies*, no. 23 (May 24, 2018): 71.

22. Coleman-Tobias, 69.

23. Joan Morgan, "Why We Get Off: Moving Towards a Black Feminist Politics of Pleasure," *Black Scholar* 45, no. 4 (Winter 2015): 40, https://doi.org/10.1080/00064246.2015.1080915.

24. "Sexual Healing," accessed July 4, 2022, https://archive.nytimes.com/www.nytimes.com/books/98/10/04/reviews/981004.04proset.html; "'By the Light of My Father's Smile': Limp New-Age Nonsense in Mexic," accessed January 6, 2021, https://archive.nytimes.com/www.nytimes.com/books/98/10/04/daily/walker-book-review.html.

25. Alice Walker, *The Color Purple* (Harcourt, 1982), 48.

26. Walker, 76.

27. Walker, 194.

28. Walker, 194.

29. Walker, 195.

30. Alice Walker, *The Temple of My Familiar* (New York: Washington Square Press, 1997), 289.

31. Transformative justice is a crip understanding of justice. According to Mia Mingus, the main imperative of transformative justice is to "respond to violence with creating more violence and/or engaging in harm reduction to lessen the violence." Transform Harm Admin, "Transformative Justice: A Brief Description—Transform Harm," https://Transformharm.Org/ (blog), January 11, 2019, https://transformharm.org/transformative-justice-a-brief-description/.

32. I will alternate between Magdalena and June to reflect Magdalena's self-naming in whatever moment of her life I am discussing.

33. For some mainstream feminist readings of spirituality and sexuality in *By the Light of My Father's Smile* see, Silvia del Pilar Castro Borrego, *The Search for Wholeness and Diaspora Literacy in Contemporary African American Literature* (Newcastle upon Tyne, UK: Cambridge Scholars Publishing, 2011); Abigail Rine, *Irigaray, Incarnation and Contemporary Women's Fiction*, xi, 184 (London, England: Bloomsbury Publishing, 2013); Maria Lauret, *Alice Walker*, ix, 290 pp. (New York, NY: Palgrave Macmillan, 2011).

34. Sianne Ngai, *Ugly Feelings*, First Harvard University Press paperback (Cambridge, Mass. London: Harvard University Press, 2007), 6 and 3. My emphasis.

35. Alice Walker, *By the Light of My Father's Smile* (New York: Ballantine Books, 1999), 72.

36. Walker, 69.

37. For an inroad into the intersections of disability studies and fat studies, see Anna Mollow, "Disability Studies Gets Fat," *Hypatia* 30, no. 1 (February 1, 2015): 199–216, https://doi.org/10.1111/hypa.12126.

38. This is quite different than Walker's Meridian Hill who finds her ill body a source of spiritual pleasure.

39. Ngai, *Ugly Feelings*, 336.

40. Ngai, 336.

41. Walker, *By the Light of My Father's Smile*, 69.

42. Walker, 168.

43. Lorde, *Sister Outsider*, 54.

44. For instance, there have been several instances of the families of victims of state violence offering forgiveness to murders without the guilty partying even asking for forgiveness. This is so common that Black forgiveness to white violence is expected, demanded even.

45. Walker, *By the Light of My Father's Smile*, 171.

46. John S. Mbiti, *Introduction to African Religion*, Second edition; Reissued by Waveland Press, Inc (Long Grove, III: Waveland Press, Inc, 2015), 124.

47. Min. Ra Ifagbemi Babalawo, . . *Ancestors: Hidden Hands, Healing Spirits for Your Use & Empowerment* (New York: Athelia Henrietta Press, Inc, 1999), 23.

48. Benjamin C. Ray, *African Religions: Symbol, Ritual, and Community*, Prentice-Hall Studies in Religion Series (Englewood Cliffs, NJ: Prentice-Hall, 1976), 140.

49. Alice Walker and Pratibha Parmar, *Warrior Marks: Female Genital Mutilation and the Sexual Blinding of Women* (San Diego: Amistad, 1996), 19.

Conclusion

1. Here, I invoke Alison Kafer's discussion of futurity in *Feminist, Crip, Queer*. Kafer writes, "I imagine futures otherwise, arguing for a cripped politics of access and engagement based on the work of disability activists and theorists." Alison Kafer, *Feminist, Queer, Crip*, 1 edition (Indiana University Press, 2013).

2. Toni Morrison, *Paradise*, First Vintage International edition (New York: Vintage International, 2014), 263.

3. Morrison, 318.

4. Morrison, 318.

5. Here, I borrow self-described Black feminist troublemaker Alexis Pauline Gumbs.

6. For some examples, see Ruha Benjamin, ed., *Captivating Technology: Race, Carceral Technoscience, and Liberatory Imagination in Everyday Life* (Durham: Duke University Press, 2019); Alison Kafer, *Feminist, Queer, Crip*, 1 edition (Indiana University Press, 2013); Dorothy Roberts, *Fatal Invention: How Science, Politics, and Big Business Re-Create Race in the Twenty-First Century* (New York; London: The new Press, 2012).

7. Kelly Fritsch et al., "Introduction to Special Section on Crip Technoscience," *Catalyst: Feminism, Theory, Technoscience* 5, no. 1 (April 1, 2019): 1–10, https://doi.org/10.28968/cftt.v5i1.31998.

8. Aimi Hamraie and Kelly Fritsch, "Crip Technoscience Manifesto," *Catalyst: Feminism, Theory, Technoscience* 5, no. 1 (April 1, 2019): 5–6, https://doi.org/10.28968/cftt.v5i1.29607.

9. Hamraie and Fritsch, 6.

10. Fritsch et al., "Introduction to Special Section on Crip Technoscience."

11. Yvonne Chireau's chapter in *Black Magic* on super natural harming traditions provides a useful overview of some examples in the US context. Yvonne Patricia Chireau, *Black Magic: Religion and the African American Conjuring Tradition*, 1. Paperback printing, The George Gund Foundation Imprint in African American Studies (Berkeley, CA: University of California Press, 2006).

12. Isiah Lavender, *Afrofuturism Rising: The Literary Prehistory of a Movement*, 2019, 26.

13. Lavender, 26.

14. Kameelah L. Martin, *Conjuring Moments in African American Literature: Women, Spirit Work, and Other Such Hoodoo*, 1st ed (New York: Palgrave Macmillan, 2013), 93.

15. Toni Cade Bambara and Thabiti Lewis, *Conversations with Toni Cade Bambara*, 2017, 131.

16. Bambara and Lewis, 132.

17. See chapter 4 "Sexual Healing: A Queercrip Spirituality of the Erotic" for a more in-depth conversation about ancestor work.

18. Kevin Everod Quashie, *Black Aliveness, or a Poetics of Being*, Black Outdoors: Innovations in the Poetics of Study (Durham: Duke University Press, 2021), 2.

19. As Jennifer C. Nash so poignantly observes, the image of mourning mothers and discourse of dying mothers, Black mothers in "crisis" animates Leftist political discourse. See Nash, Jennifer C. *Birthing Black Mothers*. Durham: Duke University Press, 2021.

20. The compendium of lives lost to state violence continues at rates seemingly impossible to retain. But we try. Al Jazeera has a useful, interactive website documenting these deaths. Al Jazeera, "Know Their Names: Black People Killed by the Police in the US," accessed July 5, 2022, https://interactive.aljazeera.com/aje/2020/know-their-names/index.html.

21. Some of the radical disabled Black activists doing this work include Leroy Moore, Talila A. Lewis, and Imani Barbarin.

22. Audre Lorde, *Sister Outsider: Essays and Speeches* (Potter/TenSpeed/Harmony, 2012), 53. My emphasis.

23. Lorde, 56.

24. See the previous chapter for my discussion of the erotic as a queercrip spiritual power.

25. Audre Lorde, *The Cancer Journals*, Special ed (San Francisco: Aunt Lute Books, 1997), 48.

26. Lorde, 48.

27. Lorde, 49.

28. Lorde, *Sister Outsider*, 57.

29. Lorde, 53.

30. Lorde, *The Cancer Journals*, 68.

31. Lorde's initial biopsy proved her first tumor to be benign; nevertheless, Lorde lived with fear of cancer, a fear that infused and motivated her work, until her official diagnosis. It was during this period that she wrote "The Uses of the Erotic: The Erotic as Power."

32. Meredith F. Coleman-Tobias, "Audre and Africa: Reconsidering Lorde's Rites/Rights," *Journal of Interreligious Studies*, no. 23 (May 24, 2018): 68–74.

33. Alexis De Veaux, *Warrior Poet: A Biography of Audre Lorde*, 1st ed (New York: W.W. Norton, 2004), 190.

34. Audre Lorde, *The Collected Poems of Audre Lorde*, 1997, 90, https://www.overdrive.com/search?q=C5230AC8-4035-4254-A564-A42ADA3C63A7.

35. Lorde, 91.

36. De Veaux, *Warrior Poet*, 222.

37. I outline Valerie Lee's theorization of "sistah conjurers" in the introduction to this book. Valerie Lee, *Granny Midwives and Black Women Writers: Double-Dutched Readings* (New York: Routledge, 1996).

38. De Veaux, *Warrior Poet*, 227.

39. Lorde, *The Cancer Journals*, 11.

40. De Veaux, *Warrior Poet*, 225.

41. Bambara and Lewis, *Conversations with Toni Cade Bambara*, 134.nationalism, and film. The intimacy of these collaborations or conversations between Bambara (1939-1995)

42. Thabiti Lewis, *"Black People Are My Business": Toni Cade Bambara's Practices of Liberation* (Detroit: Wayne State University Press, 2020), 150.

43. Toni Cade Bambara, *Deep Sightings & Rescue Missions: Fiction, Essays, and Conversations*, 1st Vintage Contemporaries Ed edition (Vintage, 2009), 21.

44. Vilissa also has publicly spoken about her turn to Black women-centered spiritual systems.

45. Vilissa Thompson, "How Technology Is Forcing the Disability Rights Movement into the 21st Century," *Catalyst: Feminism, Theory, Technoscience* 5, no. 1 (April 1, 2019): 3, https://doi.org/10.28968/cftt.v5i1.30420.

46. While technology as a liberation tool includes literacy, the pen, photography, etc. Here, I am especially signaling Black women's social media activism. For more see, Bailey, Moya. *Misogynoir Transformed: Black Women's Digital Resistance*. Intersections: Transdisciplinary Perspectives on Genders and Sexualities. New York: New York University Press, 2021 and Jones, Feminista. *Reclaiming Our Space: How Black Feminists Are Changing the World from the Tweets to the Streets*. Boston: Beacon Press, 2019.

Index

ableism, 6, 9, 23, 27, 34, 55, 56, 57, 65, 78, 85, 92, 93, 94, 95, 97, 102, 103, 105, 112, 124

ableists, 6, 16, 20, 22, 28, 46, 58, 59, 61, 69, 73, 76, 77, 79, 86, 89, 92, 93, 97, 102, 104, 109, 127

activism, 7, 10, 11, 27, 59, 60, 61, 63, 66, 69, 78, 124, 128, 132, 133, 162n46; grassroots, 68, 132; health, 9, 10, 12, 22, 27, 59; spiritual, 18

affect, 27, 40, 43, 112, 113, 117, 118, 125, 131

African traditional religions, 4

African-derived religions, 4, 12, 15, 16

Africanist, 4, 5, 12, 13, 14, 15, 16, 17, 18, 19, 20, 21, 22, 23, 24, 29, 31, 33, 44, 57, 58, 61, 65, 74, 79, 80, 84, 99, 110, 111, 113, 120, 121, 124, 125, 126, 130, 131

Afropessimism, 127

Alexander, Elizabeth, 20

Alexander, M. Jacqui, 14, 19

ancestor, 7, 8, 15, 56, 73, 77, 82, 115, 120, 121, 124, 132, 133, 139n35

anti-fat, 81, 117, 118, 120

anxiety, 39, 72, 93

Anzaldúa, Gloria, 18

Bailey, Moya, 9, 137n1; and Izetta Mobley, 9, 10

Baker, Houston A., 13

Bambara, Toni Cade, 3, 4, 10, 11, 12, 18, 19, 24, 125, 131, 132, 133, 135; *The Salt Eaters*, 3, 4, 10, 12, 15, 69, 125, 126

Baynton, Douglas, 7, 58

Bell, Bernard, 48

Bell, Christopher M., 9

Bérubé, Michael, 40

Black Arts Movement, 9, 10, 27, 69

Black Church, 23, 73, 98, 111

Black feminist studies, 7; disability studies, 6, 9, 12, 22, 34, 59; literary studies, 22; theory, 63, 108, 109, 114

Black liberation, 9, 56, 60, 61, 66, 71, 86

Black nationalism, 66, 73, 79

Black Power, 9, 10, 69, 86

Black studies, 6, 7

Black Women's Health Book, The (White), 10, 88

Body & Soul (Villarosa), 10

Brazil, 29, 31, 32

Brooks, Kinitra, 18

Bruce, La Marr Jurelle, 37, 40, 72

Butler, Octavia E., 21, 23, 89, 94, 107, 135, 147n85; *Parable of the Sower*, 23, 89, 94, 98; *Parable of the Talents*, 23, 89, 94, 95, 98, 100, 103

Campbell, Bebe Moore, 11, 27

cancer, 10, 59, 112, 113, 118, 123, 126, 128–32, 161n31

Candomble, 12

care work, 23, 57, 75, 80, 83, 87, 97, 100, 102, 103, 104, 114, 156n43

caregiving, 58, 61, 64, 66, 75, 76, 78, 97, 99, 104, 105, 114

Carter, Angela, 34, 45

Christianity, 12, 17, 18, 73, 74, 83, 116

chronic illness, 76, 77, 151n28, 153n60

civil rights, 9, 26, 59, 61, 63, 64, 65, 77, 78, 111

Clifton, Lucille, 10, 19

Cohen, Cathy, 111
Coleman Tobias, Meredith F., 113, 130
Collins, Patricia Hill, 23, 25, 90, 95, 101
conjure, 3, 12, 15, 19, 20, 38, 44, 46, 61, 83, 124, 130
controlling images, 23, 25, 27, 31, 106, 107; Crack Mother, 96; Jezebel, 25, 27, 48, 80, 82, 103, 116, 142n8; Mammy, 25, 27, 80, 81, 103; Matriarch, 66, 80, 103; Sapphire, 25, 27, 80, 103
Cooper, Brittney, 12, 111
cure, 4, 5, 15, 28, 29, 31, 33, 76, 77, 78, 106, 119

Davies, Carole Boyce, 104
De Veaux, Alexis, 130
disability consciousness, 78, 101
disability justice, 9, 12, 75
Douglass, Fredrick, 125
Down's Syndrome, 105
Du Bois, W. E. B., 58
duCille, Ann, 26, 57
Duggan, Lisa, 11, 63
Dunbar-Nelson, Alice, 10

Edwards, Erica R., 68
Ellison, Ralph, 10, 26
Enlightenment, 17, 74, 127, 145n49; Reason, 26, 36, 54, 55, 113, 145n49
Erevelles, Nirmala, 6, 9
Eshu, 15
Espiritismo, 12
eugenics, 9, 86, 124
Evans, Mari, 56

Fritsch, Kelly and Aimi Hamraie, 124
futurity, 24, 122, 124, 126, 128, 131, 160n1

Garland-Thomson, Rosemarie, 4, 54, 59, 78
Gayle, Addison, 48
griots, 33
Gumbs, Alexis Pauline, 104, 107, 148n2

Hammond, Evelyn C., 49
Harris-Perry, Melissa, 96

Hartman, Saidiya, 35
health movements, 9, 10
Henderson, Mae Gwendolyn, 20; plant medicine, 125
HIV/AIDS, 10, 11, 59, 111
Holloway, Karla F.C., 20
Holmes, Linda Janet, 11
hooks, bell, 10, 23, 75, 93; homeplace, 93, 100, 107, 117, 118; *Sisters of the Yam*, 10
Hopkinson, Nalo, 16
Hull, Akasha Gloria, 13, 19
hysteria, 34, 35, 36, 37, 40

impairment, 6, 11, 31, 40, 41, 43, 58, 60, 63, 69, 71, 83

Jarman, Michelle, 7, 9, 15, 103
Jim Crow, 22
Johnson, Georgia Douglass, 10
Johnson, Merri Lisa, 11, 63
Jones, Gayl, 21, 22, 27, 28, 40, 45, 47, 48, 55, 72, 101, 108, 135; *Corregidora*, 22, 23, 27, 28, 29, 30, 32, 33, 34, 37, 39, 40, 44, 45, 46, 47, 49, 55; *Eva's Man*, 22, 23, 27, 28, 47, 48, 49, 51, 52, 53, 55, 101, 108
Jordan, June, 10, 19, 27, 47, 85

Kafer, Alison, 30, 160n1
Keating, AnaLouise, 18
Kim, Jina B., 102
Knadler, Stephen, 58, 59, 64

La Regla de Ocha, 12
Lafargue Clinic, 10
Lavender, Isiah, III, 125
Lee, Valerie, 19; sistah conjurers, 19, 20
Lewis, Thabiti, 132
Linton, Simi, 60
Lopez, Christina Garcia, 14
Lorde, Audre, 7, 15, 19, 20, 23, 24, 55, 74, 99, 104, 110, 112, 114, 118, 122, 123, 128, 133, 135; *A Burst of Light*, 130, 131; *The Cancer Journals*, 118, 123, 129, 131
Lucumi, 12

lwa, 15, 16
Lyle, Timothy, 9
lynching plays, 10

madness, 17, 26, 27, 28, 36, 37, 40, 49, 50, 51, 52, 53, 54, 71, 72, 73, 74, 152n45; crazy, 19, 26, 27, 49, 55, 69, 71; insane, 47; mad, 19, 28, 40, 47, 49, 50, 51, 74, 113, 125, 152n45
magic, 12, 18, 35, 44, 99
Martin, Kameelah L., 13, 44, 125; conjure narratives, 44
Massiah, Louis, 126, 131
Mbiti, John, 121
McRuer, Robert, 11, 63
medical model, 5, 17, 76, 83
medical racism, 7, 49
melancholia, 36, 37, 39
mental disability, 19, 22, 23, 37, 41, 46, 49, 59, 73, 127, 142n8; intellectual disability, 102, 103, 104; mental illness, 11, 26, 29, 59, 73
Middle Passage, 111
midwifery, 15, 59
misogynoir, 3, 4, 5, 8, 9, 10, 14, 15, 22, 49, 56, 61, 65, 69, 85, 92, 94, 95, 102, 103, 105, 107, 120, 131
Mitchem, Stephanie Y., 16, 58
Mollow, Anna, 9
Morgan, Joan, 9, 114
Morrison, Toni, 18, 26, 55, 56, 58, 79, 88, 135; *Beloved*, 10, 84; *Paradise*, 23, 61, 79, 80, 81, 83, 84, 123, 124; pariah, 81, 96
Moynihan, Daniel Patrick, 66, 85

Nash, Jennifer C., 7, 154n9, 161n19
National Black Women's Health Project, 10
Neal, Larry, 10
New Age, 12, 114
Ngai, Sianne, 117; ugly feelings, 117, 118

Obeah, 12
Orisha, 16, 18, 113, 121, 130
Oshun, 121, 130
Oya, 130

paganism, 12, 72
pain, 5, 26, 33, 35, 36, 37, 39, 44, 46, 53, 63, 72, 77, 89, 95, 97, 98, 112, 117, 118, 119, 129
Pickens, Therí A., 7, 9, 18, 21
Piepzna-Samarasinha, Leah Lakshmi, 75
pleasure, 9, 24, 35, 38, 39, 46, 70, 73, 74, 82, 95, 99, 109, 110, 112–15, 116–19, 121, 122
pornography, 110
Prendergast, Catherine, 49, 50
Price, Margaret, 14
psychiatric industrial complexes, 27; institutions, 21, 60; psychiatric hospital, 4; psychiatric prison, 47, 53

Quashie, Kevin, 52, 127
queercrip, 23, 112, 113, 114, 115, 118, 122, 128, 130, 131, 134

racism, 3, 6, 7, 10, 14, 15, 23, 26, 27, 36, 49, 59, 61, 62, 64, 65, 68, 71, 73, 91, 94, 127, 131
religious model, 17, 74, 83
reproductive justice, 10, 11, 59
revolutionary, 13, 64, 65, 76, 107, 148n1
rootwork, 15, 59, 125
Ryan, Judylyn S., 13

Samuels, Ellen, 7
sanism, 19, 26, 27, 36, 49, 52, 55, 112, 142n8
Sapphire (author), 23, 89; *Push*, 23, 89, 100, 101, 102, 104, 106, 107
Schalk, Sami, 7, 9, 10, 14, 16, 18
Seboulisa, 15, 130
72-Hour Hold, 11
sexual agency, 24, 69, 91, 109, 110
sexual violence, 33, 34, 68, 71, 76, 82, 102, 108, 115, 151n34
Shange, N'tozake, 11, 26, 27
Sharpe, Christina, 35, 145n55
Sins Invalid, 22
slavery, 29, 31, 32, 35, 41, 44, 46, 65, 66, 77, 85, 103, 111, 115, 125, 127, 145n55, 149n5
Snyder, Sharon and David T. Mitchell, 21, 42
social media, 53, 109, 162n46
Society for Disability Studies (SDS), 22, 60

speculative fiction, 18
Spillers, Hortense, 5, 6
spirituality, 4, 5, 12, 13, 14, 15, 16, 17, 19, 21, 22,
　　24, 61, 64, 74, 80, 110, 112–14, 120, 124,
　　125, 128, 130, 131, 133
Stallings, L. H., 44
Stanford, Ann Folwell, 19
Steverson, Delia, 9
stigma, 5, 75, 92

"The New Negro," 9
Thompson, Vilissa, 133, 151n28
Tinsley, Omise'eke, 16
transformative justice, 115, 122, 128, 133,
　　159n31
Tyler, Dennis, Jr., 9

Villarosa, Linda, 10
Vodou, 12, 13, 16
Voodoo, 13

Walker, Alice, 10, 13, 22, 23, 58, 60, 61, 62,
　　64, 79, 82, 84, 88, 104, 109, 110, 114, 122,
　　135; *By the Light of My Father's Smile*,
　　23, 110, 114, 116, 117, 118, 120, 121, 122; *The
　　Color Purple*, 104, 106, 114; *In Search
　　of Our Mothers' Gardens*, 13, 62, 63, 88;
　　In the Temple of My Familiar, 114, 115;
　　Meridian, 23, 61, 64, 65, 66, 71, 72, 79,
　　81, 109; *Possessing the Secret of Joy*, 114
Wall, Cheryl, 25
Washington, Booker T., 58, 59
wellness, 3, 4, 10, 14, 15, 16, 20, 22, 29, 30, 57,
　　59, 65, 74, 122, 152n48
Wells, Ida B., 10
White, Evelyn C., 10
womanism, 13, 62, 63
Wonder, Stevie, 89
Woods, Jamilah, 134
Wright, Richard, 10, 26
Wright, Sarah E., 23, 89; *This Child's Gonna
　　Live*, 23, 89, 90, 91, 92, 93, 100, 107

Yaeger, Patricia, 90; throwaway, 90, 91, 94,
　　101, 102, 107
Yemonja, 130

About the Author

Dr. Anna LaQuawn Hinton is assistant professor of disability studies and Black literature and culture in the English Department at the University of North Texas. She has published in the *Journal of Literary and Cultural Disability Studies* (JLCDS) and *CLA Journal*, as well as *The Cambridge Companion to American Literature and the Body* and *The Palgrave Handbook on Reproductive Justice and Literature*. She is a disabled queer-momma Black feminist who "Loves music. Loves dance. Loves the moon. Loves the Spirit. Loves love and food and roundness. Loves struggle. Loves the Folk. (and striving to) Loves herself. Regardless."*

*Alice Walker

www.ingramcontent.com/pod-product-compliance
Lightning Source LLC
Chambersburg PA
CBHW020416230426
43663CB00007BA/1191